DATE DUE

NOV 2 5 2007			
NOV 1 3 2015			

Reflections on Freedom of Speech and the First Amendment

OTHER BOOKS BY GEORGE ANASTAPLO

The Constitutionalist: Notes on the First Amendment (1971, 2005)

Human Being and Citizen: Essays on Virtue, Freedom, and the Common Good (1975)

The Artist as Thinker: From Shakespeare to Joyce (1983)

The Constitution of 1787: A Commentary (1989)

The American Moralist: On Law, Ethics, and Government (1992)

The Amendments to the Constitution: A Commentary (1995)

The Thinker as Artist: From Homer to Plato & Aristotle (1997)

Campus Hate-Speech Codes, Natural Right, and Twentieth-Century Atrocities (1997, 1999)

Liberty, Equality, and Modern Constitutionalism: A Source Book (1999)

Abraham Lincoln: A Constitutional Biography (1999)

But Not Philosophy: Seven Introductions to Non-Western Thought (2002)

On Trial: From Adam & Eve to O.J. Simpson (2004)

Plato's "Meno," Translation and Commentary (with Laurence Berns) (2004)

Reflections on Constitutional Law (2006)

REFLECTIONS ON FREEDOM OF SPEECH AND THE FIRST AMENDMENT

George Anastaplo

THE UNIVERSITY PRESS OF KENTUCKY

Publication of this volume was made possible in part by a grant
from the National Endowment for the Humanities.

Scholarly publisher for the Commonwealth,
serving Bellarmine University, Berea College, Centre
College of Kentucky, Eastern Kentucky University,
The Filson Historical Society, Georgetown College,
Kentucky Historical Society, Kentucky State University,
Morehead State University, Murray State University,
Northern Kentucky University, Transylvania University,
University of Kentucky, University of Louisville,
and Western Kentucky University.
All rights reserved.

Editorial and Sales Offices: The University Press of Kentucky
663 South Limestone Street, Lexington, Kentucky 40508-4008
www.kentuckypress.com

07 08 09 10 11   5 4 3 2 1

Library of Congress Cataloging-in-Publication Data

Anastaplo, George, 1925-
Reflections on freedom of speech and the First Amendment / George Anastaplo.
p. cm.
Includes bibliographical references and index.
ISBN-13: 978-0-8131-2424-7 (hardcover : alk. paper)
ISBN-10: 0-8131-2424-7 (hardcover : alk. paper)
ISBN-13: 978-0-8131-9173-7 (pbk. : alk. paper)
ISBN-10: 0-8131-9173-4 (pbk. : alk. paper) 1. Freedom of speech—United
States—History. 2. United States. Constitution. 1st Amendment.
3. Freedom of speech—History. I. Title.
KF4772.A96 2007
342.7308'53—dc22   2006035386

This book is printed on acid-free recycled paper meeting
the requirements of the American National Standard
for Permanence in Paper for Printed Library Materials.

Manufactured in the United States of America.

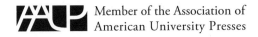

Member of the Association of
American University Presses

To
the Memory
of
My Initial First Amendment Teachers,
Alexander Meiklejohn
(1872–1964)
and
Harry Kalven Jr.
(1914–1974)

Contents

APPENDIXES

PREFACE

It has been frequently remarked, that it seems to have been reserved to the people of this country, by their conduct and example, to decide the important question, whether societies of men are really capable or not, of establishing good government from reflection and choice, or whether they are forever destined to depend, for their political constitutions on accident and force.

—*The Federalist*, No. 1

At the foundation of the series of reflections (or constitutional sonnets) offered in this volume is my treatise *The Constitutionalist: Notes on the First Amendment*, published by the Southern Methodist University Press in 1971 and recently republished, in an enhanced form with its 2004 foreword, preface, and addenda, by Lexington Books. That treatise examines at length the sources, meaning, and applications of the First Amendment text:

Congress shall make no law respecting an establishment of religion, or prohibiting the free exercise thereof; or abridging the freedom of speech, or of the press; or the right of the people to assemble, and to petition the Government for a redress of grievances.

The Constitutionalist is itself a much-expanded version of my 1964 University of Chicago doctoral dissertation, with substantial additions (drawing on instructive texts ancient and modern) in hundreds of pages of notes. Laurence Berns, the author of the 2004 foreword to *The Constitutionalist*, has suggested:

Judging roughly from the frequency of references, Anastaplo seems to have learned most from Shakespeare, from his fellow Il-

linoisan Abraham Lincoln, and from Plato. This book is a major
attempt to discover and to articulate the harmony, or at least the
compatibility, that exists between the principles of the American
polity and the principles of classical ("Greek") philosophy.

The 2004 addenda for the republished *Constitutionalist* draw upon
the two dozen reviews of the book after it was originally published in
1971. This part of the addenda includes the concluding passage in each review and, occasionally, an introductory passage as well. Thus, there is now,
within the covers of that book itself, a lively debate with my initial critics
concerning what I have ventured to say about the First Amendment. (See,
for a sequel to that 1970s debate, the addendum for this preface.)

The background and enduring principles of the First Amendment are
examined in Part One of the *Reflections* in this volume. Related materials,
including discussions of Magna Carta, the Declaration of Independence,
and the Confederate Constitution of 1861, may be found in my *Reflections on Constitutional Law*, published in 2006 by the University Press of
Kentucky.

I offer, in Part Two of the *Reflections* in this volume, suggestions
about how two dozen prominent First Amendment cases might be read
by someone who approaches both the freedom of speech tradition and
the text of the Constitution with the seriousness and the care that they
invite, require, and deserve. Technological and other developments have
made some issues, such as with respect to pornography and obscenity,
largely "obsolete," as a practical matter. (Consider, in Appendix N, one of
the "last-ditch" efforts to assert community prerogatives here. The 1989
memoranda provided there were anticipated by a 1954 memorandum,
provided in Appendix M, which also advocated a respect for due process
and the rule of law in controversial circumstances.)

Many other cases could be discussed in order to raise the questions
and to make the points dealt with in these *Reflections*. But it is hoped
that enough cases are glanced at to provide adequate applications of the
principles and issues confronted by the student of the First Amendment.
(Discussions of many more cases are available, of course, in *The Constitutionalist*, as well as in my 1995 commentary, *The Amendments to the
Constitution*.)

The importance of Hugo L. Black, as a Cold War–era champion of the
First Amendment, is recognized at the outset of the discussion of various

Supreme Court cases in Part Two. A personal note may be in order here: I met in Chicago, some years ago, Fred Korematsu of *In re Korematsu* fame, the case dealing with the Japanese Relocation Measures during the Second World War. I told Mr. Korematsu that Justice Black is widely believed to have written one of his best Opinions in my 1961 bar admission case and perhaps his worst in his 1944 case. "Unfortunately," I added, "the one he wrote about you was for the majority, while the one he wrote about me was in dissent."

I suggest, in my 2004 preface for *The Constitutionalist*, that my Second World War service as a flying officer confirmed my credentials as a citizen, deepening my ties with the Country in which my parents had settled before I was born. I then add:

> My service thereafter as a litigant meant, in effect, that the principles of the [American] regime became decisively mine, especially since others (the great majority all around me) had abandoned if not even repudiated them. Thus, whereas the Air Corps had helped me become fully a part of this Country, the [Illinois] bar admission controversy left me invoking a patriotism that most others no longer recognized. The United States became thereby, ever since the 1950s, more my Country than it was theirs, which is a remarkable state of affairs for someone who (I am told) did not know any English before he began grade school in St. Louis.

We can be reminded of what is said, in one of Euripides' plays, about the inestimable privilege of speaking freely that citizens enjoy at home (*Phoenician Maidens*, 390–92).

Vital to the principles of our regime is the importance of proper procedures upon which an effective freedom of speech in part depends. The rule of law, and especially a genuine respect for due process, can be critical here. It is such respect which is evident in the long-standing prohibition in the Anglo-American constitutional system of prior restraints (or previous restraints) of publications.

An effective freedom of speech depends, that is, on a comprehensive constitutionalism. Such constitutionalism is examined in my *Reflections on Constitutional Law* (which tracks the typical year-long course in constitutional law). It should be examined further, along of course with the Good, the True, and the Beautiful, in projected volumes (which should suggest, D.V., what is examined in specialized courses), including (using my working titles):

> *Reflections on Life, Death, and the Constitution;*
> *Reflections on Slavery and the Constitution;*
> *Reflections on Religion, the Divine, and the Constitution;*
> *Reflections on War, Peace, and the Constitution;*
> *Reflections on Race Relations and the Constitution;*
> *Reflections on Crime, Character, and the Constitution;*
> *Reflections on Property, Taxes, and the Constitution;*
> *Reflections on Habeas Corpus, the Bill of Rights, and the*
>   *Constitution.*

Changes in our lives since 1971 (when *The Constitutionalist* was first published) oblige us to wonder about the Future of the First Amendment. Serious challenges are faced, that is, by responsible citizens concerned both about what the community should *want* to do in shaping the character of citizens and about what the community *can* effectively do in circumstances radically affected by modern technology. The future here cannot help but remain highly uncertain.

As for the past, we have a distinguished journalist's recollection of "one crucial moment" during the June 1971 oral argument before the United States Supreme Court in the *Pentagon Papers Case.* A Justice asked counsel for the newspaper:

> Let us assume that when the members of the Court go back and open up this sealed record we find something there that absolutely convinces us that its disclosure would result in the sentencing to death of 100 young men whose only offense had been that they were 19 years old and had low draft numbers. What should we do?

The Justice, persisting with his inquiry, then asked, "You would say the Constitution requires that it be published, and that these men die, is that it?" Our account continues:

> [Counsel] gave an answer that troubled some First Amendment purists but that may have won the case for the newspapers: "No.

I am afraid that my inclinations to humanity overcome the somewhat more abstract devotion to the First Amendment in a case of
that sort. . . ." [*New York Review of Books*, April 7, 2005, pp. 10,
12.]

Counsel could well have added, however, the instructive reminder that the
Court's willingness to permit freedom of speech to be suppressed as much
as it was during the Cold War had probably contributed to the deaths in
Vietnam of tens of thousands, not only of the one hundred young Americans with low draft numbers conjured up by the Justice.

Concerns have been expressed about the repressive effects in this
Country of our responses to threats of Terrorism. Fortunately, we can still
discuss matters freely, if we are not obviously Muslim, especially as our
2003 Iraq Intervention appears more and more dubious. Even so, the
fearfulness evident, if not even officially promoted, among us is at times
unseemly for a Nation with our strength, heritage, and resources. I have,
in volume 29 of the *Oklahoma City University Law Review*, chronicled and
assessed our general responses during the first two years after the September 11, 2001, atrocities (with periodic updates published thereafter). Also
unseemly, of course, is the general breakdown, since the Second World
War, in that salutary discipline which should guide what we all say (as well
as do) in public.

Addendum

The lively debate I had with the initial critics of *The Constitutionalist*
about what I have ventured to say about the First Amendment can be carried further in response to a comment published in *Constitutional Commentary* (vol. 6, p. 358, n. 23 [1989]) which (so far as I can now recall) has
only recently come to my attention:

Professor George Anastaplo draws on the Declaration [of In-
dependence] to argue that "abridge" [in the First Amendment
text] should not be understood in reference to the English common law, but to the state of nature. Furthermore, he argues that
American colonists' resistance to Great Britain, which eventuated
in revolution, illustrates the intentions of the First Amendment:
"[T]he patriots were not willing to rely upon the judgment or

opinion of constituted authority, even though it was an authority to which they and their fathers had long acknowledged allegiance. The principle they *acted* upon seemed to be that the American citizen should be left free to criticize his government, even in the most decisive manner, when he believes that that government acts improperly." G. Anastaplo, *The Constitutionalist*, p. 109 (1971).

To argue that the First Amendment constitutionalized the right of revolution is remarkable, not only in light of the historical study that [Leonard] Levy provided [in his *Emergence of a Free Press* (1985)], but also in light of the distinction which John Locke made, and which the Americans drew on in the Declaration [of Independence], between legitimate governmental powers and the people's natural, or pre-political power. And since the "abridging" [in the First Amendment] extends also to freedom of the press and petitioning the government, how could these be referred to the state of nature? [See, on the "everyday political implications of the right of revolution sanctified by the Declaration of Independence," Anastaplo, *The Constitutionalist*, pp. 519–20.—G.A.]

The issue as to what I had said about "abridging" (developing thereby a suggestion originally made, so far as I know, by Malcolm P. Sharp [see *The Constitutionalist*, p. 528, n. 84]) is spoken to elsewhere in *The Constitutionalist*. Not only do I develop there what is characterized (by an always instructive scholar) in the 1989 *Constitutional Commentary* passage just quoted as my "remarkable" suggestion about the right of revolution but also I indicate there that the "abridging" of the First Amendment does not refer only to "the state of nature" (*The Constitutionalist*, p. 112 [notes omitted]):

What of the verb *abridging* [in the First Amendment]: does it connote only cutting down of previously defined legal rights, such as those that the common law establishes? Although the word may be used in this sense, it need not be limited to it, but may be used as well to refer to rights that do not have a technical legal basis and extent but rather can be said to be natural and even virtually unlimited.

Thus, there are instances in William Blackstone in which *abridge* is clearly meant to refer to a standard drawn from nature or from natural right. Nor is this usage restricted to Blackstone. It is consistent with usage prior to the writing of the First Amendment to employ *abridge* in circumstances where reference is made to the law of nature or to a standard of natural liberty to which man is entitled, of which he should not be deprived, but which is nevertheless rarely realized.

This approach to what may be called "natural liberty" or "natural right" is reflected in the Ninth Amendment, where rights are recognized which exist independently of explicit enumeration. One such right, I have suggested, is that right of revolution of which freedom of speech may be considered a continuing, if partial and restrained, exercise. And this right of revolution *is* a natural right, not dependent on any positive law or explicit acknowledgment by constituted authority. Thus, "abridging" is not limited to a context in which previously defined legal rights are involved (of which the common law would have been the principal expression). [See further, on "abridging," *The Constitutionalist*, pp. 5, 528–30, 656, 711.]

It can usefully be noticed here that Professor Levy acknowledges in the preface to his *Emergence of the Free Press* that he had made significant changes in it because of the criticisms that some of us had published about an earlier version of that book. My own review of that earlier version appeared in 39 *New York University Law Review* 735 (1964), evidently at the suggestion of Professor Edmond Cahn, who (I have been told) was prompted to do so by Justice Hugo L. Black (to whom I had sent a draft). See George Anastaplo, "Freedom of Speech and the First Amendment: Explorations," 21 *Texas Tech Law Review* 1941, 2022f (1990). Subsequent to his *Emergence* publication, Professor Levy solicited from me an article, "Political Philosophy of the Constitution" (my preferred title, "The Principles of the Constitution") for the *Encyclopedia of the American Constitution* (1986). See, for that article in its intended entirety, George Anastaplo, "Constitutionalism, the Rule of Rules: Explorations," 39 *Brandeis Law Journal* 17, 89–97 (2000). The article includes these observations, which bear on the matters discussed in this addendum (ibid., 93–94):

It seems to be taken for granted [in the Declaration of Independence] that the prudence relied upon in the Declaration and in the Constitution is generally to be promoted by free discussion of public issues, however salutary a temporary secrecy may be on occasion. Such discussion is presupposed by the relations of the various branches of government to one another and by what they say to each other. Thus, judges deliberate and set forth their conclusions in published opinions; the President, in exercising his veto power, is to give "his Objections," which objections are to be considered by Congress; the Members of Congress are protected in their exercise of freedom of speech as legislators. A continental freedom of speech and of the press was presupposed as well, even before the ratification of the First Amendment, by the repeated indications in the Constitution of 1787 that it is an ultimately sovereign people who establish and continually assess the government. The sovereignty of the People is central to the constitutional system, moderated though the People's control may be by their use of representatives and by their indirect selections of various other officers of government. . . .

See, for further discussions of these and related matters, both the bibliography in 20 *Northern Illinois University Law Review* 581–710 (2000), and the massive bibliography in political philosophy compiled by John A. Murley and published in 2005 by Lexington Books.

—George Anastaplo

Hyde Park
Chicago, Illinois
July 9, 2006

Part One

1. Plato's *Apology of Socrates*

I

The *Apology of Socrates* is one of the sacred texts upon which Western Civilization rests. The *Apology* consists of three speeches, re-created by Plato, which suggest what Socrates said in his defense during his capital trial in Athens in 399 B.C. The first speech is in response to the charges and evidence presented against him; the second is his contribution to the penalty-determination phase of the proceedings after he was found guilty; the third is in response to the sentence of death.

The indictment of Socrates, evidently initiated primarily by Anytus and Meletus, is said by him to present charges that he corrupts the youth and does not believe in the gods that the city does but rather in other *daimonia* that are novel. The reader can gather both from Socrates' remarks and from the public examination by him of Meletus what it was that had long troubled his fellow citizens about the way that he conducted himself in Athens. That Socrates continues to be troubling is indicated not only by the votes for his conviction and for his execution, but also by the instances (perhaps as many as a half-dozen altogether) when his remarks elicited or threatened to elicit outbursts from the five hundred Athenians trying the case.

It is evident both from what Socrates says and from how he is dealt with that the life dedicated to philosophy can be both liberating and dangerous (if not even, it might seem to some, suicidal). Thus, Socrates' sacrifice points up both the attractions and the risks of philosophy. Plato's dramatization of the Socratic career seems to be regarded by some as a secular anticipation of the career of Jesus.

II

Plato's *Apology* can be read as the first great document in the annals of the development of freedom of speech in the West. It is, of course, much

3

more than that—but it *is* that, at least. Thus, it can be invoked (along with Jesus' career) by such an illustrious champion of free speech as John Stuart Mill.

Perhaps the earliest predecessor to the *Apology of Socrates,* at least in "secular" literature, is the brief account in Book One of Homer's *Iliad* of the ill-fated intervention, by a common soldier, in a quarrel among the nobility. This meddler in the affairs of his betters, Thersites, is beaten for his presumptuousness. But, it can be suspected, the unlovely Thersites was not altogether without merit in what he had to say, however inept (Homer and Sophocles, among others, indicate) he may have been in how he conducted himself on that and earlier occasions.

Of course, it need not be assumed that Plato was a champion of freedom of speech as we understand it. But the account he presents of the career of Socrates, reinforced by the accounts of Xenophon, Aristotle, and others, *has* served to remind Westerners of the folly of suppressing conscientious men and women of talent. That folly is examined in a memorable fashion by John Milton in his *Areopagitica,* a pamphlet on behalf of unlicensed printing which draws on both the theological and the secular heritage of the West.

III

How *did* Socrates get into the trouble that he encountered in the year 399 B.C.? That trouble, he argues, is nothing new, for it had been decades, or half a lifetime, in the making. It all goes back, he says, to his having persisted in questioning distinguished Athenians who were regarded, not least by themselves, as wise.

This had followed upon the divinely inspired Word brought back from Delphi by Chaerephon, the surprising judgment by Apollo that no one was wiser than Socrates. Socrates, it seems, could not help so testing the god's assessment as to come to the conclusion (in support of Delphi) that those reputed to be wise believed they knew more than they did, whereas Socrates (unlike them) was aware of his ignorance. This discovery did not endear Socrates to those thus exposed, or to their partisans.

Among their partisans, it seems to be suggested, was the comic poet Aristophanes, who lampooned Socrates in the comedy *Clouds.* Even though Aristophanes shows Socrates as doing more than exposing the limitations of pretentious politicians, poets, and others of reputation, he does suggest (decades before the indictment of Socrates) the risks that Socrates ran because of teachings which openly challenged long-standing opinions. Some years after the death of Socrates, Plato (in his *Symposium*) indicates both the talents *and* the limitations of Aristophanes, a gifted man very much tethered to bodily functions.

IV

Socrates, at the time of his trial, was in his seventieth year. This meant that the Athenians *had* put up with him for decades. That he should have been indicted and tried as he eventually was testifies to radical changes in the circumstances of the city of Athens.

We are familiar with what changes in circumstances have done to the usually tolerant American public from time to time. The Civil War, with its suspensions of the writ of *habeas corpus*, and the First World War, with its Espionage Act prosecutions, come to mind. So do the crippling repressive measures resorted to among us during the Cold War.

The Athenians, during the trial of Socrates, were still suffering from the shock of the disastrous Peloponnesian War, which had cost them their remarkable empire. It did not help the supposedly apolitical Socrates that some of the talented young men who had once followed him had proved so subversive of the Athenian democracy. He probably was not taken seriously when he suggested that such men would have been even more harmful to their city if Socrates had not tried to moderate them.

V

Socrates indicates from the outset of his three speeches (and many times thereafter) how troubling, and even exasperatingly insolent, he could seem to be. His opening words display him addressing his tribunal as "men of Athens." He did this some three dozen times in his first speech, supplementing this form of address with simply "men" another dozen times in that speech.

That this is not a "respectful" form of address is evident from Meletus' uses of "judges" when *he* addresses the tribunal. Socrates makes explicit, in his third speech, what he had been doing—for he observes there that he can now address *some* of them as "judges," those who had revealed themselves as such by voting *for* him. Once again, Socrates indicates, he is wiser than most men, for he can distinguish the genuine article from the imitation.

Thus, it turned out, it was Socrates truly judging *them,* rather than submitting to being judged by them. Nor did it help his cause, as ordinarily understood, that he could suggest to the tribunal that a fit punishment for him would be permanent maintenance in the Prytaneum (that is, in the City Hall, with its guest quarters for visiting and other celebrities). It is understandable, therefore, that there should be a tradition that more of the Five Hundred trying the case voted for Socrates' execution than had just voted for his conviction.

VI

The more Socrates talked, at least in *this* forum, the more likely it was that people would be reminded of how exasperating he could be. Some might even have recognized that he was not as candid about the origins of his troubles as he purported to be. Some might have wondered, for example, how Socrates would account for why Chaerephon went to Delphi in the first place.

What *had* Socrates been doing in Athens which had led the impulsive Chaerephon to approach the priests of Apollo as he did? Must not Socrates have been challenging, in effect if not explicitly, those men usually regarded by Athenians to be wise? And must he not have already had talented young men intrigued by, if not even enjoying, what he was doing?

Perhaps the most mysterious aspect of all this is the report, evidently widely accepted in antiquity, that the Delphic oracle had indeed recognized Socrates as it did. This tale must have been particularly exasperating to those (such as Meletus) who regarded Socrates as an atheist. Some of them might even have been willing (in their patriotic piety) to indict as well the priests of Apollo for their foolishness in this matter, especially when Socrates chose to regard the Word from Delphi as virtually a command to conduct himself in the revolutionary way he did.

VII

Among the charges leveled against Socrates was that he relied upon divinities other than those recognized by the city. This probably referred to his long-standing evocation of a *daemonic* thing which, he said, always protected him from missteps. Then there were such aberrations as his occasional invocation of "the Dog," evidently an Egyptian oath.

But, during his trial, he also invoked Zeus several times and (oddly for a man) even Hera. Was this sort of talk regarded by most of the Five Hundred as a subterfuge, or at least as no more than the thoughtless expressions that people indulge in all the time? What may have ultimately counted for the Five Hundred was not what Socrates said now but what he, and perhaps even more those who "followed" him for years, had done.

If Pericles (who chanced to die during the Great Plague) had lived longer, the Athenians might have conducted themselves more prudently in waging their struggle with Sparta and her allies. Or if Socrates had not exceeded the typical life span of his day, he would never have been indicted. There is, that is, no necessity that a Socrates should be killed by his fellow citizens, however likely it may be that such a human being would always be "at risk."

VIII

That Socrates was "incorrigible" is suggested by what he says (at the end of his third speech) about how he would conduct himself in Hades (if there should indeed be any life after death). He would, he anticipates, question those he encountered there, especially about the controversies in which they had been involved on earth. It is not suggested, by the way, that *that* questioning by Socrates would be in "obedience" to any implicit divine decree.

It is evident, here as elsewhere, that much is to be said for the merits, and even for the great pleasure, of learning what is and is not. It is this capacity to learn, it seems to be suggested here and elsewhere, that permits the human being to partake of the divine. Furthermore, only thus can one know what one is doing as well as what one should probably do.

We can be reminded even here, however, of Socrates' provocativeness. For he *does* leave open a critical question, whatever may be indicated in other Platonic dialogues—the question of whether the soul of a human being survives death. The unending sleep that Socrates recognizes as a distinct possibility could seem to some of his critics to call into question, once again, the meaningfulness of whatever life human beings and their communities have on earth as pious creatures.

IX

However all this may be, the inspiration offered by the *Apology* can usefully be considered vital to the most serious purposes of the First Amendment. The claims of what *we* call "conscience" are elevated. And citizens can be encouraged thereby to speak out about the issues of concern to the community.

This is not to suggest that Socrates is a republican. Indeed, he questions, at least in the *Apology*, whether it is either safe or useful for someone with his talents and interests to engage in politics at all. But he does recall, also in the *Apology* and not without pride, the risks he had undertaken both as a soldier and as a citizen.

He had been, as a citizen, what we would call "non-partisan." That is, he risked his life by opposing (on separate occasions) democratic and oligarchic tyrannies which had made unjust demands upon him. By such responses to injustice, and the way he recalled them, he contributed significantly to the development of what we (in opposition to a dependence on "accident and force") have come to treasure as *constitutionalism*.

2. The Ministry of St. Paul

I

The Western tradition, upon which Anglo-American constitutionalism very much depends, is rooted in both the Classics and the Bible. Freedom of speech, which is so critical to American constitutionalism, claims the career of Socrates as one of its sources. Another source may be discovered, with some plausibility, in the career of St. Paul.

Paul (born Saul, of Tarsus) exhibits in his makeup the combined influences of Judaism, the Roman Empire, and the Greek language. By his time, we are told, there may have been more Jews living in other places governed by Rome than were living in the Holy Land. But, as in Paul's case, most of those Jews probably remained more or less loyal to the Way of their Fathers.

Paul himself was a particularly pious Jew. He first came to public notice, so far as we know, as a zealous persecutor of the people later to be known as Christians. It was in the course of such a campaign that he had, on the road to Damascus, the shattering revelation which turned him into perhaps the most influential missionary in the service of the crucified Jesus.

II

The Gentiles converted by Paul, he argued, should not have to become practicing Jews in order to be effectively Christian. The corporeal aspects of Judaism were not to be obligatory for Gentiles receptive to the teachings of Jesus. There could be seen here, in the Pauline dispensation, a move from a faith determined primarily by birth to a faith determined (at least in principle) primarily by choice.

This meant that the traditional Jewish reliance upon a people would not be of use for the Christian community. At first, of course, all or al-

9

most all Christians were Jewish both in their origins and in many of their observances. But it was not long before Christian Gentiles outnumbered Jewish Christians.

This history leaves us with questions about the meaning of a "people." The Christian departure from traditional Jewish arrangements corresponds to what the United States has done in distinguishing itself from the other nations in the world. This Country is made up, that is, almost completely of immigrant peoples who are bound together by creed or doctrine, not by blood.

III

The movement from Judaism to Christianity is most obvious with respect to rituals and food. Eventually, many Christians would come to be largely unaware of what the daily life of Jews required. Even so, it *is* Judaism from which Paul moved—and upon which he built.

Preaching would become at least as important in the life of the Christian community as *prophecy* had been among the Jews. Lowered in importance, for Christians, would be the political life of the community. One manifestation of these changes is the elimination of *the Law* as that by which the religious community is primarily guided.

The movement is, then, from deeds to words. Thus, the Hebrew Bible opens with an account of the deeds of Creation. The Greek Bible has its culminating Gospel open with an account of the all-encompassing Logos.

IV

It can be instructive to notice the distinctive vocabulary of Christianity, especially in its Greek origins. Overarching the movement from the Old Way to the New is the movement from a rigorous monotheism to a triune divinity. This is a development more apparent in the post-biblical literature of Christians than it may be in their earliest texts.

The Christian grounding in the Greek language means, among other things, that a vocabulary is used which had been shaped somewhat by the philosophical tradition. This may be seen in the recourse to *phusis,* or *nature,* a term which does *not* have its equivalent in the Hebrew Bible. Nor is it found in the Gospels, which are closer in spirit than "later" texts are to the Judaic tradition.

Nature comes into its own in the Book of Acts and in the Epistles. There, for the most part, Greek-speakers are addressed in language familiar to them. Wherever *nature* is relied upon, even if only tacitly, conventions (however long-standing) can in effect be called into question.

V

The shift in vocabulary associated with Christianity is not limited to departures from the ways and thought of the Jews. That shift can include departures as well from Classical Greek. This may be seen in what happens, in the Greek Bible, to the word *parresia.*

Parresia, as outspokenness, was regarded in Classical texts, depending on the circumstances, as either commendable or questionable. In fact, *parresia* tended to be something to be avoided by the Greek citizen seeking a proper balance in one's life, a condition that the dedicated Christian regarded as insufficient for the good of one's soul. The Christian, or would-be Christian, was urged to witness frankly to what he believed.

Thus, one should be outspoken in one's faith so much that political consequences, including how the authorities might deal with one, should be disregarded—and all this with a view to one's eternal salvation. Such frankness of speech is particularly called for in the affirmation of one's faith, even to the extent of openly calling into question the deeds and the doctrines of those in authority. There may be seen, in this endorsement of frankness in the face of authority, an attitude associated with modern freedom of speech.

VI

The emphasis on the personal, instead of on the political and social (and even on the intellectual), leads to considerable reliance by Christians on the *conscience.* This term also emerges in the Book of Acts and the Epistles. It, too, is a term not relied upon either by Judaism or by Classical Greece.

Thus, Aristotle could discuss at considerable length the moral life of citizens without ever having to use such a term as *conscience.* The Classical Greeks made much instead of *honor* and *shame,* which means that the typical citizen looks outward, rather than inward, for guidance. Perhaps reliance on the conscience was likely, if not even necessary, inasmuch as

Christians repudiated that primacy of the political and social order found both among the Ancient Jews and among the Classical Greeks.

Conscience may be related to the sense of *pollution* that Jews attempt to avoid, but pollution itself is very much dependent on the rules that govern how Jews should live. Conscience is very much a personal guide, even though it is likely to be shaped and nurtured by one's religious community. Such an emphasis is very much in accordance with the Christian elevation of the *self* as something entitled to a perhaps unprecedented respect ultimately independent of any assessment or control by the community.

VII

One consequence of an emphasis upon the *self* may be to make much of self-preservation. Such preservation can be either spiritual or physical. As circumstances change, therefore, human beings can find themselves concerned more about their personal well-being *here and now* than about their personal well-being *through eternity.*

A further consequence, when self-centeredness is made much of, is a depreciation of the status of *prudence.* There may still be that cunning or canniness in the service of self-interest, which is exhibited by "the wise guy." But this does little more than mimic that prudence which is grounded, ultimately, in a respect for that Common Good which is informed by a somewhat philosophical understanding.

The political order, however much it may be influenced by chance, is thereby taken seriously by the prudent (and somewhat self-regarding) human being as essential for securing the Common Good. The perspective of the Christian tends to be significantly different, with the things of this world regarded as of little enduring significance. One may be encouraged to obey the earthly rulers one happens to have, at least so long as one is not called on either to do obviously dreadful things or to disavow one's faith.

VIII

Even so, the non-political (if not even the *anti-*political) emphasis of early Christians developed in an empire very much governed by laws which took "this world" seriously. The importance of the rule of law in the Roman Empire is exhibited during Paul's career. He was, for example, evidently very much aware of the prerogatives of his Roman citizenship.

It is remarkable that Paul was able, on more than one occasion, to invoke those prerogatives. Nothing is said in these biblical accounts about how one established one's Roman citizenship—but it is clear (or so it is said) that once it was established, one had to be treated with far more consideration than were the "natives" that the Romans ruled all over their empire. This could even mean, for example, that one would, if execution was called for, be beheaded rather than be crucified.

The Roman Catholic Church, it can be said, inherited and adapted to its spiritual purposes the legal apparatus of the Roman state. This could mean, among other things, that the Protestant Reformation was somewhat "political" in its campaign for independence. One of the consequences of the Reformation may have been that enhanced emphasis upon the Self seen in the development among us, since the late nineteenth century, of the Right to Privacy.

IX

To make much of the Right to Privacy seems to make more of the Self than of the Citizen. Such a development would have seemed strange both to the Ancient Jew and to the Classical Greek. They both tended to exhibit a far greater dependence upon a community, for any meaningful existence for the typical human being, than do their successors.

Paul's declaration of independence from the conventional allegiances of his day may be seen in his insistence that the old distinctions between Jew and Gentile and even between male and female no longer mattered. All that matters, wherever one may be, is one's personal relation with the Resurrected Christ. To this relation one should testify freely, without regard for political or legal consequences.

We can be reminded here of the *parresia* that Christianity elevated to a duty in the service of personal salvation, a duty which countenanced if it did not even encourage martyrdom. "Freedom of speech," as it developed in the Anglo-American tradition, is perhaps too political for Pauline tastes. It may even be said to be "natural" that an emphasis upon "the Pursuit of Happiness" has contributed, at least among us, to a subordination of the traditional and patriotic "freedom of speech" to the much more modern and ostensibly liberating "freedom of expression."

3. Thomas More and Parliamentary Immunity (1521)

I

A 1521 petition to King Henry VIII, by Sir Thomas More as Speaker of the House of Commons, is said to be the earliest document in which parliamentary freedom of speech is recognized. It is also said that there had been, theretofore, the *practice* of respecting parliamentary immunity. Such immunity may even be intrinsic to (as well as vital for) the workings of any legislative body that is entrusted with serving the good of a community.

The precise term "freedom of speech" is not used in More's petition (which is set forth in Appendix D of this volume). The closest to this term may be seen in the assurance requested that a Member of the House of Commons might be able "boldlye in every thinge incident among us to declare his advise" without having to fear the consequences of the royal displeasure. "Freedom of speech" did come to be used to identify, in English constitutional documents and discussions, the parliamentary privilege.

It was from this English tradition that the right of freedom of speech evidently found its way into American constitutional law. First, it was the immunity that was taken for granted in Colonial legislatures and other councils. Then, as the ultimate sovereignty of the American People came to be recognized, freedom of speech also came to be recognized as essential to an effective exercise by the People of their ultimate authority, an authority repeatedly asserted in American documents.

II

If freedom of speech is indeed rooted in English parliamentary experience, it is obviously (one might even say, naturally) associated primarily with political discourse. It is such discourse that is intended to be protected when traditional parliamentary immunity is provided for in the Articles of Confederation and thereafter in the Constitution of 1787. It is also taken for granted by both the legislatures and the citizens of the several States, even when not explicitly recognized in State constitutions.

It might be sensed that the right to freedom of speech is implicit as well in the negotiations associated in 1215 with Magna Carta. After all, the Barons had told their King, in no uncertain terms, what troubled them about the way he had conducted himself. And, of course, they then had the military forces necessary to assure themselves that they could safely do (at least for the time being) what they were attempting.

Perhaps the most momentous exercise of freedom of speech on this continent was when the People of the Thirteen Colonies collected their grievances in the Declaration of Independence. They were confident that they could and should speak freely about what troubled them about the recent doings of the British government. Such an exhibition on their part was one aspect of the independence that they insisted upon on that occasion.

III

Two decades before Thomas More became Speaker of the House of Commons, he had served in that body. This was during the reign of Henry VII, who was evidently displeased by what the young More ventured to say in opposition to a royal proposal. It is said that because of this the More family, and especially Thomas More's father, were treated unkindly by that King.

But by the time of the latter part of the reign of Henry VIII, Thomas More was in good standing at the Palace. His elevation to the Speakership was evidently in compliance with the King's desire. The massiveness of royal power is reflected in the obsequiousness employed by Thomas More in this petition, with one-third of his lines including flattering references to the King.

Obsequiousness was evidently the order of the day, as may be seen also in how Thomas More spoke to and of Cardinal Wolsey when the Cardinal was Chancellor. This could be followed by the harsh language shamelessly used against Wolsey by More when the Cardinal fell from royal grace. The latent power of the Throne may even be seen in Magna Carta, with its inclusion of a royal pardon as part of what the temporarily subdued King John was obliged to concede.

IV

The power of Henry VIII was reflected in the choice of Thomas More as Speaker of the House. Later it could be seen in the selection of More as Chancellor, the most powerful temporal post in the kingdom after the King. In fact, the very existence of any particular Parliament has always depended upon a royal summons.

The obsequiousness of Henry's subjects evidently pleased him, especially when a variety of flattering appellations could be developed. Even so, the King may have been tacitly instructed thereby in *how* he should conduct himself. Was it not being suggested, in effect, that he should so act as to deserve what was said of him?

Perhaps the most extreme form of flattery under which Henry suffered could be seen in the six marriages he contracted. Although that kind of flattery can be gratifying, at least for a while, one may eventually be moved to wonder whether one is loved for oneself alone, rather than for the powers and gifts at one's disposal. One can be reminded here of the girl, immortalized by William Butler Yeats, who wanted to be loved for herself alone, and not for her wonderful yellow hair.

V

Critical as parliamentary freedom of speech is, it does recognize (and, indeed, may be requested because of) the considerable power exercised by the Monarch (or Executive). The ambition, so to speak, of freedom of speech may ultimately be directed at the subjugation of the Executive. It is this that we see done in various ways by the Constitution of 1787.

Thus, the existence of our Congress does *not* depend on the summons or pleasure of any President. Rather, it depends, for the most part, on constitutional directives, subject to authorized modifications by Congress, which is itself ultimately subject to the People. In addition, it even depends upon Congress who becomes President as well as who remains President—that very Congress which can enact legislation without the consent of (that is, despite any veto by) the President.

At the core of this arrangement is the sovereignty of the People. That sovereignty is evident not only in various election processes but, even more, in the ultimate authority of the People to make and to unmake (that is, to amend) the Constitution of the Country. This means that the National freedom of speech extends to the consideration of how a people should organize itself and thereafter live.

VI

It is evident, from the opening part of the Thomas More petition, that the Speaker anticipates that he might, on occasion, have to return to the House with a report of royal displeasure. This is discreetly put by him as seeking clarification from the House. But, it seems, the Commons is expected to recognize on such occasions what the King *requires* to be done.

The American Congress is hardly likely to be so vulnerable, especially since it does have the power to override Executive vetoes. Thus, as a practical matter, it may not be the Congress as a whole which needs protection of freedom of speech; rather, that is needed most by unpopular Members of either House of Congress, Members that the Congress would not be likely to protect by threatening the Executive with retaliatory measures. Such unpopular Members need the assurance of protection from Executive oppression which the traditional parliamentary immunity offers.

It is, however, an immunity that does not protect the unpopular Member from *all* retaliation. He may still be expelled from a House of Congress "with the Concurrence of two-thirds." And, of course, such a Member may be replaced, at the next election, by his constituents.

VII

We have noticed the obvious power of Henry VIII, power reflected in the constant flattery to which the King was evidently accustomed. But the limitations of even this King's power are suggested by the difficulty he had controlling the succession. His many marriages reflect his desire to guide events beyond the grave.

Of course, he did not recognize that he chanced to have in one of his daughters the makings of probably the greatest of the English Monarchs. And, it seems, neither he nor Elizabeth could see how vulnerable the Throne could become. The second Monarch after Elizabeth lost his head—and the English Monarchy has never been the same since.

Charles I got into the fatal trouble he did when he tried to raise money without having to depend upon an unreliable Parliament. He was not the last English-speaking Executive who believed that he knew better than a parliamentary body what his country needed. A recent instance of Executive presumptuousness could be seen in the Iran arms/Contra aid shenanigans in this Country.

VIII

We can return to Thomas More, the patron saint, so to speak, of the freedom of speech. He is celebrated now, even canonized, for the opposition he manifested (although not, at the outset of his troubles, in explicit language) to the King's ecclesiastic ambitions. Both the King and he should have known better than to allow their differences to develop as they did.

More himself was not without serious faults, aside from those that the King attributed to him. Thus he, as Chancellor, was quite harsh in his attacks on "heretics." When one sees such men in power, one can suspect that their past obsequiousness has not been good for their character.

One can be reminded, upon recalling Thomas More in power, of how Isaac Newton (two centuries later) conducted himself as Master of the Royal Mint. He was ruthless in his extirpation of counterfeiters—and yet he had personally expended considerable time and resources attempting to bring about transformations in metals through alchemy that would have made conventional counterfeiters seem mere triflers by comparison. Similarly, Thomas More's merciless campaign against heretics helped reinforce the notion of "heresy"—and it contributed perhaps to his running the risk of eventually appearing to be a dangerous heretic himself.

IX

The history of Magna Carta is useful to keep in mind when considering how freedom of speech, in Parliament and out, came to be established. Magna Carta *was* accepted by King John in 1215, but thereafter (when he was once again physically safe) he repudiated it. There was, in fact, a sequence of royal acceptances and repudiations before Magna Carta became firmly established in the hearts, souls, and laws of the English people.

Much the same can be said to have happened with freedom of speech, both in legislative bodies and in communities at large. Eventually it could come to be regarded as obviously necessary in a republican regime. It could also come to be exercised freely from time to time by those who even used it to argue for its curtailment when it was exercised by troublesome people.

It is left, then, to consistent champions of freedom of speech to make the arguments needed for its viability, including the argument that appearances can be deceiving. Particularly to be recognized, then, is the fact, as Thomas More put it, that just "as much folly is uttered with painted polished speache, so [also] many, [who are] boystyous and rude in language, see deepe indeed, and give right substanciall councell." Among the substantial counsels available are those offered by men and women who use polished speech in making the case for risking the boisterousness that is sometimes needed to shake us out of our complacent (if not even dangerous) self-satisfaction.

4. John Milton's *Areopagitica* (1644)

I

"As everyone knows," we have been reminded by Barbara K. Lewalski, "[John] Milton's argument [in the *Areopagitica*], couched in poetic imagery and high rhetoric, has become a cornerstone in the liberal defense of freedom of speech, press, and thought." This document is particularly important with respect to freedom of the press, as traditionally understood. Freedom of speech, insofar as it *is* different, can be said to depend, for its cornerstone, upon the traditional parliamentary immunity, an immunity reaffirmed in such declarations as the English Bill of Rights of 1689.

The "high rhetoric" referred to begins with the title and epigraph for this pamphlet. Reference is made in its title to the Areopagus, an important Athenian tribunal. The reader can be reminded thereby of a speech by Isocrates, the *Areopagiticus,* which had been directed to that tribunal, an institution to which the English Parliament is implicitly likened by Milton.

His epigraph from Euripides draws on a speech attributed to Theseus, the legendary founder of Athens. The argument thereafter draws freely upon Classical and other literary sources, as Milton implicitly likens himself to a citizen of the Athenian democracy. Milton's learning is evident throughout, but in such a way as to make him less accessible to the typical reader today than is, say, the Socrates of Plato's *Apology,* a speaker in fact before an Athenian tribunal.

II

The principal concern expressed by Milton is with respect to the Licensing Act enacted by Parliament in 1643. This concern took the form, in liberty of the press discussions during the ensuing century, of opposition to previous, or prior, restraints of publications. Such restraints often tended, in effect, toward a system of censorship.

Systematic censorship is attacked as destructive of honest, and useful, criticism of public measures. Costs and delays can be expected, as well as unfortunate accommodations by authors to the current orthodoxy, with matters likely to deteriorate as the quality of the censoring declines, something to be expected, if only because of the tedium of a censor's duties. And if there are indeed corrupting materials being dealt with routinely by the system, what is the effect of systematic review of such materials likely to be on the character of the typical censor?

Milton's efforts did not win an immediate repeal of the Licensing Act. On the other hand, he himself, an influential member of the dominant political movement of the day, was not prosecuted for having published his pamphlet without a license, even though his name is presented boldly on its cover. But, it seems, the printer and bookseller were far more vulnerable, which may account for why their names were omitted from the title page.

III

The boldness of Milton is not limited to his presuming to publish without a license. His language throughout is that of a human being determined to be, and to seem to be, free. There is not here, despite the closing paean to Parliament, the determined obsequiousness, in the face of authority, of Thomas More's generation a century earlier.

Particularly criticized by Milton, and others of like mind, is any *system* which subjects writings to official scrutiny before publication. Thus, William Blackstone, more than a century later, could still consider the prohibition of prior, or previous, restraints the most important feature of liberty of the press. The repudiation of prior restraint means, in effect, that the activity of publishing will be treated like most other activities of which the law takes notice.

Thus, the publisher (or printer) would always have the benefit, in his dealings with government, of due process of law, something which can inhibit considerably even the most determined "thought police." It should not be forgotten that a licensor can suppress scores of publications with far less effort and publicity than can be expected during the prosecution of a single offending printer because of the contents of what has been published (not simply because he has published without a license, which can be fairly easily established). Of course, some printers have always been willing to subject themselves to pre-publication review in order to make it highly likely that they would not be troubled thereafter for whatever they do publish.

IV

The traditional arguments against prior restraints usually acknowledged that prosecutions could properly be directed against the publication of offensive matter. Such offensiveness could consist of treasonable utterance, sedition, fraud, blasphemy, obscenity, and the like. This is aside from private actions for libel, unfair competition, infringement of copyright, and the like.

Milton, too, recognizes that post-publication prosecution might sometimes be in order. He can refer to some publications as so offensive to piety and morality as to be worthy of punishment. He can even seem to permit pre-publication suppression of Papist materials, somewhat in the spirit of those (during the Cold War) who argued that members of the Communist Party of the United States should not be permitted in this Country the freedom that they would deny to others if they should ever gain power here.

But Milton does not say how the authorities would be able to suppress in advance the suppressible if there should not be a systematic review of all potential publications. Besides, however much Milton's arguments are directed primarily against the institution of censorship, it is evident that those arguments also have the effect of questioning many of the other restraints upon public discussions. This meant, for example, that Papists too could be the beneficiaries of the spirit of openness generated in part by Milton in his *Areopagitica* (as also by his arguments in favor of relaxing restrictions on divorce).

V

The openness promoted by Milton seems to rest, to a significant degree, upon the veneration he personally has for books. So deeply ingrained is this among us as well that we can have a visceral reaction to such scenes as those depicting Germany's Nazis presiding over piles of burning books. One might wonder, however, whether contemporary technological developments, such as the Internet, place both books and the proper supervision of public utterances in even more jeopardy.

Milton is moved to exclaim, "[A]s good almost kill a Man as kill a good Book; who kills a Man kills a reasonable creature, Gods Image; but hee who destroyes a good Booke, kills reason it selfe, kills the Image of God, as it were in the eye." This kind of talk should be compared with the insistence by Plato's Socrates that an unchanging text is markedly inferior to ever-adapting conversation. Milton does not address this argument, but he does take issue with what he considers to be the Platonic endorsement of a systematic censorship of publications.

Insofar as Milton is significantly poetic in his argument here, he can remind us of the ancient quarrel between poetry and philosophy that Socrates spoke of. To the extent that Milton *is* poetic in his arguments here about public policy, is he not as attractive and hence as common-sensical as sound public policy requires? That is, his language may have helped him secure and retain more of an audience than would have been likely if he had relied on unadorned prose, however difficult his poetic language may sometimes seem today.

VI

What, nevertheless, is the commonsensical response to Milton's rapturous accounts of the power of truth? One such account includes his celebrated observation, "Let [Truth] and Falshood grapple; who ever knew Truth put to the wors, in a free and open encounter." Of course, there *is* the question of what the conditions are for "a free and open encounter."

Among the relevant conditions here is the information, bearing on any issue of the moment, that is generally available. Even more important is the caliber of the people engaged in the "grappl[ing]." After all, it *is* recognized in the epigraph taken by Milton from Euripides that some "free-born" citizens may not be qualified to speak usefully on a particular occasion.

It is not a concern of Milton, in this "Speech," to prescribe the proper training of the citizen body, except to the extent that exercises of liberty may help equip citizens to deal sensibly with the issues of the day. No doubt, the religious practices of the community (if they are decent) are counted on to continue to have a beneficent effect on the character of citizens. But is a steady supervision of what is said and shown needed to maintain, or if need be to elevate, the character required for responsible self-government?

VII

It may be, however, that the deepest truths are reliably accessible to only a few. This could mean that the most meaningful encounters depend upon carefully selected contenders. This could also mean that some communities are better equipped than others for the robust debate that Milton considers useful.

He himself does seem to recognize the special competence of the English for the kind of constitutional system advocated. But there is little if anything said about how England got to be the way it is—or about how whatever favorable condition it happens to enjoy can be maintained. Does, for example, its geography help it to become and to remain what it is, a community somewhat isolated from Continental fevers, the kind of advantage which chanced to be shared by the United States during its formative centuries?

It may be difficult to exaggerate here the importance in these matters of the English language, not least because of the influence of William Shakespeare. That freedom-minded influence, which includes that playwright's lessons about the Roman Republic, may be reflected in the use of Roman terms and names (such as the Publius of *The Federalist*) by the founding generations in this Country. The significance here of Shakespeare is illustrated by a comparison of his sympathetic handling of Brutus and Cassius with the ferocious treatment of them by Dante (as betrayers of Julius Caesar) in the concluding canto of his *Inferno*.

VIII

Milton recognizes that England is regarded with respect, in Europe, for its liberty. It is from the Continent that there have come the practices and institutions that threaten English liberties, with the repressive measures associated then with the Roman Catholic Church being particularly troubling. It is noteworthy that Milton visited, in Italy, the legendary Galileo, who was spending the last years of his life under house arrest after running afoul of the Inquisition.

Milton, in his critique of the Church and its Inquisition, is himself very much a Christian. Particularly significant is his repeated reliance on *conscience* (more than a half-dozen times), something which (we have seen) does not have to be relied upon by pre-Christian authorities. Such intellectual authorities would perhaps have been concerned lest an emphasis on something like conscience tend to lead both to undue self-centeredness and to an undisciplined variety.

These authorities might also have questioned any Miltonic suggestion that one should welcome, if not deliberately devise, tests of the soul. They might even endorse the prayer that one not be led into temptation. They might go so far as to suggest that a well-ordered community recognizes the temptations that its citizens might encounter—and makes reasonable efforts to minimize them.

IX

A decent community also recognizes that its most talented members should be treasured. It was recognition of Milton's stature as a poet which evidently helped protect him, during the Restoration (beginning in 1660), from the harsher retribution suffered by other leaders of his political movement. It had been that movement which had culminated in the execution of Charles I in 1649.

Restoration or not, the seeds of a new way, both political and intellectual, had been sown. Even on the Continent, although it was not generally grasped at the time, the persecution of Galileo may have been the last major spasm of a fading system. And in England, the Restoration was followed, three decades later, by still another Revolution, which left parliamentary government permanently in control of the affairs of the country.

That "Glorious Revolution" proclaimed itself through the Bill of Rights of 1689. This declaration, very much in the spirit of Milton's *Areopagitica,* included among its provisions the insistence that "it is the Right of the Subjects to petition the King and all Committments [that is, arrests] and Prosecutions for such Petitioning are Illegall." Complementing what we have heard about the *Areopagitica* serving as the "cornerstone" upon which freedom of speech can rest is what is reported by Roy Flanagan about its conspicuous elevation: "The great dining hall at Victoria College of the University of Toronto contains the full text of *Areopagitica* as a ribbon of gold-leaf single-lined band running around the entire room."

5. William Blackstone, Patrick Henry, and Edmund Burke on Liberty (1765–1790)

I

William Blackstone brought his four-volume *Commentaries on the Laws of England* to a close with the chapter "Of the Rise, Progress, and Gradual Improvements, of the Laws of England." He proposed "to mark out [there] some outline of an English juridical history, by taking a chronological view of the state of our laws, and their successive mutations at different periods of time." This 1769 Blackstonian account, of "an English juridical history," provided many American lawyers (for a century thereafter) an instructive, if not even an authoritative, account of English (and hence American) constitutional history prior to 1776.

"The several periods, under which I shall consider the state of our legal polity," Blackstone wrote, "are the following six":

> 1. From the earliest times to the Norman conquest [in 1066]: 2. From the Norman conquest to the reign of king Edward the first [1272–1307]: 3. From thence to the reformation [1509–1603]: 4. From the reformation to the restoration of king Charles the second [in 1660]: 5. From thence to the revolution in 1688: 6. From the revolution to the present time [1769].

This concluding chapter of the *Commentaries* ends with the observation: "The protection of THE LIBERTY OF BRITAIN is a duty which they owe to themselves, who enjoy it; to their ancestors, who transmitted it down; and to their posterity, who will claim at their hands this, the best birthright, and noblest inheritance of mankind." An American scholar, Thomas A. Green, calling this concluding chapter "a Whig panegyric," described it in language echoing Blackstone's enthusiasm:

Sweeping in scope, majestic in style, this final paean to the elegance, wisdom, and humanity of English laws displays both Blackstone the optimistic and complacent eighteenth-century gentleman and Blackstone the proponent of measured reform. It was the duty of the nobility and gentlemen in Parliament "to sustain, to repair, to beautify this noble pile."

The American lawyers who relied on Blackstone had reservations, of course, about his respect for, if not even his dependence upon, both the Monarchy and the Church of England. The six-stage history that Blackstone laid out has come to be supplemented, on our side of the Atlantic, by a seventh stage: the emergence of the American Republic grounded in Anglo-American constitutionalism. That emergence was heralded by adventurous Englishmen such as Patrick Henry.

II

Blackstone's historical account traces the development in Great Britain of an effective recognition of liberty under law. This development has consisted in large part, he argues, of a restoration of the liberty that had prevailed "from the earliest times" among the Saxons—that is, before "the Norman Conquest." One can wonder whether this is one of those salutary "pious fictions" that Blackstone endorses for a healthy system of law.

Perhaps this use of the Saxons serves for him as a respectable means for drawing upon a vision of "the best regime." Certainly, the specialness of English liberty is insisted upon. The suspicion of Continental influences, of which the vigorous Normans had been carriers, is something that continues down to our day, as may be seen in the tentativeness of the English, with respect both to the European Union and to European currency.

A generation after Blackstone, the suspicion of Continental influences found expression in the Napoleonic Wars. Another way of putting the differences here is to distinguish the Civil Code from the Common Law. Once Americans had separated themselves politically from the English, with the help of the French, they too could exhibit toward Continental influences many of the reservations that they had acquired with their language and their political heritage from the English.

III

A major stage in the restoration of the liberty "natural" for Englishmen was the recourse to Magna Carta. That Charter, originally exacted from King John in 1215, had to be affirmed several times by Monarchs before it was permanently established. It is seen by Blackstone as, at least in part, a repudiation of Continental impositions upon the English Constitution.

Various provisions of Magna Carta are reviewed, some of which (such as "grievances incident to feudal tenures"), although "of no small moment at [that] time," can now seem to the inattentive "but of trifling concern." Other provisions, of course, are generally still recognized as vital to the English regime. Thus, Blackstone can conclude his review of the provisions of Magna Carta thus: "And, lastly, (which alone would have merited the title that it bears, of the *great* charter), it protected every individual of the nation in the free enjoyment of his life, his liberty, and his property, unless declared to be forfeited by the judgment of his peers or the law of the land."

Further on, Blackstone criticizes the use of force against Monarchs. But, in making as much as he does of Magna Carta, he does not choose to notice that "the great charter of King John" had been coerced from him by the Barons at Runnymede. However important that charter was, much remained to be done to return England to the condition it was said to have been in before William the Norman imposed himself upon the Saxons.

IV

Among the reforms yet to be made was "the reformation of religion, under Henry the eighth, and his children [1509–1603]." The "usurped power of the pope [was] now for ever routed and destroyed, all his connexions with this island [England] cut off, the crown restored to it's supremacy over spiritual men and causes, and the patronage of bishoprichs [was] once more indisputably vested in the king." These changes meant (it is said) that "the old Saxon constitution with regard to *ecclesiastical* polity [was substantially] restored."

Even so, despotism could reassert itself, particularly during the reign of Henry VIII. It was then that "the royal prerogative was . . . strained to a very tyrannical and oppressive height." Even worse, Blackstone reports, the royal prerogative's "encroachments were established by law, under the sanction of those pusillanimous parliaments, one of which to it's eternal disgrace passed a statute, whereby it was enacted that the king's proclamation should have the force of acts of parliament, and others concurred in the creation of [an] amazing heap of wild and new-fangled treasons."

The great Elizabeth also comes in for reproach: "For, though in general she was a wise and excellent princess, and loved her people, though in her time trade flourished, riches increased, the laws were duly administred, the nation was respected abroad, and the people happy at home, yet, the encrease of the power of the star-chamber, and the erection of the high-commission court in matters ecclesiastical, were the work of her reign." Blackstone continues, "She also kept her parliaments at a very awful distance: and in many particulars she, at times, would carry the prerogatives as high as her most arbitrary predecessor." And he can assess Elizabeth thus:

> It is true, she very seldom exerted this prerogative, so as to oppress individuals; but still she had it to exert: and therefore the felicity of her reign depended more on her want of opportunity and inclination, than [on] want of power, to play the tyrant.

V

However well-behaved Elizabeth generally was, Blackstone observes, "these were not those golden days of genuine liberty, that we formerly were taught to believe: for surely, the true liberty of the subject consists not so much in the gracious behaviour, as in the limited power, of the sovereign." It is "true liberty"—an ordered and predictable liberty, with the legislature dominant—for which, too, the Constitution of 1787 provides. Indeed, much of the history of English, and later of Anglo-American, constitutional development, is reflected in that Constitution and its Bill of Rights of 1791.

Thus, various provisions in such instruments were designed to limit claims of executive prerogatives, with special emphasis upon the President as an officer whose primary duty is to execute laws enacted (with *or without* his approval) by Congress. Particularly to be noticed is the suppression of recourse to "wild and new-fangled treasons," a recourse which is particularly ominous for a proper freedom of speech. It is the usefulness of an unfettered parliamentary freedom of speech that Thomas More, as Speaker of the House of Commons, spoke of in his 1521 petition to Henry VIII.

Well before American constitutional developments, there had been, after Henry, Elizabeth, and their much-tossed-about successors, critical developments in Britain. Particularly to be noticed is the Habeas Corpus Act of 1679, which provided "a second magna carta as beneficial and effectual as that of Runing-Mede." Blackstone goes so far as to suggest, "*Magna carta* only in general terms, declared, that no man shall be imprisoned contrary to law: the *habeas corpus* act points him out effectual means, as well to release himself, though committed even by the king in council, as to punish all those who shall thus unconstitutionally misuse him."

VI

Blackstone notes, "The point of time at which I would chuse to fix [the] *theoretical* perfection of our public law, is the year 1679; after the *habeas corpus* act was passed, and that for licensing the press had expired: though the years which immediately followed it were times of great *practical* oppression." There had been, after the death of Elizabeth in 1603, seven decades of turmoil before the "theoretical perfection" of public law could be realized. Included in that turmoil had been what the "popular leaders" had done, "with deliberate solemnity," when they resorted to "the trial and murder of their king."

We have noticed that Blackstone did not register any disapproval of the Barons' coercion of their King at Runnymede. Reprehensible as the execution of Charles I (in 1649) was for Blackstone, far worse for him would have been what the French Revolutionaries did during the decade after his death (in 1780). The respectable English response to the French upheaval is reflected in how Edmund Burke (the noted British parliamentarian) spoke about this subject, criticizing at length what the French did in breaking as they did with their political heritage.

Thus Burke could, in the Blackstonian spirit, acclaim the English Revolution in these terms (in his *Reflections on the Revolution in France*):

The Declaration of Right (the [1689] act of the 1st of William and Mary, sess. 2, ch. 2) is the cornerstone of our constitution, as reinforced, explained, improved, and in the fundamental principles for ever settled. It is called "An act for declaring the rights and liberties of the subject, and for *settling the succession* of the crown." . . . [T]hese rights and this succession are declared in one body, and bound indissolubly together.

Further on, Burke describes how much English liberty depends upon respect for continuity:

Our oldest reformation is that of Magna Charta. You will see that Sir Edward Coke, that great oracle of our law, and indeed all the great men who follow him [down] to Blackstone, are industrious to prove the pedigree of our liberties. They endeavor to prove, that the antient charter, the Magna Charta of King John, was connected with another positive charter from Henry I. and that both the one and the other were nothing more than a re-affirmance of the still more antient standing law of the kingdom.

And so Burke can insist that all this "demonstrates the powerful prepossession towards antiquity, with which the minds of our lawyers and legislators, and of all the people whom they wish to influence have been always filled; and the stationary policy of this kingdom in considering their most sacred rights and franchises as an *inheritance.*"

VII

Eventually, the French were to confirm Burke's worst fears by executing both their King and Queen, along with many others. But well before these fateful steps the French Assembly had seemed to Burke to be ill-fitted for responsible leadership and reform. It is critical, he argued, to notice "the materials of which in a great measure [the National Assembly] is composed, which is of ten thousand times greater consequence than all the formalities in the world."

It can be instructive, considering the composition of the congresses and conventions that chanced to be so critical both to the Independence movement and thereafter to Constitution-making in the United States, how Burke speaks of the composition of a critical body in France. He reports in his *Reflections,* "After I had read over the list of persons and descriptions elected into the *Tiers Etat,* nothing which they afterwards did could appear astonishing." He then explains:

> Among them, indeed, I saw some of known rank; some of shining talents; but of any practical experience in the state, not one man was to be found. The best were only men of theory. But whatever the distinguished few may have been, it is the substance and mass of the body which constitutes its character, and must finally determine its direction.

It is rare, Burke argues, that someone of "a supreme degree of virtue" can "prevent the men of talents disseminated through [an assembly that is viciously or feebly composed in a very great part of it] from becoming only the expert instruments of absurd projects!" Particularly troubling for Burke, and eminently challenging when one thinks about how American political bodies have tended to be made up, is a discovery recorded thus in his *Reflections*:

> Judge, Sir, of my surprize, when I found that a very great proportion of the [French] Assembly (a majority, I believe, of the members who attended) was composed of practitioners in the law. It was composed not of distinguished magistrates, who had given pledges to their country of their science, prudence, and ingenuity; not of leading advocates, the glory of the bar; not of renowned professors in universities;—but for the far greater part, as it must in such a number, of the inferior, unlearned, mechanical, merely instrumental members of the profession.

It can be instructive to compare Burke's assessment of the French lawyers ("the fomenters and conductors of the petty wars of village vexation") with what Alexis de Tocqueville was to say, two generations later, about the vital contribution of lawyers to democracy in America, a contribution which reached its peak perhaps in the career of the most illustrious lawyer nurtured in Illinois.

VIII

The significance of lawyers in public life on this continent may be seen, a generation before Burke's *Reflections,* in the career of Patrick Henry of Virginia. It was a career which anticipated, in some particulars, that of Abraham Lincoln, three-quarters of a century later. The Patrick Henry entry in the *Dictionary of American Biography* recalls:

> At the age of twenty-one Henry [who had been born in 1736] lost his house and furniture by fire and he and his wife turned to . . . store-keeping. In two years they were hopelessly in debt but known to everybody in the county. . . . With ruin staring him in the face and with three or four children about him, Henry now turned his thoughts to law. In the spring of 1760, with a little knowledge of "Coke upon Littleton" and a speaking acquaintance with a digest of Virginia acts, he appeared before Sir John Randolph and three other members of the bar and obtained license to practise law. He returned home, studied diligently the customary book of forms, closed out his store, took quarters with his father-in-law, who kept a tavern at Hanover Courthouse, [Virginia,] and opened his door to clients. He won immediate success.

Five years later, Patrick Henry was elected to the Virginia House of Burgesses. Thereafter, the *Dictionary* entry reports, the Stamp Act, enacted by the Parliament at Westminister, circulated among the burgesses:

> Patrick Henry . . . offered (May 29, 1765) seven radical resolutions to the committee of the [House of Burgesses]. . . . Henry pressed his resolutions in a speech which closed with the famous comparison: "Caesar had his Brutus—Charles the first, his Cromwell—and George the third—may profit by their example. . . ." The resolutions passed the committee amidst an uproar unprecedented in that staid Assembly.

The resolutions of the twenty-seven-year-old Patrick Henry "became the basis of violent agitation [against the British] from Boston to Charleston."

Relations between the Colonies and the Mother Country so deteriorated that Henry offered to a Virginia convention three resolutions, "one of which provided that 'this Colony be immediately put into a posture of defense'; and that a committee be appointed 'to prepare a plan for the embodying, arming, and disciplining such a number of men as may be sufficient for that purpose.'" He pressed his resolutions with one of the great speeches of his life (on March 23, 1775), in which occurred his famous exclamation, "[G]ive me liberty, or give me death!" This is one of the most memorable exercises of freedom of speech in American history, an exercise that did not depend for its legitimacy or effectiveness on the First Amendment.

IX

Patrick Henry, as an apostle of liberty, is very much in the tradition drawn on by both Blackstone and Burke. He could say, in this 1775 speech, that he considered the question to be "nothing less than a question of freedom or slavery." Thereafter in this speech he could insist:

> There is a just God who presides over the destinies of nations, and who will raise up friends to fight our battles for us. The battle, [Mr. Speaker,] is not to the strong alone, it is to the vigilant, the active, the brave. Besides, sir, we have no election [choice]. If we were base enough to desire it, it is now too late to retire from the contest. There is no retreat but in submission and slavery. Our chains are forged. Their clanking may be heard on the plains of Boston! The war is inevitable—and let it come!! I repeat it, sir, let it come!!!

Again and again, Virginia slaveholders revealed (as Henry had here) that they had no illusions about the awfulness of slavery, at least for the enslaved. Further on in the speech, Henry could ask, "Is life so dear or peace so sweet, as to be purchased at the price of chains and slavery?" Yet he could warn, as in one of his speeches in the 1788 Virginia Convention considering the ratification of the proposed Constitution of 1787:

> This [proposed government] is a consolidated government . . . and the danger of such a government is, to my mind, very striking . . . our rights and privileges are endangered, and the sovereignty of the States will be relinquished . . . and . . . [the proposed government] may, if we be engaged in war, . . . liberate every one of your slaves.

We can see, in how Patrick Henry conducted himself, an anticipation of the Secessionists nurtured by John Calhoun, with slavery the vital interest to be protected. Sometimes, it seems, these defenders of slavery were themselves always uncomfortably aware of the dubious status of slavery in the Anglo-American constitutional system, something that is recognized by Blackstone (in the first volume of his *Commentaries*):

> [The] spirit of liberty is so deeply implanted in our constitution, and rooted even in our very soil, that a slave or a negro, the moment he lands in England, falls under the protection of the laws, and with regard to all natural rights becomes *eo instanti* a freeman.

It should be evident, upon considering the careers of such gifted lawyers as William Blackstone and Patrick Henry, that there is considerable merit to Edmund Burke's suggestion (in his *Reflections*) that a country should "be animated by a spirit of rational liberty," something that can be said to be implicit in Abraham Lincoln's call for "a new birth of freedom."

6. The Declaration of Independence (1776); the Northwest Ordinance (1787)

I

The Declaration of Independence *is* for the United States its founding document. It is this not only because it asserts the independence (that is, the very existence) of the United States, but also because it suggests the principles upon which its regime rests. Critical to those principles was the recognition that "a decent Respect to the Opinions of Mankind require[d] that [this People] should declare the causes which impel[led] them to the Separation" that they were announcing.

It is assumed throughout the Declaration that it is important to have, and to give, reasons for what a people and its governments do, especially when grave measures are resorted to. It is not enough for a people simply to exert themselves in an act of will, however important it may be that the government that emerges be adequately empowered. Facts must be "submitted to a candid World," as part of the effort to apply to their circumstances the applicable "Laws of Nature and of Nature's God."

It is evident throughout the Declaration that there are indeed standards by which governments should be judged. There are standards as well by which a people may be judged when they presume to challenge an established government. The Declaration, as it prepares to close, recalls that numerous attempts *had* been made to alert their "British Brethren" to repeated mistreatment by their government of the American Colonies.

II

The standards drawn on in the Declaration are those which "a candid World" should recognize as applicable to these circumstances. It can be wondered, of course, how far the "World" that is addressed extends. Thus,

36

much of the Declaration was probably incomprehensible among those peoples not yet influenced by European ways.

Even in most of Europe, various of the grievances collected in the Declaration would probably have been unpersuasive, grounded as they were in English constitutional law. These include the grievance at the core of the array collected, that there had been an imposition of taxes "without [their] Consent." This was a complaint made both in England and in North America well before 1776.

Most of the grievances collected in the Declaration refer to both actions and inactions by the British Government following upon the Colonists' refusal to pay the taxes imposed on them by Parliament. It is insisted in the Declaration that the Colonists are not undertaking to repudiate long-established relations "for light and transient Causes." No cause, it is assumed, is more important than that which resists arbitrary interference with the control of that property upon which an effective "Pursuit of Happiness" depends.

III

A constitution for the United States is implied in the Declaration of Independence, a constitutional system that includes a recognition of long-established ways of conducting the public business. It is assumed throughout the Declaration that citizens should be able to discuss fully and frankly what their governments are doing. This can be thought of as not only a *right* but also as a *duty.*

Various institutions are taken for granted throughout the Declaration. These include those which assure "the Benefits of Trial by Jury." This and like terms, used in invoking various standards and rights, do not have to be defined for anyone familiar with both the English language and Anglo-American constitutional history.

The implication in the Declaration of a constitution for the United States extends to the evident assumptions about how governments should be organized. The proper workings of legislatures and courts are implicit in the grievances which recall what had been done to long-established legislative and judicial institutions on this continent by the British Government. And, of course, the proper ordering of an executive is implied in what is said about the misconduct of the King and his Ministers.

IV

A model is provided, in the Northwest Ordinance, of how a superintending power should treat its colonies. Thus, it can be said, the Congress demonstrated in its 1787 provisions for the Northwest Territory how Parliament should have dealt with its American territories well before Independence. Critical to what the Congress did was to announce the expectation that the people of the Northwest Territory would someday form States equal in principle to the original Thirteen.

The Northwest Ordinance is, in effect, the first local Constitution for the people of Ohio, Indiana, Illinois, Michigan, and Wisconsin. It was enacted by the Congress (sitting in New York City) established by the Articles of Confederation. This was done while the Federal Convention (sitting in Philadelphia) was drafting the Constitution.

In effect, the Confederation Congress dictated to the Federal Convention how the Territories of the United States should be managed. Thus, there were not to be, in North America, any permanent colonies of the United States. The provision, in Article IV of the Constitution governing the establishment of new States, accepts in effect what the Northwest Ordinance provides.

V

There is also provided in the Northwest Ordinance (the Ordinance of '87) guidance as to what an American bill of rights should include. This may be seen in Section 14, the concluding section of the Ordinance, thereby making this the last word at this time by this Congress on the subject of the Territory. The six articles collected in this section are called "articles of compact between the original States [of the United States] and the people and the states in the said territory [the Northwest Territory]," having been introduced (in Section 13) as "extending the fundamental principles of civil and religious liberty."

It is significant that the rights affirmed in Section 14 do not need to be defined, so familiar are they to the People of the Country, wherever they may live. Perhaps even more significant may be the evident assumption that *all of the States in the United States* should be respectful of the rights enumerated in Section 14. It took a century and a half of experience, including a civil war, before this assumption came explicitly to be recognized and implemented by the Courts of the United States.

The ultimate primacy of the legislative branch of government is indicated again and again in the Northwest Ordinance. Particularly instructive here is what is said (in Section 5 of the Ordinance) about the legislating that the appointed governors and judges may do in the Territory before proper legislatures can be constituted: these officers of governments may, subject to Congressional veto, "adopt and publish [in a Territorial] district, such laws of the original States, criminal and civil, as may be necessary, and best suited to the circumstances of the district." The presuppositions and implications of this provision (to which we will return) are remarkable for what they suggest about what the Founders considered to be legitimate statesmanship.

VI

The first article in Section 14 of the Ordinance of '87 provides: "No person, demeaning himself in a peaceable and orderly manner, shall ever be molested on account of his mode of worship or religious sentiments in the said territory." This echoes the primacy, in the Magna Carta of 1215, of a concern for the liberty of the Church, something insisted upon in both the opening and closing passages of that document. And this anticipates the primacy, in the first article of the Bill of Rights of 1791, of religious liberty.

Such liberty, it seems to be recognized, is fundamental to the happiness of human beings. It is a recognition reinforced in this Country by recollections both of festering European conflicts and of the reasons why many had emigrated to this continent. The diversity in religious allegiances among the States also called for forbearance in these matters.

The importance of religion is recognized as well in the third article of Section 14, which opens with the directive: "Religion, morality, and knowledge, being necessary to good government and the happiness of mankind, schools and the means of education shall forever be encouraged." This is followed, in the same article, by the exhortation about the "utmost good faith [that] shall always be observed towards the Indians." Here, as elsewhere, the rule of law is insisted upon, with the expectation that justice and liberty would be enhanced thereby.

VII

Of course, the pious hopes (with respect to the Indians and others) expressed in New York could not always be realized on the frontiers of the Country. Circumstances would very much affect what duties and rights would be respected, and by whom. Even so, much of what was anticipated by the Ordinance of '87 could be seen fulfilled in the admission to the Union of five States from the Northwest Territory between 1803 (Ohio) and 1849 (Wisconsin).

The circumstances to be confronted by these new States included the already-incurred obligations of the United States. Students of these matters in England must have been intrigued by the Congressional insistence in the Northwest Ordinance that new States had to assume a share of the National debt. They might even have wondered how this requirement differed from what Parliament had tried to do with its Colonies before 1776, Colonies that had been "asked" to help pay for the debt run up by the English, partly on behalf of their Colonies, during the French and Indian War.

Of course, American partisans would have been likely to counter with references to the equal powers promised the new States, along with their equal obligations. This *is* a remarkable feature of American expectations, that all States are to be on an equal footing in the National councils. This kind of expectation is carried even further, at least in principle, in what is done to and with immigrants in this Country, wherever they chanced to come from.

VIII

The concluding article of Section 14 of the Northwest Ordinance begins (in language drawn on later for the Thirteenth Amendment to the Constitution): "There shall be neither slavery nor involuntary servitude in the said territory, otherwise than in punishment of crimes whereof the party shall have been duly convicted." The Northwest Territory, it should be remembered, was at that time the major territory of the United States. That slavery should be forbidden in this fashion suggests the fundamental opposition to that institution implicit in the regime established pursuant to the Declaration of Independence, an opposition even reflected in such dubious provisions in the Constitution as the permission to import slaves from abroad until 1808.

The indefinite (but not permanent) continuation of slavery is anticipated in the Fugitive Slave provision, also found in Article VI of Section 14 of the Ordinance of '87. Without such a provision, the institution of slavery wherever it was already established would have been more and more difficult, if not even virtually impossible, to maintain. Most leaders, including some vigorously opposed to slavery, were originally agreed that the Countrywide elimination of slavery should be controlled and gradual.

The prohibition of slavery in the Northwest Territory, which was far more effective than the plea on behalf of the Indians (in Article III of Section 14 of the Ordinance of '87), was critical for the future of the United States, however distorted the 1787 territorial policy was by the Louisiana Purchase of 1803. Indeed, the Northwest Ordinance can be said to have proved decisive for the outcome of the Civil War, insuring as it did so great an increase in the number of Free States. Not only did massive armies and resources come out of the Old Northwest Territory, but also the leading political and military leaders of the Union.

IX

However familiar the rights may be that are confirmed in Section 14 of the Northwest Ordinance, they do not include something as familiar to us as "freedom of speech, or of the press." We have seen that the free exercise of religion *is* protected in Article I of Section 14 of the Ordinance of '87. The establishment-of-religion issue, also addressed in the First Amendment, is something which is left to the States to deal with as they choose, keeping in mind the Section 14 exhortation about the necessity of "[r]eligion, morality, and knowledge" for "good government and the happiness of mankind."

Even though nothing is said directly about freedom of speech or of the press in the Northwest Ordinance, it is evident that it is taken for granted throughout. The Ordinance itself is an exalted product of political discourse in the United States. In addition, it is provided, in Article V of Section 14 of the Ordinance, that the institutions of government to be established in the new States "shall be republican."

The extent to which the Territorial institutions *are* to be like those in the already existing States is suggested by the Section 5 limitations we have noticed upon the legislating that the appointed officers may do in the Territory before proper legislative bodies can be established. The importance, in 1787, of freedom of speech throughout the Country is suggested by the vitality of the legislature sitting in New York and in the convention sitting in Philadelphia. A reliance upon a productive freedom of speech would be evident during the deliberate consideration thereafter, by the People of the new Nation, of the proposed Constitution for the United States.

7. Constitutionalism and the Workings of Freedom of Speech

I

The legislative immunity of Members of Congress, confirmed in Article I, Section 6, of the Constitution, provides a reminder of what a sovereign People in turn require and are entitled to. We have seen that parliamentary immunity is essential if Congress is to be able to face up adequately to the more controversial issues of the day. That immunity is reinforced by such provisions as those for the fixed terms of Members of Congress and for "Compensation for their Services, to be ascertained by law."

The freedom of speech by Members of Congress is guarded some-what against abuse by the power of each House to "punish its Members for disorderly Behavior, and, with the Concurrence of two thirds, expel a Member." And, of course, Members are restrained in what they say by what they fear that their constituents may in turn "say" at the polls. Do public opinion and the prospect of social ostracism encourage citizens at large also to be responsible in *their* use of freedom of speech?

The Constitution itself was a product of the exercise by the People of their powers. This exercise was preceded by years of discussion of how the English government had conducted itself, and thereafter various American governments as well. Once a permanent Constitution was drafted, there was, naturally enough, considerable, often frank, discussion of its defects and merits.

II

It can be instructive, in thinking about freedom of speech in this Country, to consider what can be learned from the Constitution itself about the workings of that freedom. Suppose, that is, a document such as the Constitution (known to have been used by a people) provided the only evidence one had of what had gone on in a country. What, besides the institution of parliamentary immunity, can be instructive here?

The Preamble to the Constitution of 1787 reflects, and in effect affirms, the powers and interests of the People. The ends of government are identified and insisted upon. Such ends are understood to be within the power of the People to provide for—and to assess how well they *are* provided for.

The ends of government identified in the Preamble culminate in "the Blessings of Liberty," which are to be secured at once and ever after. Other ends, such as "Justice," "domestic Tranquility," "common defence," and "the general Welfare" can be provided for without any evident qualifications comparable to the use of "Blessings" with "Liberty." Is it recognized, that is, that there may be drawbacks, if not even curses, associated with Liberty, unfortunate consequences that must be risked if a people is to be truly self-governing, especially if that people does not have the benefit of divine revelation to guide what it does?

III

The power of the People, drawn upon in the Preamble, is very much in evidence in Article I of the Constitution. There may be seen in the opening sections of that article directions for how Congress is to be established and maintained. There may be seen as well the expectation that the People are quite competent in doing what has to be done if sensible Congresses are to be developed.

The House of Representatives first comes to view. "[T]he Electors in each State," it is ordered, "shall have the Qualifications requisite for Electors of the most numerous Branch of the State legislature." It is taken for granted, of course, that there exist legislatures in the States comparable to the Congress that is provided for here.

State legislatures will be directly responsible for selection of the Members of the Senate of the United States. The age limits associated with a range of offices suggest that various levels of maturity are likely to be associated with age and hence experience. Here, too, it is evident that no authoritative divine revelation can be depended upon, that citizens have to be given time to learn what is needed for their effective performance of the duties they may be assigned.

IV

The President is also chosen by the People, but not as directly as the Members of the House of Representatives are. His mode of selection resembles more that used for the selection of Senators. Here, too, the actions of the People are indirect.

It is left to Congress to identify the President selected, and thereafter to finance and otherwise to provide for what he can do. It is also left to Congress to determine whether a President may be removed from office. No doubt, Members of Congress, in determining how to proceed against a President, are expected to be aware of their constituents' opinions.

Congress is ultimately independent of the President in still another way, for it can enact laws overriding Presidential vetoes by an enhanced majority. The place of discussion in our constitutional system is recognized by the provision that the President should provide objections if he chooses *not* to sign a bill presented to him by Congress. That is, it is assumed that he would have reasons which Congress is entitled to learn and to assess.

V

Vital to the political system incorporated in the Constitution is the Republican Form of Government Guarantee in Article IV. Each State of the Union is to have such a regime. It is reasonable to suppose that substantial guidance, as to what a republican form looks like, is provided by the system of government ordained for the United States.

Critical to republicanism is the reliance upon periodic elections, a requirement reinforced by the repudiation in the Constitution of all titles of nobility in this Country. Such elections, in order to be meaningful, have to be made by citizens who can discuss freely the merits of candidates, including those officers seeking reelection. A dependence upon an effective, Countrywide freedom of speech seems to be taken for granted.

Also taken for granted, it seems, are various privileges and immunities of citizens that the States are obliged to respect in some circumstances. It is not made explicit what these include, but the 1791 Bill of Rights is suggestive here. The Fourteenth Amendment has come to be understood, plausibly enough, to have made applicable against the States most of the restrictions placed upon the General Government by the Bill of Rights.

VI

Critical to any bill of rights is respect for orderly government. This is reflected, for example, in the prohibition of recourse to *ex post facto* laws by any government in the United States. This can be consistent with respect for rules and standards ordained by nature and apparent to any sensible human being.

Particularly important for effective discussion is a reliable respect for due process of law. It is this which is taken for granted in the case against prior restraint of publications. Due process is also taken for granted generally in the reliance upon a decent judicial system.

Thus, the People know what to expect from their governments in a variety of circumstances. This is not to deny that conditions may develop which make it unbearably hazardous to rely upon the normal processes and expectations. In those rare conditions (when normal processes are substantially interfered with) a suspension of the writ of *habeas corpus* remains available, a remedy that is so radical that it is rarely relied upon explicitly by any government that wants to retain the allegiance of its people.

VII

Any survey of the Constitution of 1787, with a view to determining its assumptions about its form of government, should take account of its provisions with respect to slavery. Those provisions can be understood, as of 1787, to have left slavery under a cloud. It was an institution to be tolerated, but with the expectation by some (perhaps even by most) that it would eventually be eliminated.

Such elimination can be said to have been anticipated by a recognition (in Section 9 of Article I) of Congressional authority to prohibit the importation of slaves after 1808. But that there would have to be, before complete elimination of slavery in the United States, uncomfortable political compromises in the Country is indicated by the reliance upon the Fugitive Slave Clause. In this and other ways, the Framers of the Constitution accommodated themselves to unfortunate conditions that they happened to inherit.

Another historical accident to be reckoned with was the substantial political equality (at least on paper) of the States, no matter what their differences in population or wealth chanced to be. This contributed to the challenges posed by the existence of slavery in the United States. The limits of constructive discussion were evident in the growth of passions, North and South, which proved almost fatal to the survival of the Union.

VIII

Even so, the language of the Constitution helped sustain those, during the Civil War and thereafter, who insisted upon a continued Union under a continent-wide Republican Form of Government. That language was reinforced by the guidance provided by the Declaration of Independence and confirmed, especially with respect both to republicanism (pro) and to slavery (con), by the Northwest Ordinance. The authority of the language of the Constitution itself is confirmed by the degree to which that language was relied upon by the framers of the Confederate Constitution of 1861.

Among the features carried over from 1787 to 1861 was a reliance upon oaths of office. Words do matter, it is thereby recognized. This can be particularly important for judges who are not subject to systematic assessments by the People, however much courts can be effectively regulated by the Congress when it is determined to do so.

Oaths cannot be reinforced, however, by any "religious Test." Other uses of words are anticipated by provisions in the Constitution for copyrights and for contracts. And, "from time to time," the President shall "give to the Congress Information of the State of the Union," still another reminder of the words relied upon for effective government.

IX

It is evident throughout the Constitution that the powers of the People are paramount. This is evident in the Preamble, where the People's ordaining is authoritative. This is evident as well in the concluding article of the Constitution, where it is provided, "The Ratification of the Conventions of nine States shall be sufficient for the Establishment of this Constitution between the States so ratifying the Same."

Conventions in the several States, *not* the State Legislatures, were relied upon for ratification. These were, more than the State Legislatures, assemblies immediately chosen by the people in each State to consider ratification. Discussion of the proposed Constitution by the people in each State was presupposed.

Discussion was also anticipated with respect, thereafter, to any proposed amendments to the Constitution once it was ratified. Although such amendments are typically developed by the Congress and thereafter ratified by the State legislatures, they may also be developed and thereafter ratified by State Conventions, which means that the People can exercise thereby the powers delegated as well to the Congress and to the State legislatures. In this way, too, the People reserve to themselves the power and the means for discussing the changes they want to consider in the Constitution of 1787, just as they had done during the years of debate that had culminated in the Declaration of Independence of 1776.

8. The Virginia Statute of Religious Freedom (1786)

I

The Virginia Statute of Religious Freedom is regarded as one of the great American constitutional documents. It may well be the most influential document ever issued on its own by one of the States in the Union. On the other side of the ledger, so to speak, are the also quite influential Secessionist declarations issued by eleven States, including (unfortunately) Virginia, in 1860–1861.

The 1786 Virginia Statute (set forth in Appendix E of this volume) is anticipated by the 1776 Virginia Declaration of Rights. Rights are identified in 1776 as "pertain[ing]" to "the good people of Virginia," and to "their posterity," and as such (it is further asserted) they are "the basis and foundation of government." Among these rights is one found in Section 12 of the 1776 Declaration, using language that had already become familiar: "That the freedom of the press is one of the great bulwarks of liberty, and can never be restrained but by despotic governments."

It is thereafter declared, in Section 15 of the 1776 Declaration of Rights, "That no free government, or the blessings of liberty, can be preserved to any people, but by a firm adherence to justice, moderation, temperance, frugality, and virtue, and by frequent recurrence to fundamental principles." This is immediately followed, in Section 16 (the final section in this 1776 declaration), by the expression of a caution about how the virtues of citizens are to be developed and maintained:

[R]eligion or the duty which we owe to our Creator, and the manner of discharging it, can be directed only by reason and conviction, not by force or violence; and therefore all men are equally entitled to the free exercise of religion, according to the dictates of conscience, and that it is the mutual duty of all to practise Christian forbearance, love, and charity towards each other.

Nothing was said on that occasion about what is known as the establishment of religion.

II

What a State establishment of religion could include is evident in the Massachusetts Declaration of Rights of 1780. There, too, the free exercise of religion is affirmed, following upon this recognition: "It is the right as well as the duty of all men in society, publicly, and at stated seasons, to worship the SUPREME BEING, the great Creator and Preserver of the universe." Thereupon it is declared,

And no subject shall be hurt, molested, or restrained, in his person, liberty, or estate, for worshiping GOD in the manner and season most agreeable to the dictates of his own conscience; or for his religious profession or sentiments, provided he doth not disturb the public peace, or obstruct others in their religious worship.

The 1780 Massachusetts Declaration goes on to insist that "the happiness of a people, and the good order and preservation of civil government, essentially depend upon piety, religion and morality." But these, it is also insisted, "cannot be generally diffused through a community but by the institution of the public worship of GOD, and of public instructions in piety, religion and morality." This means, among other things, that "the people of [the] commonwealth have a right to invest their legislature with power [to promote] the public worship of GOD."

Among the measures that may be ordered by the legislature are "the support and maintenance of public Protestant teachers of piety, religion, and morality, in all cases where such provisions shall not be made voluntarily." It also seems that the legislature may "enjoin upon all the subjects an attendance upon the instructions of the public teachers [of piety, religion, and morality]." Even so, this subject is not left without the assurance, "And every denomination of Christians, demeaning themselves peaceably, and as good subjects of the commonwealth, shall be equally under the protection of the law: and no subordination of any one sect or denomination to another shall ever be established by law."

III

The kind of State establishment of religion permitted, if not even required, by Massachusetts in 1780 is decisively repudiated by Virginia in 1785. The Virginia Statute opens with the insistence that "Almighty God hath created the mind free." The uses here of "temporal punishments or burdens, or [of] civil incapacitations, tend only to beget habits of hypocrisy and meanness."

Critical to this 1785 assessment is the reminder that "the Holy author of our religion, who being Lord both of body and mind, yet chose not to propagate [our religion] by coercions on either, as was in his Almighty power to do." Thus, in effect, the authors of this Declaration seem to identify themselves as Christians. It is hardly likely that any of our State legislatures today would go (or would even want to go) as far as is done here in drawing explicitly upon Christian doctrines.

False religions, it is argued, have always been "established and maintained" by "fallible and uninspired men" in governments. Even to force a man "to support this or that teacher of his own religious persuasion . . . depriv[es] him of the comfortable liberty of giving [or withdrawing] his contributions to . . . particular pastor[s]." Thus, it is suggested, it is more efficient, morally and spiritually, if pastors have to compete for and earn a people's support.

IV

It is argued that "to compel a man to furnish contributions for the propagation of opinions which he disbelieves, is sinful and tyrannical." That is, the objection here draws upon both religious and political standards. This combination may be seen, further on, in the insistence "that our civil rights have no dependence on our religious opinions, any more than our opinions in physics or geometry."

Thomas Jefferson prepared the epitaph found on his tombstone at Monticello, an epitaph which did not need to include the political offices he was generally known to have held. He identified himself, instead, as "Author of the Declaration of Independence, and of the statute of Virginia for religious freedom, and father of the University of Virginia." Is not an identification with the University of Virginia appropriate for anyone who can somehow or other liken "religious opinions" to "opinions in physics or geometry"?

This kind of language, reflecting the ascendancy of modern physics then recently dramatized by the career of Isaac Newton, anticipates the scientific studies to which religions and the faithful would be subjected during the following century. The systematic study of nature thereby promoted extended to the development of a system of "the natural rights of mankind." All this culminates in an enactment (in 1786), "That no man shall be compelled to frequent or support any religious worship, place, or ministry whatsoever, nor shall be enforced, restrained, molested, or burthened in his body or goods, nor shall otherwise suffer on account of his religious opinions or belief; but that all shall be free to profess, and by argument to maintain, their opinion in matters of religion, and that the same shall in no wise diminish, enlarge, or affect their civil capacities."

V

The culminating enactment, in the 1786 Virginia Statute of Religious Freedom, does not retain any of the language of piety found in the long preamble to this document. In this respect, at least, it sounds like something that could be adopted by an American State today. There can be seen here a further development of that rationalizing tendency with respect to the Divine evident in the reference in the Declaration of Independence to "the Laws of Nature and of Nature's God."

Something of that tendency (inappropriate perhaps for the God of Revelation) may be seen in an invocation of "the natural rights of mankind." It can be said to be carried even further in the concluding words of the Virginia Statute of Religious Freedom, where there is an invocation of *natural right—not,* it should be noticed, either of *natural rights* (just used) or (even more significant perhaps) of *natural law.* It can be wondered how many in the 1786 General Assembly appreciated these distinctions.

This *natural right* may be distinguished from the earlier use, in this 1786 Statute, of "civil rights" and "natural rights." It is used at the end where others might have used "natural law," also suggesting thereby enduring standards, but standards which are more likely *in our tradition* to be based on theological (even Christian) authority than is "natural right" (which can be said to go back to pre-Christian, or philosophical, authorities). It is not likely that the typical member of the General Assembly connected this concluding invocation of natural right with what had been said earlier in the Statute about coupling "religious opinions" with "opinions in physics or geometry."

VI

The preamble to this 1786 Statute had spoken of a desire to avoid corruption of "the principles of . . . religion." It is recognized how people might be bribed, in effect, to "profess or [to] renounce this or that religious opinion." The analysis here seems to be ultimately political rather than theological.

This assessment is reinforced by what is said in opposition to the use of civil power "to restrain the profession or propagation of principles on supposition of their ill tendency." This, it is further said, "is a dangerous fallacy, which at once destroys all religious liberty." The civil magistrate thus empowered, it is natural to expect, is likely to "make his opinions the rule of judgment, and approve or condemn the sentiments of others only as they shall square with or differ from his own."

The preamble to the 1786 Virginia Statute closes with two assurances. The first, which is critical to the case for due process of law and against systems of censorship, is this: "[I]t is time enough for the rightful purposes of civil government, for its officers to interfere when principles break out into overt acts against peace and good order." The second assurance (perhaps even a pious hope), which has had its most eloquent formulation in John Milton's *Areopagitica,* takes the form of the expression of confidence "that truth is great and will prevail if left to herself, that she is the proper and sufficient antagonist to error, and has nothing to fear from the conflict, unless by human interposition disarmed of her natural weapons, free argument and debate, errors ceasing to be dangerous when it is permitted freely to contradict them."

VII

It is recognized, in the 1786 Virginia Statute of Religious Freedom, that it can be a matter of chance which religious opinions are dominant from place to place. Who *is* in control and where can depend upon the vagaries of "history." One can be reminded of this when it is recalled that the Puritans who ended up in an austere region along the Atlantic coast had evidently hoped, upon leaving Europe, to settle much farther south.

Such observations can lead one to wonder how much any people can ever control its social and economic developments. Even more critical (indeed, even sobering) is the question of how much one's personal understanding of the most important matters also depends on chance. Liberation in these matters may not be the same as empowerment, for genuine empowerment requires considerable, sustained discipline.

"History" can depend upon surprising combinations of anomalies. It is curious, for example, that the most stirring public language during the first decade of the United States—the language found in the Declaration of Independence and in the Virginia Statute of Religious Freedom— should have originated among the slaveholders of Virginia. It is language which contributed to the eventual abolition of slavery on this continent, something to which the most astute and the most public-spirited of the Virginians may have (however cautiously) deliberately contributed.

VIII

Another way of making distinctions here is to notice the religious heritage of New England. There does not seem to have been in Virginia anyone of the stature, in theology, of Jonathan Edwards. Nor does there seem to have been in Virginia anything comparable to the Great Awakening that inspired New England religiosity during the first half of the eighteenth century.

That religiosity would eventually find political expression in the abolitionist movement. Its classic literary expression seems to have been John Bunyan's *The Pilgrim's Progress.* This may have reinforced tendencies toward individualism, if not even toward the self-reliant frontier spirit.

Another text of considerable influence in early America seems to have been Plutarch's *Lives,* rivaled in its prevalence here (it is said) only by the Bible and perhaps Shakespeare's plays. Plutarch, like Virgil's *Aeneid,* promoted civic-mindedness, with the Roman Republic providing an important model for American citizens. It is this spirit which can be said to enliven both the Declaration of Independence and the Virginia Statute of Religious Freedom.

IX

The First Amendment, ratified within a decade of the Virginia Statute, has long been understood to stand for the free exercise of religion Nationwide, even though its text explicitly restrains only Congress. The Amendment is also explicit in providing that "Congress shall make no law respecting an establishment of religion." This means, among other things, that Congress should not interfere with any *State* establishment of religion, such as that (we have noticed) provided for in the 1780 Massachusetts Declaration of Rights.

The way of the future *here* was charted not by the "hands off" Establishment Clause of the First Amendment, but rather by the Virginia Statute of Religious Freedom. This 1786 Statute (as is evident in its concluding lines) takes on the majesty of the great legislative enactments, such as the Habeas Corpus Acts of 1641 and 1679, enactments which, although technically within the power of Parliament to repeal, have come to be regarded as profoundly influential expressions of English constitutional law. The enduring influence of the 1786 Virginia Statute may be seen in subsequently developed State constitutions, such as the first Illinois Constitution (of 1818), which includes the provision (in its Article VIII)

> That all men have a natural and indefeasible right to worship Almighty God according to the dictates of their own consciences; that no man can of right be compelled to attend, erect, or support any place of worship, or to maintain any ministry against his consent; that no human authority can, in any case whatever, control or interfere with the rights of conscience; and that no preference shall ever be given by law to any religious establishments or modes of worship.

A resurgence of public religiosity in this Country may be seen in the inclusion in the Preamble for the 1861 Confederate Constitution of pious language that has no counterpart in the Constitution of 1787: "invoking the favor and guidance of Almighty God." But the way of the future was that seen, three decades earlier, in the amendment (in 1833) of Section III of the 1780 Massachusetts Declaration of Rights, repudiating such establishment features as the provisions for "the support and maintenance of

Protestant teachers of piety, religion, and morality." Here, as in the Illinois Constitution of 1818, the emancipating spirit of the Virginia Statute of Religious Freedom may be encountered.

9. The Emergence of a National Bill of Rights (1789–1791)

I

The Constitutional Convention finished its work in September 1787. By July 1788, eleven of the original Thirteen States had ratified the proposed Constitution, more than enough to set the new constitutional machinery into motion. In the spring of 1789, the First Congress met pursuant to the directions laid down in the Constitution and by the retiring Articles of Confederation Congress.

Among the many matters to be considered during the First Session of the First Congress was the preparation of proposed "Bill of Rights" amendments to the Constitution. The lack of a separate bill of rights in the proposed Constitution had been made much of by the opponents to ratification in 1787–1788. Proponents of the proposed Constitution, who did not want any delay that might put its ultimate ratification at risk, had argued that no bill of rights was needed, that the rights that would be recognized thereby were already well-established in the United States, and that enumerating some rights might make those not mentioned vulnerable.

Besides, it was pointed out, several of the State constitutions had no bill of rights either, and yet the people there did not feel threatened. But, opponents of the Constitution argued, a National government is far less subject to control by the People than are State governments and, as such, is more in need of a bill of rights. It was evident that the arguments used by various parties to this Ratification controversy were suspect, just as it was likely that the Framers of the Constitution would have provided a separate bill of rights in September 1787 if it had been anticipated how much would be made of its absence.

II

James Madison promised his Virginia constituents that he, as a Member of the House of Representatives, would push for a bill of rights in the First Congress. One difficulty he faced there was the lack of interest even among some of those who had been so vigorous in their criticisms of the Constitution during the Ratification Campaign. It became obvious that some of those critics had used the lack of a bill of rights merely as something with which to defeat ratification of a Constitution that they opposed primarily because of its substantial empowerment of the General Government.

It also became obvious that the Federalists (that is, Madison and those of like mind), who controlled the First Congress (just as they had controlled the Constitutional Convention), did not intend to reduce any of the powers of the new General Government. This is apparent upon examining the lists of proposed amendments fashioned by the minorities in State ratifying conventions who opposed ratification. Those proposals which would have substantially curtailed the powers of the General Government were *not* included by Madison in the array of amendments he either introduced in June 1789 or developed thereafter.

Attempts *were* made by the anti-Federalist minority in the House of Representatives to curtail the powers of the General Government. Particularly significant was their effort to insert "expressly" in what is now the Tenth Amendment. The attempt failed to restrict thereby the General Government as Article II of the Articles of Confederation had done, setting the precedent that has continued to our day—that no constitutional amendment has ever curtailed any substantial power of the General Government provided by the Constitution of 1787.

III

The integrity of the Constitution of 1787 has been further recognized by the way that amendments have been arranged. The original set of amendments proposed by Madison, in June 1789, was offered as a series of statements to be incorporated at various places in the body of the Constitution. Thus, the Constitution was to be treated as a statute is when it is amended.

This incorporation approach was assumed during the opening stages of the discussion of proposed amendments in the House of Representatives. It should be noticed that, so far as we know, the Senate (as representatives of the States) waited upon amendment proposals from the House of Representatives. It seems to have been assumed that any bill of rights would be primarily an assertion of the rights of the People at large—and that that would be better left to the House of Representatives to initiate and to develop.

However that may have been, incorporation of the Bill of Rights in the body of the Constitution would have had the advantage of helping to clarify what was intended by each of its provisions. It was evident, for example, that most of the proposed provisions (which were to be inserted here and there into Article I) exhibited concerns about how Congressional powers were to be exercised. It was evident, as well, that the Congress was regarded as the ultimately dominant branch of the General Government.

IV

The incorporation approach was relied upon by the House of Representatives for two months into its deliberations—that is, well into the middle of August 1789. Then something happened. That is, it was decided that all amendments should be *added* to the 1787 document, not incorporated in it.

Perhaps one argument made earlier finally took hold, the argument that to incorporate amendments would be to have the Signers of the Constitution of 1787 implicitly endorsing language that they had not personally known. We can notice in passing that when the Confederate Convention of 1861 framed *its* constitution, using the 1787 Constitution as its "first draft," it did incorporate into the body of *its* document, at various places, one form or another of the twelve amendments that had been ratified theretofore. And this expanded document these 1861 framers *could* sign.

The 1789 Congress, when it abandoned the incorporation approach, had to revise the language of the proposed amendments so that they could stand alone as supplements to the Constitution. One consequence of this shift was to make most of the proposed amendments seem general in scope—and, as such, perhaps applicable to *all* governments in the United States. It was such general applicability that *Barron* v. *Baltimore* (1833) considered (and denied) and that the Fourteenth Amendment authoritatively revived.

V

Of course, it was obvious that the House of Representatives, even after it regarded amendments as supplements and converted most of them to a general form, did not intend them to be of a general applicability. Otherwise, it would not have had to include in the list of proposed amendments sent to the Senate, as its fourteenth article of amendments, this provision: "No State shall infringe the right of trial by Jury in criminal cases, nor the rights of conscience, nor the freedom of speech, or of the press." This can be said to be comparable to Section 10 of Article I, where there are repeated, as applicable against the States, a few provisions which had been already set forth (in general language), in Section 9 of Article I, but which were nevertheless understood to be restrictions only upon the Congress.

When, however, the amendments proposed by the House were reviewed by the Senate (sitting, as usual then, behind closed doors), this fourteenth article of the House-proposed amendments was removed by the Senate, evidently acting thereby as *the* protector of State governmental interests. But, it can be *argued,* the Senate inadvertently made most of the remaining proposed amendments seem to be applicable against the States as well when it acted as it did. This is a particularly dramatic illustration of how a draftsman, by changing one part of a text, can have unintended consequences elsewhere in that text.

Of course, it can also be argued, its fourteenth proposition was as far as the House of Representatives of the First Congress ever intended to go in further restricting the States by means of a National Bill of Rights. On the other hand, it *had* been vigorously argued that all of such rights as are now found in the Bill of Rights had long been part of the constitutional heritage of the English-speaking peoples whether or not explicitly recognized in the Constitution of 1787 or in any other American document. However this may have been, were there in 1789 any astute observers who recognized what the States' Rights advocates in the Senate had inadvertently risked doing to their cause by removing the fourteenth proposition from the House's array of amendment proposals?

VI

The House's fourteenth proposition is further instructive in that it singles out a few rights as particularly important for the States to respect.

These are the right of trial by jury in criminal cases, the rights of conscience, and the freedom of speech and of the press. The States were already restrained, by Section 10 of Article I of the Constitution of 1787, with respect to bills of attainder and *ex post facto* laws.

The people of a State would have been protected both as subjects and as rulers by the fourteenth proposition. As subjects, they would have had (pursuant to the rejected fourteenth proposition) the safeguards of a jury trial and of freedom of conscience. As rulers, they could criticize any government and offer their opinions about what should be done.

All this can be said to have been anticipated, however, by the insistence, in Article IV of the Constitution of 1787, that each State must have a Republican Form of Government. Perhaps *the* model for such a form is suggested by the way that the General Government itself is organized by the Constitution of 1787, however limited the precedent of the allocation of seats in the United States Senate may have been. But it is a form of government, so far as the States are concerned, that can be quite limited in its conduct of foreign affairs, and that in turn may affect the threats that such a government might be expected to deal with.

VII

The Senate, insofar as it acted to protect State interests by deleting the House's fourteenth proposition, may have been shortsighted. Particularly significant were the consequences, during the first half of the nineteenth century, of the severe curtailment in the Southern States of discussions of the problems of slavery. The inevitable case against slavery was pretty much left, therefore, for "outside agitators" to develop.

Some of the guarantees that there may have already been in Southern State constitutions were evidently of quite limited effect during the decades preceding the Civil War. Whether anything could ever have been done then by recourse to the Federal Courts can be doubted. But this evidently could not even be attempted without something like the House's fourteenth proposition to work with.

The limitations of any constitutional provision are suggested by the failure of the General Government, for two centuries now, to make much explicit use of the Republican Form of Government Guarantee. It took the Civil War to begin to establish the conviction Nationwide that the governments of the States should be obliged to be as respectful as the General Government is required to be of the long-standing rights of the English-speaking peoples. It is a curious chance, if not even apparently providential, that one consequence of that war was to produce (in 1868) an amendment which bears the same number (fourteen) as the proposition originally offered to the Senate (in 1789) by the House of Representatives as a significant restraint upon the States.

VIII

We have noticed that a recognition of the long-standing rights of the English-speaking peoples is evident in the Ninth Amendment. The insistence there upon rights not enumerated, we have also noticed, was provided as an assurance to those who were concerned lest the enumeration of some rights in a bill of rights might implicitly surrender others (including both rights already recognized and others likely to be developed). We can again be reminded thereby of the substantial body of venerable constitutional doctrines, including constitutional processes drawn upon both by the Constitutional Convention and by the First Congress.

Still, there *is* something to be said for the concern that had been expressed about *any* enumeration. This can be seen in the pre–Civil War immunity of State governments (with respect to slavery issues) that we have noticed, an immunity that disregarded a long-established understanding about the right to criticize government. It can be seen as well in what has been done—but even more in what has *not* been done—with the Ninth Amendment for more than two centuries now.

The principal explicit use of the Ninth Amendment has been with respect to emerging "privacy" rights (grounded ultimately in traditional property interests), and often at the risk of having judges condemned as "activists." Perhaps the Ninth Amendment serves as well as a reminder that there are principles and standards upon which constitutions draw and by which they can be judged. Such a reminder is provided, in an authoritative way, by the Declaration of Independence and thereafter by the Preamble for the Constitution of 1787, as well as by the provisions for amending of the Constitution (which are quite different, in this respect, from the Law provided by, say, Moses).

IX

The collaboration between the House of Representatives and the Senate produced, on September 25, 1789, a set of twelve proposed amendments to the Constitution, with all but two of them ratified as of December 15, 1791. The two not ratified, about the makeup and the pay of the Congress, were not of the caliber of those we now acclaim as the Bill of Rights. The States can be said to have known what they were doing when they settled upon ten of the twelve proposed amendments.

Even so, it can also be said that nothing changed in December 1791 or whenever people, Countrywide, learned that a bill of rights had indeed been ratified. That is, people did not suddenly consider themselves empowered or protected in ways that they had not been before. After all, these *were,* for the most part, rights that these people had long exercised, even well before Independence.

Indeed, if such rights are *not* well-grounded in the experience and expectations of a people, they are not apt to be taken seriously and used prudently. We can be reminded of how vital a heritage can be when we recall that the year that the Bill of Rights was ratified was also the year that Wolfgang Amadeus Mozart died. Both Mozart and the Framers of 1787–1791 drew upon a great heritage in laying down programs for generations to develop.

10. The Organization of the First Amendment

I

The First Amendment is the only article in the Bill of Rights that is explicitly directed at the Congress. Two other proposed amendments, the first and the second of the twelve proposals sent to the States in September 1789, also clearly dealt with the Congress. Those two, which were amendments to the structure of the Constitution rather than elements of the future Bill of Rights, were not ratified by the States at that time.

The First Amendment itself is divided into two parts. It can be said, loosely speaking, that the first part deals with the religious life of the community, the second part with its political life. These two parts are readily, and frequently, connected (as may be seen in Appendix F of this volume).

It was insisted, from the onset of deliberations about these matters in the First Congress, in June 1789, that no "national religion" should be "established." This concern became the preliminary element in the First Amendment as it was developed in the First Congress. We can be again reminded by this arrangement of the insistence upon the liberty of the Church at the beginning (as well as at the end) of Magna Carta almost six centuries before the First Amendment was fashioned.

II

Why may provision for the religious life of the community go first in such formal assertions of rights and liberties? This primacy could be seen not only in the Magna Carta of 1215 and in the Bill of Rights of 1791, but also in the bill-of-rights-like article in the Northwest Ordinance of 1787. It had been known for centuries that religious difference threatened political stability in one European country after another, something that could be testified to by the denominational diversity of the earliest immigrants to this continent, more perhaps than by the immigrants of the past century who seem to have been more secular in their objectives.

It is emphasized at the outset of the First Amendment that Congress should itself make "no laws respecting an establishment of religion." No such restriction was placed, or even suggested to be placed, upon the States, in some of which there were (as we have seen) various degrees of an "establishment" (that is, the support of one or more denominations *in preference to others*). Indeed, the language of the First Amendment insisting that Congress should make no law *respecting* establishments precluded all Congressional interference with any establishment that any State chose to sponsor.

The First Amendment continues, after its "hands off" directive with respect to establishments, with the command that Congress should make no law "prohibiting the free exercise [of religion]." The first draft of *this* part of the amendment (as may be seen in Appendix F of this volume) had decreed that "the full and equal rights of conscience [should not] be in any manner, or on any pretext, infringed." It seems to be left open to Congress, however, to interfere with any State prohibitions of the free exercise of religion, however uncertain it may be whether such Congressional interference can moderate any State establishment measure which has the effect of putting "free exercise" in jeopardy.

III

Very early in the development of the First Amendment there was a joinder of the speech/press/assembly provision with the establishment/exercise provision. These two sets of provisions do seem to have an affinity. Both recognize how vital it can be to the soul what one believes, says, and does about the most important matters, spiritual and temporal, by which human beings are guided.

Whatever power Congress may have to restrain State abridgments of the freedom of speech and of the press is not in any way restrained by the First Amendment. Such State abridgments might have to be dealt with, for example, by the General Government in fulfilling its Article IV obligation to guarantee to every State in the Union a Republican Form of Government. This is consistent with the long-standing (but currently neglected) opinion that "freedom of speech, or of the press" is primarily concerned with political discourse.

We have seen that that opinion is *suggested*, to say the least, by the historic origins of the term "freedom of speech." It is that which Members of Parliament, and thereafter American legislators (Colonial, State, and National), have been assured in order to be both empowered and encouraged to discuss public affairs freely and fully. And if a people come to be regarded as sovereign, as is routine in the United States, then that People must be as encouraged, protected, and hence empowered as legislators have to be in order to be most effective.

IV

These considerations bear upon what is and is not protected by the First Amendment. What *is* protected is the most vigorous questioning of how the affairs of the Country are to be conducted. This questioning can include, of course, such activities as the way that wars are fought.

Even more critical is that question which presumes to challenge the sensibleness, if not even the propriety, of the particular war in which the Country may be engaged. The patriotism of such critics can be challenged in turn. Whatever protection the First Amendment provides, it cannot insulate the speaker from the most vigorous criticism of what he says, when he says it, and how.

Thus, the freely speaking citizen can be, in turn, severely condemned as uninformed, as reckless, if not even as subversive, by other freely speaking citizens. That is, there may not be among the citizens at large the kind of discipline there is apt to be among a well-regulated parliamentary body, that discipline which helps keep exchanges among Members from becoming "personal." This makes it critical that citizens be assured, if they are to brave such personal criticism, that at least there will be no governmental measures "abridging [their] freedom of speech."

V

It might be wondered, if the freedom-of-speech protection provided by the First Amendment *is* as extensive as the traditional parliamentary privilege, why anything needed to be added protecting "[freedom] of the press." After all, the parliamentary privilege should protect the writing as well as the speaking done by Members in their parliamentary capacity.

One reason for providing for the press is to make certain that nothing is inadvertently surrendered of the traditional right here.

Besides, it is because "freedom of speech" can properly be substantially limited to the protection of *political* discussion that freedom of the press should be reaffirmed. After all, we can see in Appendix F of this volume, freedom of the press was identified (on June 8, 1789) as "one of the great bulwarks of liberty," an identification which draws, in effect, on a tradition highlighted by John Milton's *Areopagitica.* That 1644 pamphlet did make the most celebrated argument against censorship, or the licensing of printing.

If there *is* a system of licensing, a publication can be held up without the authorities having to acknowledge that it is its *political* content (rather than something else) which is offensive. Thus, the traditional freedom of the press permits one to run the risk of immediate publication, no matter how unpopular (or otherwise costly) that may be. Any prosecution thereafter would have to confront not only whatever extensive protection is provided to political discussion but also the procedural and other safeguards available in traditional criminal trials.

VI

What, then, does "freedom of speech" *not* protect, whether spoken or printed? Among the questionable things that can properly be policed are obscenity, fraud, slander and libel, and various kinds of advertising (including that advertising once denied to lawyers, doctors, and other professionals). Such talk has not traditionally been considered the kind of political discourse which should have virtually unlimited protection.

But to say that such talk (once made public) does not merit First Amendment coverage does not mean that it has no protection at all. Punishment of nonprivileged expression is controlled by the protection offered by the guarantees associated with due process, property, and the rule of law generally. And, of course, freedom of speech permits the unlimited questioning of any governmental campaigns against obscenity, fraud, and the like.

Such governmental campaigns may well be directed toward the development and protection of the moral standards upon which effective republican government depends. Those standards depend, at least in part, upon the talk that becomes pervasive in a community. This is something that can be of particular concern today, when there seem to be no effective limits placed either upon what can be said or upon how and where it may be said.

VII

The importance of freedom of speech can be better grasped when it is recognized how much chance can determine what is officially disfavored from time to time. This can remind us of how much a community's passions can distort its judgment. The prosecutions reviewed in *Schenck* v. *United States* (1919), *Debs* v. *United States* (1919), and *Dennis* v. *United States* (1951) reveal exaggerated concerns (as about "terrorism" today) that may be difficult to understand years afterward.

Of course, there are risks run when political speech is virtually unlimited in scope. But consider the implications of Article V of the Constitution, where it is recognized that comprehensive amendments to the Constitution may be proposed, considered, and even ratified. This is somehow in the spirit both of the Preamble and of the Ninth Amendment, which can be said implicitly to recognize the sovereign power of the People of the United States.

The significance in all this of the power to suspend access to the writ of *habeas corpus* should be noticed. The General Government is told, in effect, that no political speech should be suppressed unless "the situation" is indeed considered grave enough to call for suspension of the writ of *habeas corpus*. Such a suspension was, it seems, never seriously considered in the circumstances which led to the prosecutions undertaken in the *Schenck, Debs,* and *Dennis* cases (discussed in Part Two of these *Reflections*).

VIII

We have considered why the two sets of concerns (one spiritually oriented, the other politically oriented) addressed in the First Amendment are brought together as they are. We have considered as well why "freedom of speech" does not make "freedom of the press" superfluous. A similar inquiry about the assembly/petition provision should also be instructive.

Some might consider the assembly/petition provisions little more than a special case of the speech/press provisions. But there may be seen at work here the kind of precaution evident in the decision to provide separately for freedom of the press. Besides, effective use of freedom of speech may be curtailed by discouraging the assembling of citizens (such as in Tiananmen Square, in June 1989) who want to consult one another with a view to telling their government what is wrong with how public affairs are being conducted.

On the other hand, the integrity of the political process may be undermined by the tendency these days to extol *not* "freedom of speech [and] of the press," using the constitutional language, but rather (as we have seen) "freedom of expression." The traditional "freedom of speech" is somehow very much involved with citizenship and political concerns; the now fashionable "freedom of expression" looks much more to individualism and personal concerns (if not even to mere private gratification). One consequence, if not a cause, of this shift *is* the depreciation both of citizenship and of those community measures that contribute to the proper shaping of the moral character of citizens (measures which are discussed in the memoranda provided in Appendix N of this volume).

IX

We can be reminded by the House of Representatives Proposition No. 14, of August 24, 1789, of what were evidently considered the most critical rights at that time. "No State," it was suggested, should "infringe the right of trial by Jury in criminal cases, nor the rights of conscience, nor the freedom of speech, or of the press." Trial by jury, it seems, was looked to as providing significant protection for the personal liberty of citizens against governmental abuse, especially if the government is unpopular.

Thus, citizens are apt to be "on the defensive" when they rely on trial by jury to protect them. They are more apt to be "on the offensive" when they exercise their right to freedom of speech. Perhaps both offensive and defensive modes are evident in reliance upon "the rights of conscience."

It remains to be seen what *we* consider proper for the community to do, acting through its governments, to shape the moral character of citizens. The technical problems here are illustrated by the drastic decline in movie-house audiences in this Country during the past half-century, even as access steadily grows to television, videos, the Internet, and the like. That is, there no longer seem to be, at least in the United States, as much common *theater* experience which, week in and week out, helps shape us by routinely having us show one another as audiences how we should respond (with both tears and laughter) to various kinds of "situations."

11. The Sedition Act of 1798

I

Ulysses S. Grant, in his remarkable post–Civil War memoirs, spoke of France as "the traditional friend and ally of the United States." Monarchical France had indeed been a critical supporter of Americans during their Revolution. But France's own revolution, a decade later, very much disturbed the more conservative elements in this Country.

Particularly threatening was the Terrorism that was believed to be exported by the new French regime. It seems, in fact, that both the term "Terrorism" and the more fearful mode of responding to it go back for us to the 1790s. One consequence of the fear in this Country, especially among the Federalists, of French meddling in American affairs was the Sedition Act enacted by Congress in 1798 (which is set forth in Appendix G of this volume).

We can be reminded here of the concerns in this Country, after the Second World War, about the Soviet Union, which had been a critical ally during *that* war. On this postwar occasion, too, a fear of foreign subversive doctrines was critical. The Communist Party of the United States, along with "fellow travelers," became the target of anti-sedition measures, including a pervasive (and hence influential) system for testing the loyalty of all employees of the General Government.

II

Thomas Jefferson's Republican Party seemed more receptive than the Federalists to French notions about "the Rights of Man." Jefferson himself never got over the love he developed for Paris during his mission there (in Monarchist times) as the American Minister. The Jeffersonians came to see the Sedition Act of 1798, and its companion Aliens Acts, as in large part an improper effort on the part of the Federalists to retain their control of the General Government.

"The Sedition Act, aimed at 'domestic traitors,'" the *Encyclopedia of the American Constitution* reports, "made it a federal crime for anyone to conspire to impede governmental operations or to write or publish 'any false, scandalous, and malicious writing' against the government, the Congress, or the President." Little, if anything, was done with the Aliens Acts, which did depend on a state of war having been declared for their full effect. "The Sedition Act, on the other hand," it is also reported, "was widely enforced."

It is recorded as well by the *Encyclopedia,* "Twenty-five persons were arrested, fourteen indicted (plus three under common law), ten tried and convicted, all of them Republican printers and publicists." In the three most notorious cases, "the defendants were fined upward to $1,000 and imprisoned for as long as nine months." Partisan judges, it seems, were able to get juries to do what was "required."

III

The significance, across the centuries, of the lack of a comprehensive loyalty-testing program for General Government employees should be noticed. It is difficult to exaggerate the effects of such a program developed in this Country in the 1940s and 1950s. Those post–Second World War effects depended, in large part, upon the fact that many people worked for the General Government, unlike the condition in the 1790s.

It is hard to determine what the effects were, in the Country at large, of the Sedition Act of 1798. There *were* the dozen convictions for sedition. But it seems to have been widely believed that partisan political considerations guided the authorities involved (including the judges).

It is now also believed by some historians that the Federalist Party lost ground in the 1800 elections because of the Sedition Act of 1798. It is certainly true that the Jeffersonians (the first Republican Party) secured control both of the Presidency and of the Congress. This was, in 1800, the beginning of the permanent decline of the Federalist Party in this Country.

IV

No doubt, the Sedition Act of 1798 was considered oppressive by people accustomed (from even before Independence) to American-style liberty. The Federalists, on the other hand, were inclined to speak of the Sedition Act as *relaxing* that law of seditious libel inherited from England. It was for them, therefore, a progressive measure, not an assault upon the proper liberties of a free people.

The English lawyer would have noticed with interest two provisions in Section 3 of the Sedition Act of 1798. One was that "it shall be lawful for the defendant, upon the trial of the cause, to give in evidence in his defence, the truth of the matter contained in the publication charged as a libel." The English law had been that the truth of what had been said was irrelevant if the sentiments emitted tended to undermine the effectiveness of government.

The other noticeable provision in the 1798 Act was the concession that "the jury who shall try the cause, shall have a right to determine the law and the fact, under the direction of the court, as in other cases." The much-disputed English law had been that a judge would determine whether an utterance had been seditious, leaving to the jury merely the determination of whether the defendant had indeed been responsible for the utterance under consideration. Another way of putting the Federalists' argument here is to say that the Sedition Act of 1798 recognized the principles contended for in the 1735 case of the New York printer John Peter Zenger.

V

The most significant challenge to the Sedition Act of 1798, aside from the 1800 elections, came in the Virginia and Kentucky legislative resolutions of 1798–1799. James Madison is associated with the Virginia Resolutions, Thomas Jefferson (who was at the time Vice-President) with the Kentucky Resolutions. A particularly instructive response to these Resolutions was made in a Minority Report filed in the General Assembly of Virginia in 1799 (a report drafted, perhaps, by John Marshall, and found in Appendix I of this volume).

Questions are raised in the Virginia Resolutions (which may be found in Appendix H of this volume) about the powers of the General Government, with an emphasis placed upon the federal arrangement being a "compact." It is insisted by the Virginia Assembly that the Sedition Act

exercises . . . a power not delegated by the constitution, but on the contrary expressly and positively forbidden by one of the amendments thereto; a power which, more than any other, ought to produce universal alarm, because it is leveled against that right of freely examining public characters and measures, and of free communication among the people thereon, which has ever been justly deemed, the only effectual guardian of every other right.

It is noticed, in this context, that various States had, upon ratifying the Constitution, insisted that a Bill of Rights should be added to it.

It is significant that two Southern States could thus present themselves, in these Resolutions, as the critical defenders of the privileges of the people, and especially the right to freedom of speech and of the press. By the time of the Civil War, however, that right had come to be suppressed in one Southern State after another as desperate efforts were made to protect their vital interests in slavery from being undermined by abolitionist doctrines. By that time, also, the talk by Southerners about the Constitution as a *compact* was so pronounced that it became ever more difficult for them to regard the United States as a Country or Nation independent of its constitutional arrangements.

VI

The elections of 1800 *have* been seen as a repudiation of the Sedition Act of 1798. With that repudiation has come the now-orthodox legal opinion that there are not, at least so far as the General Government is concerned, any common law crimes. Also repudiated is the Federalist contention, expressed in the January 1799 Minority Report in the Virginia Assembly (and decades earlier by William Blackstone), that the "liberty of the press" signifies only "a liberty to publish, free from previous restraint" and hence does not include "the liberty of spreading with impunity false and scandalous slanders which may destroy the peace and mangle the reputation of an individual or of a community."

Particularly significant here *were* the elections of 1800. They came to be regarded as a popular repudiation of the Sedition Act of 1798, so much so that Congress refused to legislate against sedition again until the First World War, more than a century later. Even more important was the fact that the 1800 elections were followed by a perhaps unprecedented peaceful transfer of power from one political party to another in the modern world.

This transfer of power is celebrated in Thomas Jefferson's First Inaugural Address as President (set forth in Appendix J of this volume), which includes his proclamation, "We are all Republicans, we are all Federalists." This is followed by his Miltonian sentiment, "If there be any among us who would wish to dissolve this Union or to change its republican form, let them stand undisturbed as monuments of the safety with which error of opinions may be tolerated where reason is left free to combat it." This is, in effect, a sequel for Jefferson to the Declaration of Independence, as he insists here upon a liberation from the unmanly fears and the oppressive restraints of the old political order.

VII

No matter how soundly constituted and how well explained a political order may be, chance aberrations can be expected from time to time. A salutary lesson is offered here by the Sedition Act of 1798, which did not close without providing "That this act shall continue and be in force until the third day of March, one thousand eight hundred and one, and no longer." That was the last full day of the then-current term of President John Adams.

This is a lesson put to good (but perhaps not enough) use in the USA PATRIOT Act of 2001. The passions of a day can lead to unprecedented measures, some of which may turn out to be unfortunate. Even so, it can be difficult to repeal such measures, especially when patriotic sentiments are invoked in their support—and so it is prudent to provide, from their outset, an automatic expiration date.

If these measures are truly needed, they can be periodically reenacted. The precaution evident in the 1798 legislation drew, in effect, on the political wisdom of English parliamentarians. That the British continue to be aware of the problems here is testified to by the March 2005 compromise struck in Parliament, after a standoff between Commons and Lords, permitting some controversial passages in the Security Act under consideration to be effective for only a year.

VIII

Although the Sedition Act of 1798 was condemned as "unconstitutional" by its critics, it was *not* expected by them that the United States

Supreme Court would be reviewing it for its constitutionality. *Marbury* v. *Madison* (1803), with its insistence upon the power of Judicial Review of Acts of Congress, did not appear until the next decade. Thus, the response to the Sedition Act was to be *political,* not *judicial,* as would have been (and still usually is) the response to such legislation in Great Britain as well.

It eventually became routine, of course, to expect American Courts to review various kinds of legislation for constitutionality. Has not this tended to relieve Congress of its own duty to review all proposed legislation for constitutionality, something that only it can do in a comprehensive manner? The limitations of the Supreme Court here are evident, for example, in *its* inability to review the prosecution of wars that have been initiated without the constitutionally required declarations of war by Congress.

In the final analysis, of course, the integrity of a constitutional process depends upon the morale and the wisdom of the People. Constitutional provisions, including a pronouncement as august as the First Amendment, depend ultimately for their vitality upon the character of the People at large, something which was recognized by those who argued during the Ratification Campaign of 1787–1788 that the great rights of the English-speaking peoples were assured for the American People whether or not incorporated in a National bill of rights. Some support for this argument may be provided when we notice that the First Amendment is referred to, in the Virginia Assembly Minority Report of 1799, as "the 3d amendment," which suggests a curiously relaxed attitude about precisely what had happened to the twelve proposed amendments of 1789, among which were those we now know as the Bill of Rights (with its ten articles).

IX

It is fairly clear, in any event, that there has long been a National consensus that the Sedition Act of 1798 was an unwarranted interference with American self-government. This has not depended upon any Supreme Court Opinion. In fact, when the Court first addressed this kind of issue (in *Schenck* v. *United States* [1919] and, a week later, in *Debs* v. *United States* [1919]), it repudiated in effect what the People at large had come to believe about the Sedition Act of 1798.

That popular belief is reflected in what Justice Oliver W. Holmes says in his dissent in *Abrams* v. *United States* (1919), that he "had conceived that the United States had shown its repentance for the Sedition Act of 1798, by repaying fines that it imposed." This was said by him in response to the 1919 "argument of the Government that the First Amendment left the common law as to seditious libel in force." It is unfortunate that Justice Holmes had not sufficiently recalled these and related matters six months before when he wrote his disastrous Opinion for the Court in *Schenck* v. *United States.*

The reassuring vitality of the American regime may be seen even during political episodes that are troubling. Thus, the Fifth Congress, which enacted the anti–French Revolution Sedition Act (on July 14, 1798—the day now celebrated as Bastille Day!) had, a few weeks earlier (on June 25, 1798) enacted the Aliens Act of 1798, which included the concession,

> That it shall be lawful for any alien who may be ordered to be removed from the United States, by virtue of this act, to take with him such part of his goods, chattels, or other property, as he may find convenient; and all property left in the United States by any alien, who may be removed, as aforesaid, shall be, and remain subject to his order and disposal, in the same manner as if this act had not been passed.

This concession echoes the assurances in English law about the property of foreigners, assurances going back to at least Magna Carta, which are now at the heart of that reliable market economy upon which enduring liberty may in part depend in a continental republic.

12. John Stuart Mill's *On Liberty* (1859)

I

"The subject of this Essay," John Stuart Mill explains at the outset of his *On Liberty*, is "Civil, or Social Liberty: the nature and limits of the power which can be legitimately exercised by society over the individual." An important branch of this subject is, he says, "the Liberty of Thought, from which it is impossible to separate the cognate liberty of speaking and of writing." The Liberty of Thought and Discussion, to which chapter 2 of *On Liberty* is devoted, is "a subject which for now three centuries has been so often discussed."

Mill's "three centuries" take us back to the time of Thomas More, the author (as Speaker of the House of Commons) of the celebrated petition justifying parliamentary immunity, the precursor of our "freedom of speech." A century after More there had appeared the even more celebrated *Areopagitica* of John Milton, the pamphlet that argues for unlicensed printing. Mill's essay (the third in this trilogy of noteworthy liberty-minded English texts) is so celebrated that it can be identified in our own time (by Hilail Gildin) as virtually an appendix to the Declaration of Independence and the Constitution of the United States.

More's primary concern had been to insure the intimidation-free political discussion needed for effective parliamentary operations. Milton's primary concern had been to liberate publications from any system of routine censorship, publications that would include discussions of religious as well as of political subjects. Mill carries this campaign even further, arguing not only for the absence of prior restraint but also for immunity from subsequent official prosecution (if not also for immunity from persecution by public opinion) for what one says on any subject whatsoever.

II

Two great martyrs to the cause of "the Liberty of Thought and Discussion" are recalled by Mill: Socrates and Jesus. Socrates, we are reminded, "was put to death by his countrymen, after a judicial conviction, for impiety and immorality." The impiety, we are told, consisted of his "denying the gods recognized by the State"; the immorality consisted of his "being, by his doctrines and instruction, a 'corruptor of youth.'"

Mill then passes on "to the only other instance of judicial iniquity, the mention of which, after the condemnation of Socrates, would not be an anti-climax." He speaks thus of "[t]he man who left on the memory of those who witnessed his life and conversation such an impression of his moral grandeur that eighteen subsequent centuries have done homage to him as the Almighty in person." This man, Mill goes on to say, was condemned and executed as a "blasphemer."

Mill insists that those who had contributed to the condemnations of Socrates and Jesus had not been "bad men." They were "not worse than men commonly are, but rather the contrary; [they were] men who possessed in a full, or somewhat more than a full measure, the religious, moral, and patriotic feelings of their time and people." Mill does not venture to suggest, however, what either Socrates or Jesus would likely have thought of the virtually unlimited Liberty of Thought and Discussion that he advocates in his essay.

III

Perhaps, it might be argued, both Jesus and Socrates would have accommodated their sometimes vigorous denunciations of dubious doctrines to the more relaxed manners of modernity. Thus, it is evident in Mill's essay that the Roman Catholic Church, which had been portrayed by Milton as a particularly troubling practitioner of censorship, is no longer as repressive as its adversaries had once regarded it. Indeed, Mill can, in support of his case for the freedom to make the most unpopular arguments, remind his readers of the Church's use of the institution of the Devil's Advocate in the canonization process.

If even those proposed for sainthood may not be spared any possible criticism, why should the men and measures of one's day be shielded from critics? Of course, someone such as Thomas More would argue that it had

been his Church, in the time of Henry VIII, which had stood for freedom
of conscience in the face of oppressive political demands. On the other
hand, we have noticed, More himself, when in power, was evidently ruthless in his pursuit of heretics.

A willingness to suppress offensive opinions, Mill argues, presupposes
the infallibility of those in control. He indicates that the opinions of his
day that are particularly vulnerable to official sanctions are religious in
character, opinions which tend to be guarded in the United States more
by "free exercise of [religion]" protection than by "freedom of speech" protection. Also vulnerable in his day, Mill indicates, are opinions endorsing
tyrannicide, an extreme political remedy that can be said to be sanctioned,
at least in principle, by the Declaration of Independence.

IV

Mill's willingness to extend the protection he endorses to a wide, perhaps even to a virtually unlimited, range of subjects suggests that he does
not ground himself in traditional English constitutionalism. He speaks as
very much a modern, aware of considerable scientific progress, rather than
as an old-fashioned legal scholar. Thus he can use Newtonian physics as an
illustration of a discipline that is firmly established in his day.

Repeated challenges are needed, Mill argues, even for those who do
know the truth about a matter. Only if one is stoutly challenged from time
to time is one likely to understand fully what one believes. Otherwise, one
"knows" the truth no better than do those who accept errors that they
mistake for the truth.

The motives of the challenger do not matter, however inferior they
may be to those who are challenged. Whatever the challenger's motives, he
can be thought of as a benefactor. A challenger's motives may impede his
own pursuit of the truth, preventing *him* from benefiting in the way that
the person challenged can be helped who is intent upon learning what is
right and what is wrong about what he himself believes.

V

Mill, in his *On Liberty* essay, questions a critical premise in Milton's
Areopagitica—the premise that truth will prevail over error in a free and
open encounter. The truth, Mill laments, can be eclipsed among a people

for long periods of time. Its discovery and thereafter its maintenance require constant effort.

He recognizes, of course, that the truth does have advantages, that it *is* more apt than error to be revived from time to time. In extolling the truth as he does, however, Mill does not seem to recognize that there may be truths that only a few can grasp. One may well wonder whether that should make Mill cautious about the virtually unfettered liberty that he champions.

Caution here may even lead one to resort to salutary deceptions for the sake of those who may not understand either what threatens or what benefits them. Such a subterfuge may be, as well, a defensive maneuver on the part of anyone who is vulnerable at the hands of those who cannot recognize either how good he is or how inferior they are. Perhaps Mill's dedication for this essay, in which his late wife is extolled, should have reminded him both that there are markedly superior people in the world from time to time and that they can be quite vulnerable.

VI

Of course, the vulnerability of the best is recognized early on in what Mill says about Jesus and Socrates. But he does not seem to recognize as well that both of these men insisted that the best that they had to offer is not for this world. We recall that Socrates, for example, had observed at his trial that he would have perished long before if he had engaged in politics.

The vulnerability of the best is recognized by Mill in still another way when he recalls the career of Marcus Aurelius, a Roman ruler with the greatest gifts and of the noblest character. Yet he, as Emperor, had been a persecutor of Christians. But, we can wonder, had he, as a man with political duties, been properly concerned with whether "primitive" Christianity would be socially responsible?

This is a concern that can be aroused in one who observes how Christian outspokenness (*parresia*) has disregarded the prudent accommodations that make an enduring community possible. Were the early Christians doctrinally, if not also temperamentally, inclined to elevate the "personal" far above the "political," something that the Church was *not* inclined to do once it succeeded to various institutions of the Roman Empire? Marcus Aurelius' own undue deference to the "personal" took the disastrous form of his settling the imperial succession upon his abominable son, putting a halt thereby to an unprecedented series of good Emperors.

VII

The significance of the political (as well as of the modern right to privacy?) may be seen in the heritage to which More, Milton, and Mill have been able to contribute. Milton, for one, believed that the English are particularly open to liberty. He was reinforced in this belief by what he had observed during a Continental trip, which had included (we have noticed) a visit to Galileo, who was ending his life under house arrest.

What shapes a people to have the dominant inclinations it may chance to have, whether it is for liberty or for love or for piety? For example, the centuries of discipline to which the Israelites were subjected can be said to be manifest in their remarkable descendants to this day. Does Mill, with his insistence upon liberty, recognize what had been required to establish and to maintain the English-speaking peoples whom he addresses?

Particularly to be noticed in the "program" that produced (or at least permitted) Anglo-American constitutionalism is the influence of William Shakespeare. However receptive Shakespeare was to Roman republicanism, he would probably have had reservations about the elevation of that "individual" made so much of by Mill. It could be instructive to speculate about which of Shakespeare's characters most resembles Mill's devotee of liberty, with Brutus and Cassius (and perhaps Coriolanus) suggesting the elevation of liberty into self-sacrifice (if not even into the suicidal) and with Richard III and Iago (and perhaps Caliban) suggesting the degradation of liberty into licentiousness (if not even into anarchy).

VIII

Mill, in developing his advocacy of liberty, is obliged to acknowledge the limitations of his principles. Thus, he recognizes that the system he describes should not be expected to benefit barbarians, arguing that despotism is "a legitimate mode of government in dealing" with such people, "provided the end be their improvement, and the means justified by actually effecting that end." Mill adds, "Liberty, as a principle, has no application in any state of things anterior to the time when mankind have become capable of being improved by free and equal discussion."

Thus, Mill does not assume that civilization develops automatically (or "naturally") among a people. There may even be the problem of determining what *is* a people and where it should be situated. Thus there is, it seems, no natural goodness that can be depended upon to assert itself everywhere sooner or later.

Indeed, one must wonder whether Mill is sufficiently aware of that reversion to barbarism of which even an advanced people is capable, something we have seen horribly displayed in our time. This bears on the question of the discipline needed to maintain the good. Liberty, it can be said, is in the service of excellence, just as equality is in the service of justice—with both liberty and equality subject to adjustments (if not even to prudent manipulations) by the truly good.

IX

The noteworthy concession that Mill makes about how a primitive people should be disciplined is matched by another noteworthy passage about the discipline that might be needed in England itself. He recognizes, that is, that "even opinions lose their immunity when the circumstances in which they are expressed are such as to constitute their expression a positive instigation to some mischievous act." It is here that Mill goes on to concede, "An opinion that corn-dealers are starvers of the poor, or that private property is robbery, ought to be unmolested when simply circulated through the press, but may justly incur punishment when delivered orally to an excited mob assembled before the house of a corn-dealer, or when handed about among the same mob in the form of a placard."

In such circumstances, it seems, an assembly, even in England, becomes like the barbarians in need of firm rule for their own good (as well as for the good of others). We can be reminded here of our own clichés (taken from the *Schenck Case* discussed in Part Two of this volume) about "a clear and present danger" and about "falsely shouting fire in a theatre." But Mill would remind us as well of what he said in his "corn-dealer" passage about leaving "unmolested" the circulation of incendiary talk "through the press."

Thus, whatever reservations we may have about Mill's evident lack of concern for the maintenance of that discipline which properly shapes and thereafter governs a not-primitive people, we can find him useful as a curb on those who are (as we have seen since September Eleventh) unduly fearful. That is, Mill can be put to good use by anyone who truly knows what he is doing. It can therefore be said of Mill's arguments what he himself says about "popular opinions, on subjects not palpable to sense," that they "are often true, but seldom or never the whole truth."

13. Freedom of Speech and the Coming of the Civil War

I

Once a generation of Americans had become accustomed to an everyday exercise of liberty in a constitutional regime characterized both by self-government and by the rule of law, the recognition of universal equality that seemed to have been endorsed in the Declaration of Independence became harder to ignore. *Liberty* thus came to be invoked in the United States by those (anticipated by John Woolman, much earlier) who condemned slavery and wanted to abolish it altogether. Liberty was also invoked by those who defended slavery and wanted not only to maintain it but also to expand it into ever more Territories of the United States.

The decisive responses to abolitionist demands can be said to have come out of South Carolina. The most authoritative of these expressions appeared first in the form of speeches by Senator John C. Calhoun and then (two decades later) in the form of a declaration of secession and independence by the State of South Carolina. The decisive responses, in turn, to Southern arguments and actions were made (beginning in early 1861) both by Northern volunteers and by President Lincoln, probably the most articulate champion thus far of the Declaration of Independence.

Abraham Lincoln rose to National prominence in large part because of his reasoned opposition in 1858, especially during the Lincoln-Douglas Senatorial debates in Illinois, to the doctrines advanced by the United States Supreme Court in *Dred Scott* v. *Sandford* (1857), a case that seemed to deny power in the General Government to keep slavery out of the Territories of the United States. Such a restraint upon the General Government challenged what Lincoln and others regarded as critical to the Declaration of Independence and the Constitution of 1787, the understanding that slavery should be regarded as having been placed by the Founders in the course of ultimate extinction Nationwide. One consequence of the Civil

War was to give the Declaration of Independence a new luster both in this Country and abroad, not least perhaps because of the way that Southerners, too, very much relied on parts of it in 1860–1861 (even as they ignored its "created equal" language).

II

Calhoun, in a speech in the Senate on February 6, 1837, condemned the growing number of abolitionist petitions being submitted to Congress, petitions which he believed Congress should refuse to accept, however much the petitioners invoked the assembly and petitions provisions of the First Amendment. Such petitions and the political movements associated with them were regarded by the most influential Southerners as a determined assault upon the distinctive, and vital, social institutions of the South. The South was thought of by Southerners, as the slavery issue intensified, as both distinctive and separable, something that would become evident to everyone (they warned) if irresponsible talk in the North was not curbed.

Already, by the 1830s, it was apparent that the South was being obliged to assume a defensive stand with respect to slavery. And this, in turn, stimulated Southerners to justify their sense of separateness by talk of the Constitution as merely a "compact" and of the Union as no more than a "confederation." The term *federal* appealed to them much more than the term *national.*

And so Southerners talked more and more of what they, as once independent States (if not even as Nations), had bargained for, and relied on, when they agreed in 1787–1789 to the current Constitution. Such talk could not easily be made to apply, however, to the States carved by Congress out of the Territories of the United States, that score of States which followed upon the original Thirteen. The ambiguous status of such States is reflected in the motto found on the seal of Illinois, which became a State in 1818: "State Sovereignty, National Union."

III

So South Carolina, the eighth State to ratify the Constitution of 1787, took the lead in the effort to vindicate what it considered the prerogatives of the States. *The* model for its "fire-eaters" of December 1860 and their

Declaration of Secession was Calhoun (who had died in 1850), someone who could condemn Northern abolitionists as "blind fanatics." He offered himself as a champion of liberty and as a defender of "free and stable political institutions."

Southerners, Calhoun argued, have to defend themselves against the aggression of the more irresponsible Northerners. "I do not belong," he proclaimed in 1837, "to the school which holds that aggression is to be met by concession." Rather, he counseled "the opposite creed, which teaches that encroachments must be met at the beginning, and that those who act on the opposite principle are prepared to become slaves."

Calhoun, in this vivid repudiation of Southern enslavement, echoes Patrick Henry in his great "Give Me Liberty, or Give Me Death" speech of 1775, when he proclaimed, "[H]e considered [the question before this house] as nothing less than a question of freedom or slavery." Calhoun said, in effect, that Southerners should not permit themselves to be treated by the North the way that Southerners had to treat Africans. He thereby recognized, here and elsewhere, that slavery is an unfortunate condition for any people, whatever the necessities of the case may be.

IV

But Calhoun went on to argue, in this speech as elsewhere, that slavery is beneficial for people such as the Africans. In this he anticipated what John Stuart Mill would say two decades later, in his *On Liberty* essay, about the benevolent despotism needed by barbarians if they are ever to enjoy the benefits of civilization. In this argument Calhoun was evidently not moved by, if he was even aware of, protests, such as those by John Wesley in 1774, that Africans had had decent communities in their homelands which the depredations of slave traders had callously devastated.

It is, in a way, reassuring that Calhoun could suggest the arguments he did for the "positive" good of slavery, an institution which (he argued) benefited both slaves and masters. It is somewhat reassuring, that is, that he felt *a need* to justify continuing, as the Founders had, the institution of slavery without continuing also their assessment of it as no better than "a necessary evil" to be temporarily put up with. Both fear and greed seem to have led Southerners, early in the nineteenth century, to move away from an assessment of slavery that did look to its eventual abolishment—but this they evidently could not do without justifying themselves, in their intention to continue slavery indefinitely, as just and decent.

Certainly, Calhoun could not bear to have slavery spoken of by the abolitionists as "sinful and odious." Thus, he could argue, not without some justice, that the elderly and infirm among the slaves tend to be better treated than their counterparts among the free laborers in the North. Thus, also, we see again and again (I argue in a volume being prepared on life, death, and the Constitution) the desire of everyone (including even monsters such as Adolf Hitler and Josef Stalin) not only to seek what they believe to be good but also to appear to do so—a complicated desire which may provide support for the proposition that there may be, for human beings, some things that are good and right by nature.

V

No argument has to be made by us for the benefits of freedom of speech and of the press. But this freedom *is* like medicine that is hardly likely to do one much good if it is not capable, in some circumstances, of doing one harm. And the great harm that decades of agitation, North and South, eventually did may be seen in the South Carolina Declaration of the Causes of Secession in December 1860, after it had become evident that Abraham Lincoln would be the next President of the United States.

Lincoln observed, in 1861, that Secession had followed upon the corruption of language for some years. This meant, among other things, that the South could not face up squarely to what it was doing, something reflected in what Lincoln said (in his Message of July 4, 1861): "It might seem, at first thought, to be of little difference whether the present movement at the South be called 'secession' or 'rebellion.'" But, he argued, "The movers . . . knew they could never raise their treason to any respectable magnitude by any name which implies *violation* of law."

Much is made by the 1860 South Carolina Convention of the failure of Northern States (thirteen of them are listed) to respect their obligations under the Fugitive Slave Clause in Article IV of the Constitution of 1787. It is evident here as elsewhere that the critical issue *was* slavery, something that President Lincoln insisted upon in his Second Inaugural Address and that General Grant recognized in his *Memoirs*. Care in the use of language may be seen in how the South Carolina Convention never used *Nation* when referring to the United States, but only when referring to the States that may secede from the federal compact and thereby join the other nations of the world.

VI

The South Carolina Convention borrowed liberally from the Declaration of Independence, taking care however (as we have seen) to ignore its "created equal" language. It was apparent to the Convention that Lincoln and his party were hostile to slavery, and this was so no matter how careful Republicans had been in giving repeated assurances that slavery would not be touched by them *where it already was.* Southerners sensed, that is, that if the Lincoln policy with respect to the Territories was insisted upon, the future of slavery even in the Old South would be precarious.

The States for which the South Carolina Convention spoke were identified as "slave-holding States." The other States are not identified as "Free States," but rather as "non-slave-holding States." Again and again, one can see, slavery was something that was very awkward to be talked about, especially by those who would not concede that it should be eventually abolished.

A continued Union was deemed impossible once the nonslaveholding States "[had] assumed the right of deciding upon the propriety of [the South's] domestic Institutions; and [had] denied the rights of property established in fifteen of the States and recognized by the Constitution." Particularly resented, it seems, was something that had offended John Calhoun (and, later, Alexander H. Stephens), the fact that the Northern States "[had] denounced as sinful the Institution of Slavery." The Convention concluded its December 1860 cataloging of grievances with its lament that "Sectional interests and animosity will deepen the irritation and all hope of remedy is rendered vain, by the fact that public opinion at the North has invested a great political error with the sanctions of a more erroneous religious belief."

VII

A tidal wave of "erroneous religious belief[s]" must have seemed to some South Carolinians to have inundated them when they encountered, later on, the most powerful Northern song of the war, "The Battle Hymn of the Republic." Its closing stanza must have seemed particularly heretical:

> In the beauty of the lilies Christ was born across the sea,
> With a glory in His bosom that transfigures you and me:
> As He died to make men holy, let us die to make men free,
>   While God is marching on.

And, if this was not bad enough, there was the quite popular "John Brown's Body" (sung to the same tune), the glorification of a man who had been hung for treason by the United States as recently as December 1859 because of his attempt to free slaves at Harpers Ferry, Virginia.

Fifteen States had been identified by the 1860 South Carolina Convention as slaveholding. Following South Carolina's lead, Mississippi, Florida, Alabama, Georgia, Louisiana, and Texas also "seceded" by February 1, 1861, forming thereafter the Confederate States of America. Thus, of the first seven States to "secede," only two of them chanced to have been among those original Thirteen that, it could be argued with *some* plausibility, had entered (in 1787–1789) into a compact known as the Constitution.

It was not until after the firing upon Fort Sumter, a National fort in Charleston Harbor, five weeks after the Lincoln inauguration, that Virginia, North Carolina, Tennessee, and Arkansas also "seceded." We are told, by the *Encyclopedia of the American Constitution,* "A proslavery rump session of the Missouri legislature and a convention of Kentucky Confederate soldiers declared their States seceded, but both States as well as the [two] other [slaveholding] border States [Delaware and Maryland], remained in the Union." It is indicative of the precision to which Lincoln (a fancier of Euclid) was inclined that he could, in his July 4, 1861, Message to Congress, speak of "the border States, so called—in fact, the middle States," indicating thereby (as he did many times thereafter) that he would consider the entire Country (of thirty-four States) to be virtually indivisible.

VIII

Calhoun had spoken, in 1837, of the "incendiary opinion" about slavery insisted upon by Northern abolitionists. We can see anticipated here the "fire in a theatre" talk seven decades later in *Schenck* v. *United States* (1919). Again and again, Southerners insisted that the Congress of the United States was not authorized to meddle with slavery—and hence that the provocative abolitionist petitions should never be received by either House of Congress or in any other way officially recognized.

It could be argued, of course, that the efforts to implement not only the Fugitive Slave Clause but also the Three-Fifths Clause, upon which Southern slaveholders depended, made slavery a legitimate topic for Congress to consider. It would have to be determined, from time to time, who indeed was a slave, a question that had already been addressed in *Dred Scott*. But once questions had to be entertained about who *was* a slave (with State laws urged by Southerners as decisive), it could be virtually impossible thereafter to avoid the question of who *should* be a slave.

In addition, the Amendment Power of the People of the United States, recognized in Article V of the Constitution, meant that the continued traffic in slaves, Countrywide, could be assessed from time to time, just as later the continued traffic in alcoholic beverages was assessed (and prohibited) by a Constitutional amendment. Besides, the recognition in the Constitution of a power in Congress after 1808 to prohibit the importation of slaves testified to the Founders' opinion that slavery was a legitimate object of National concern. Thus, the Calhounian insistence, in effect, that no one outside of the South could properly even *think* about slavery in the United States reflected the desperation of Southerners who really did not know what to do about slavery, an institution that did seem to go against the grain of the liberty-oriented constitutionalism generally relied upon by the English-speaking peoples.

IX

Even so conservative, property-respecting a judge as Lord Mansfield had recognized, in *Somerset's Case* of 1772, that slavery was in principle questionable (an understanding developed in the *Reflections* I have prepared on slavery and the Constitution). This assessment had been confirmed by what the Founders themselves *did* about slavery in 1787 in the Northwest Ordinance. This perpetual prohibition of slavery in the Northwest Territory was laid down by a Congress, under the Articles of Confederation, which had far fewer powers than Congress was to have under the Constitution of 1787.

Calhoun, in 1837, very much resented what the pulpit, the schools, and the press in the North were doing to turn their people against slavery. But, Lincoln argued in his First Inaugural Address, there had been nothing in what Northerners had been doing or saying which justified the current Southern invocation of that right of revolution recognized by the Declaration of Independence. Indeed, Lincoln himself was to learn in the course of his Presidency how abusive a free-speaking people can be toward those in authority.

A general freedom of speech and of the press was maintained in the North throughout the Civil War, despite the occasional suspension here and there of access to the writ of *habeas corpus*. So powerful were the critics of the Lincoln Administration that it at times seemed unlikely that Abraham Lincoln would be reelected in 1864. The intimate relation between freedom of speech and the necessary political processes of the Country was again and again evident even during that soul-wrenching period of genuine "clear and present danger" for the United States.

PART TWO

1. The Naive Folly of Realists:
A Defense of Justice Black (1937–1971)

I

A distinguished legal scholar recently assessed the career of Hugo L. Black as a constitutional fundamentalist. This assessment recognized Justice Black as the preeminent judicial champion of the First Amendment. He was also recognized as one of the great United States Supreme Court Justices.

This discussion by a would-be realist questioned the assumption that there is an "original understanding" of constitutional provisions to be relied upon. Or, if there is such an understanding, it was questioned whether it can be known. Or, if it can be known, it was questioned whether it can or should be relied upon by those in authority.

It is not denied by such scholars, who can be quite competent, that there are better and worse constitutional determinations. Nor is it denied that the Supreme Court should attempt to advance the Good. But it is questioned whether there is any "original understanding of the Constitution" by which judges, or anyone else in authority, can and should take their bearings.

II

Three important facets of Justice Black's career were reviewed, beginning with that reading by him of the First Amendment which would invalidate virtually all suppression of "freedom of speech." But, it was argued, whatever the merits of such invalidation, as a matter of public policy, it cannot be regarded as *the* understanding of the Framers. Thus, it was observed, the Alien and Sedition Acts were enacted within a decade of the ratification of the First Amendment, with the Federalists defending them as constitutional.

Next to be reckoned with was Justice Black's reading of the Fourteenth Amendment as a barrier to any racial segregation in this Country. However desirable this desegregation may be, it was argued, it cannot be regarded as the understanding of the Framers of the Fourteenth Amendment. Thus, it was recalled, the Houses of Congress which proposed the Fourteenth Amendment had then, and continued to have, racially segregated seating in their visitors' galleries.

Also to be reckoned with was Justice Black's reading of the Commerce Clause. This, it was argued, has permitted a far more detailed regulation of the economy of this Country than could ever have been contemplated by the Framers. Particularly to be noticed here is the kind of New Deal regulation that was ratified in *Wickard* v. *Filburn* (1942), where the way a farmer used his modest acreage was supervised in some detail (and perhaps not always sensibly) by the Government of the United States.

III

Each of these three facets of the Black career can usefully be touched upon here. There is no doubt that the New Deal regulation of the economic life of this Country was far more extensive than anything attempted by the early Congresses. But that does not settle the question of how much economic regulation the Commerce Clause was intended to permit.

Consider, for example, what is done today in developing the military forces of the United States. This illustrates how a power, originally exercised to acquire and use sailing ships and muskets, can properly be used to develop and employ submarines and intercontinental missiles. Comparable developments can be expected as the General Government attempts to minister to the economic life of the Country.

After all, it would have been a curious state of affairs if the Nationalists who framed the Constitution had not provided *their* General Government the scope of powers to deal with the economy of their Country that all other governments elsewhere that they knew about had long had. And, it should be recalled, it was noticed in the unanimous Court's Opinion (not by Justice Black) in *Filburn* that the scope of the reading *there* of the Commerce Clause had been anticipated more than a century earlier by Chief Justice John Marshall and his colleagues. That Chief Justice, it should also be recalled, *was* of the Founding generation.

IV

The next facet of the Black career to be touched upon here is his contribution to the desegregation efforts by the United States Supreme Court. Of course, racial segregation continued long after the Fourteenth Amendment was ratified. And it *is* likely that various of those responsible for that Amendment did not expect such segregation to be immediately removed by this change in the Constitution.

We should be reminded here of the history of other constitutional documents of remarkable scope. Consider, for example, the long-run implications of the demands made by the Barons upon the King in Magna Carta. Intrinsic to those demands were standards that could eventually be applied in turn to the Barons' relations with their own subjects.

Consider, also, the scope of the "created equal" language in the Declaration of Independence. Abraham Lincoln's deeply instructive career very much depended upon a reading of that language as dooming slavery in the United States. That this is *not* a reading unanticipated by the Framers is suggested by the decisive prohibition of slavery found in the Northwest Ordinance of 1787, an absolute prohibition that contributed significantly to the eventual abolition of slavery in the United States.

V

Last in this review of three facets of the Black career is his championing of freedom of speech and the First Amendment. What *do* the Alien and Sedition Acts of 1798 suggest about the original understanding of the First Amendment? What *should* be made of the fact that a Federalist Congress enacted them?

Federalists, it should be remembered, were on both sides of this controversy. After all, James Madison contributed significantly to the Virginia Resolutions condemning those Acts—and in doing so, he invoked the fundamentals of the regime. Whatever his personal standing by then as a "Federalist," he *had* been one of the *Federalist* contributors and thereafter one of the principal Framers of the First Amendment.

In addition, it can be said, with some plausibility, that resentment of the Alien and Sedition Acts was critical to the decline in power of the Federalist Party, beginning with the 1800 elections. The reading of the First Amendment by the generation that ratified it seems to have been decidedly against those Acts, which were soon (and for more than a century and a half thereafter) generally regarded as having been unconstitutional. It is this response, grounded in a general understanding of the principles of our regime, that Justice Black was nourished by in his championing of the First Amendment.

VI

This, then, is how the Black career can begin to be understood, a career very much grounded in the constitutional principles and expectations of the American regime. This is an understanding that makes more of the influence of "ideas" than of "forces" in the way that a People conduct their affairs. The realist, on the other hand, does tend to make more of "forces"—and in doing so, he may not recognize the unexamined opinions which move him.

Thus, the realist, however principled he may personally be, does not recognize the significance of principles in the ordering of communities. Of course, people often do not understand what it is that they are saying and doing. That is, they may need help in recognizing the ideas implicit in what they say and do.

Among the things people do is to establish and to amend constitutions, either explicitly or implicitly. That it is reasoning beings who do such things means that ideas are fundamental to how they think. And as reasoning beings they can learn that passions may impede the deliberations upon which they depend.

VII

The passions that are at work in human affairs can enliven and enrich our lives. But they can also mislead us, leaving us more subject to chance than we either want or recognize. We are all familiar with the kind of speculation which begins, "What *could* I have been 'thinking' when . . . ?"

Questionable passions are very much in evidence at various times in the history of the United States. They may be seen, for example, in the excitement that produced the Alien and Sedition Acts, the sedition prosecutions of the First World War period, and our domestic excesses of the Cold War. They may be seen, as well, in various of the responses among us to the September Eleventh attacks.

The most critical display of passions in the history of the United States was that following upon the efforts, in 1860 and thereafter, of the South Carolina "fire-eaters" and others of like mind elsewhere in the Country. The very presuppositions of the regime were challenged by them. Indeed, they can be said to have been "realistic" in recognizing that the principles of the regime, grounded in the Declaration of Independence, were indeed such that it was only a matter of time before there would be repudiated Nationwide the way of life by which Southerners happened to be trapped and to which they considered themselves obliged to be dedicated.

VIII

Thus, it should be evident that not all dedications are created equal. One is not apt to recognize this if one, in the mode of realists, makes more of forces than of ideas in the ordering both of the human soul and of human communities. Here, as elsewhere in our speculations, we should notice the dubious character of contemporary legal realism.

The realist *can* be quite competent, making considerable use of the intelligence with which he is endowed. But he can also be simply wrong-headed, not least when he makes more of legal precedents than of the principles that those precedents strove to discover and to develop. In these matters judges are very much in need of help if they are to understand what they try to do.

This may be seen, for example, in the judicial suicide, or at least the judicial self-mutilation, exhibited in *Erie Railroad Company* v. *Tompkins* (1938). This is one of the more conspicuous monuments these days to legal realism. But the *Erie* doctrine (discussed at length in my *Reflections on Constitutional Law*) simply does not recognize and defer to what common law judges, lawyers, and scholars have known and done for centuries in the service of an awareness of the requirements both of justice and of reasonable expectations.

IX

Justice Black dramatized his constitutional fundamentalism by "always" carrying a pocketbook-size copy of the Constitution, which he would ostentatiously consult on occasion. Of course, the realist is inclined to see such a reliance on the Constitution (if sincere) to be naive. Perhaps even more naive, for the realist, is the belief among us that any *serious* judge relies on the Constitution to a significant degree.

One of the most prominent realists in our history was Stephen A. Douglas, a statesman who insisted (for the sake of domestic tranquility) that *permanent* concessions had to be made to the slavery interests in the United States. He was, that is, more than willing to adjust his readings both of the Declaration of Independence and of the Constitution to re- assure Southerners about such "politic" accommodations. Abraham Lin- coln, on the other hand, insisted again and again that there are principles upon which the American regime depends, principles which called for the eventual elimination of slavery in this Country.

Justice Black's valedictory statement, as a member of the Supreme Court, was his contribution to the disposition of the *Pentagon Papers Case* in June 1971, the case involving a purloined "Top Secret" Defense De- partment study that the *New York Times* and the *Washington Post* had tried to publish. His Concurring Opinion on that occasion opened with these challenging observations:

> I adhere to the view that the Government's case against the *Wash- ington Post* should have been dismissed and that the injunction against the *New York Times* should have been vacated without oral argument when the cases were first presented to this Court. I be- lieve that every moment's continuance of the injunctions against these newspapers amounts to a flagrant, indefensible, and con- tinuing violation of the First Amendment.

Three months later there could be heard at Hugo Black's funeral one of the passages which he selected to be read on that occasion, a passage from a Dissenting Opinion he had written ten years earlier that concluded, in the spirit of the First Amendment, "We must not be afraid to be free."

2. *Schenck* v. *United States* (1919); *Abrams* v. *United States* (1919)

I

Schenck v. *United States* may be the most important case interpreting and applying the Speech and Press provisions of the First Amendment. *Schenck* dealt with what may have been the first significant legislation bearing directly on these provisions since the Sedition Act of 1798. The United States Supreme Court never had occasion to review any convictions under the Sedition Act.

Six months after *Schenck,* the Supreme Court disposed of the appeals in *Abrams* v. *United States,* appeals that challenged much harsher applications of the Espionage Act of 1917 than those seen in *Schenck.* The *Abrams* convictions, too, were upheld, with only two dissenters, following upon the unanimity of the Court in *Schenck.* The patriotic passions aroused by the First World War were thus vindicated, just as had been done by the Sedition Act of 1798 in response to the passions said to have been stirred up in this Country by the dreaded Terrorism of the French Revolution.

An even greater threat to the very survival of the Country was faced during the Civil War, which did see suspensions of the writ of *habeas corpus* but no significant legislation attempting to suppress criticisms of the General Government. The "unschooled" Abraham Lincoln, it seems, had been far more tolerant of criticism of him and his policies than Woodrow Wilson (a former academic) was to be. Testifying to the vigorous and generally uninhibited political discourse in the North during the Civil War was the conduct of free elections there, both in 1862 and in 1864, contests so free that it seemed for a while that Lincoln would not be reelected.

II

Schenck and *Abrams* confirmed, in effect, that the most vigorous criti-

101

cisms of American participation in the First World War had properly been subject to suppression. Serious reservations about that war had been suppressed in Britain as well. The toll exacted by the conflict was much more severe there than in the United States, as may be seen in the rolls of the local dead memorialized in country churches all over Great Britain.

It is hard now to overestimate the spiritual as well as the physical damage caused by the First World War, a war which almost wrecked European Civilization. Among its consequences was the empowerment of Josef Stalin, Adolf Hitler, and their movements. It may also have made the Second World War virtually inevitable.

One can wonder, upon reviewing the appalling carnage of the First World War, whether anyone "in charge" knew what he was doing. And yet, a few years before the war, the German Kaiser had been the most exalted foreign guest, housed even in Windsor Castle, for the funeral in London of an English king, his uncle. Not long after, however, would begin what turned out to be the devastating Thirty Years War of the twentieth century.

III

War passions became so inflamed during the First World War that suggestions about a negotiated peace, such as had been possible to end conflicts in nineteenth-century Europe, could not be tolerated. Even so gifted a politician as Winston Churchill was swept up by the passions of that fateful decade. Those passions were such that the privileged classes in Britain sacrificed their sons along with those of the working classes.

There were more serious reservations about the war in the United States. For one thing, more than one-fifth of the population here was of German descent. The unpopularity of the war, at least in some quarters, is attested to by the report that three hundred thousand men evaded the draft, which would be equivalent to about a million men today.

Besides, Woodrow Wilson had won reelection in November 1916 on a platform which included the assurance that "He kept us out of war." One can be reminded of the victory by Lyndon Johnson over Barry Goldwater in 1964, a victory that was widely expected to keep the United States out of the Vietnam War. Within a year of Wilson's reelection, however, the President was asking Congress for a declaration of war, a declaration that was based in large part on pre–November 1916 grievances.

IV

Thus, the anti-war utterances complained of by the government in the *Schenck Case* were hardly unfamiliar. The principal count against the *Schenck* defendants, as stated by the United States Supreme Court, "charge[d] a conspiracy to violate the Espionage Act of June 15, 1917 . . . by causing and attempting to cause insubordination, &c., in the military and naval forces of the United States, and to obstruct the recruiting and enlistment service of the United States, when the United States was at war with the German Empire." The Court then explained that "the defendants wilfully conspired to have printed and circulated to men who had been called and accepted for military service under the [Conscription] Act of May 18, 1917, a document set forth and alleged to be calculated to cause such insubordination and obstruction."

The leaflet in question was "set forth" in the indictment and may be found in the Briefs and Records of the Supreme Court. But it is *not* found, even in substantial quotations therefrom, in the *Schenck* Opinion of the Supreme Court written by Justice Oliver W. Holmes. In fact, the only places where this leaflet can be found these days are in publications for which I have been responsible (including in Appendix K of this volume)—and this I have done in order to display the innocuousness of what the defendants had said, something that the admirers of Justice Holmes also seem to be somehow aware of, considering how they (like him) avoid quoting from the troubling leaflet when they recall his participation in the *Schenck Case.*

The political folly, as well as the constitutional impropriety, of the attempt at suppression in *Schenck* should be evident upon inspecting this leaflet, which calls upon its readers to "Assert [Their] Rights." Prominent politicians are quoted in the effort to enlist opposition to the Conscription Act. In short, the defendants (who were anything but original) were continuing the debate that had occupied the Country for several years, culminating in their somewhat naive appeal, "Come to the headquarters of the Socialist Party, 1326 Arch Street [in Philadelphia], and sign a petition to congress for the repeal of the Conscription Act."

V

Such sentiments as those expressed in the *Schenck Case* leaflet could have been published (and may even have been published) at that time without risk in the Country's larger newspapers. An attempt by the Administration to have a press censorship provision included in the Espionage Act had failed, which meant that vigorous criticism of the government continued. Perhaps, therefore, the only practical effect of the *Schenck Case* was to set an unfortunate precedent in First Amendment law.

It was a precedent that was enlivened by memorable language in the Holmes Opinion for a unanimous Court. The more unpopular critics of government had, for decades thereafter, to contend with his "clear and present danger" formula. This was reinforced by his likening of some exuberant arguments to that of someone "falsely shouting fire in a theatre."

Thus, the language used by Justice Holmes can be understood to have done far more to weaken the security of the United States than anything that the *Schenck* defendants and their successors in the docket ever tried to do. In fact, it might even be lamented that people such as Schenck had not been far more successful than they were not only in the United States but even more in Europe. It was almost as if a death wish dominated the Western soul, a suicidal impulse that could be exorcised only by tens of millions of casualties over a half-century, casualties that resulted from the passions of what the *Schenck* circular aptly described as "war-crazy nations."

VI

The language of the pamphleteers in *Abrams* was bolder than that in *Schenck*. But in that case, decided six months after *Schenck,* Justice Holmes dissented and was joined by Justice Louis D. Brandeis. Once again, Justice Holmes used memorable language.

It remains something of a mystery why Justice Holmes shifted his position as he did. And this time, in support of his dissent, he quoted at length from the defendants' writings, exhibiting thereby how inconsequential they had been. Perhaps the much more severe sentences in *Abrams* (imposed upon defendants who were Russian Jews) forced Justice Holmes to reconsider what he had somewhat cavalierly done in *Schenck* (although the severe sentence in *Debs* v. *United States* [1919] had not been enough to move him even when a prominent culprit was involved).

The Justice did not, however, repudiate his *Schenck* Opinion, upon which the *Abrams* Court relied. The way was now open for the so-called Red Scare of 1919–1920 (following upon the Russian Revolution), which anticipated the even more severe Red Scare after the Second World War. Eventually, *Schenck* could be carried to its extreme in *Dennis* v. *United States* (1951), which contributed to that intimidated public opinion which permitted the nightmarish involvement of the United States in the Vietnamese Civil War, an experience replicated in Iraq.

VII

Timing in these matters can be critical. This could be seen, decades later, in the death of Chief Justice Fred M. Vinson before the critical issues could be addressed by the Supreme Court in *Brown* v. *Board of Education* (1954). That permitted the installation of a Chief Justice with the personality and the talents (as well as with recollections of mistakes *he* had made during the Japanese Relocation days) that were needed for a statesmanlike handling of the *Desegregation Cases,* someone who could thereafter impress Laurence Berns as "a kind of living argument for democracy."

The effect of chance timing could be seen as well in the sequence of the Holmes Opinions in *Schenck* and *Abrams.* Had Justice Holmes been moved earlier, as he was in *Abrams* (where he could dismiss the defendants' talk as "a silly leaflet"), the Court would probably have had to content itself with a mediocre Opinion in *Schenck* that would have had far less of an effect than the Holmes rhetoric did for decades. Nothing that Justice Holmes might say in *Abrams* and thereafter could disarm the weaponry he had irresponsibly fashioned during the *Schenck*-stage of his First Amendment pronouncements.

Of course, the timing of the Russian Revolution, which itself was one of the disasters brought on by the First World War, was critical to the initial judicial pronouncements on the First Amendment in the United States. We have seen that the French Revolution, with its purported spawning of Terrorism, contributed to the development of the Alien and Sedition Acts of 1798. Fortunately, however, the 1798 Sedition Act was limited by Congress to two years, a prudent precaution whenever unusually repressive legislation responds to the excitement of the moment.

VIII

There was something comic about the two-bit *Schenck* and *Abrams* operations. Because of the defendants' quite limited resources, the critical *Schenck* text had been placed on the blank side of an already printed leaflet. Also, many copies of the critical *Abrams* leaflet were distributed by being thrown "from a window of a building where one of the defendants was employed" in New York City.

Also comic (and somehow similar) was the months-long Chicago Seven Conspiracy Trial (1968–1969), a spectacle to which a remarkably intemperate judge woefully contributed. All this had been anticipated by the folly of the city authorities who so conducted affairs that the Democratic Convention protesters would do the greatest possible harm to the protestors, to the Democratic Party, and to those authorities. Hubert Humphrey left Chicago as the badly damaged Presidential candidate of the Democratic Party, having exhibited during the Convention his incapacity for governance by not vigorously reining in his would-be supporters in the Chicago city government.

Of course, there is always, or almost always, something to be said for "the other side" in such controversies. Thus, the Mayor of Chicago could not bear to see his city "trashed," especially while the whole Country was watching. Thus, also, an elderly student of mine—an intelligent, quite decent lady—revealed at her death that she had over the years written speeches for the *Chicago Seven* trial judge, someone whom she had personally found courteous and honorable, quite unlike the unfortunate *persona* that he evidently could not help displaying on the bench.

IX

Today, far more severe criticisms are made (without any risk of prosecution) about our governments, even during wartime, than were made by the defendants in the *Schenck* and *Abrams Cases* as well as by defendants in the Cold War cases, such as *Dennis*. There does not seem to be much effective official curtailment at this time of even the most vigorous attacks upon official policies. Sometimes, indeed, our governments seem simply oblivious to any sustained criticism that calls their motives, their talents, or their methods into question.

Much criticism originates today in sources that are hard to identify, especially when the Internet is used to circulate fanciful, even scurrilous, messages. This may be seen, for example, in how conspiracy theories are now circulated worldwide. One result of these developments could eventually be to make all "talk" risk-free because little of it can be taken seriously.

Thus, it can sometimes seem a healthier state of affairs when people such as the defendants in *Schenck* and *Abrams* were taken seriously enough as "threats" to move the government of their day to prosecute them. Of course, those defendants did take themselves with a proper seriousness as well, as may be seen in how much (well over one-half) of the space in the *Schenck* leaflet is devoted to pronouncements about the Constitution. Appeals are made therein to "the citizens of Philadelphia, the cradle of American liberty," appeals which include the touching reminder (not associated with radical rhetoric these days?) that it was in *their* city that there "was signed the immortal Declaration of Independence."

3. *Debs* v. *United States* (1919);
Gitlow v. *New York* (1925)

I

One week after *Schenck* v. *United States* (1919), the United States Supreme Court confirmed the conviction (pursuant to the Espionage Act of 1917) of Eugene V. Debs for attempting to obstruct recruitment for the armed forces of the United States during the First World War. Justice Oliver Wendell Holmes again wrote for a unanimous Court, observing, "The chief defenses upon which the defendant seemed willing to rely [included] that based upon the First Amendment to the Constitution, disposed of in *Schenck* v. *United States*." Debs had been sentenced to ten years' imprisonment, Schenck to six months.

Debs was born in Terre Haute, Indiana, in 1855; he died in Elmhurst, Illinois, in 1926. He is identified in the *Encyclopedia Britannica* as a "labor organizer and Socialist Party candidate for U.S. President five times between 1900 and 1920." Debs, after "conduct[ing] a successful strike against the Great Northern Railroad (April 1894) for higher wages," "was further projected into the [national] limelight when sentenced to six months in jail (May–November 1895) after a federal injunction halted the Chicago Pullman Palace Car Company Strike, which he was helping to direct."

"During his [1895] prison term at Woodstock, Illinois," we are further told, "Debs was deeply influenced by his broad reading—including the works of Karl Marx—and subsequently became increasingly critical of traditional political and economic concepts, especially capitalism." It is also said, "Neither an intellectual nor a hardheaded politician, Debs won support through his personal warmth, integrity, and sincerity." The character of the man is suggested by the final exhortation in his June 16, 1918, speech at Canton, Ohio, which was critical to his indictment and which Justice Holmes quotes, evidently without sensing the nobility thereby revealed: "Don't worry about the charge of treason to your masters; but be concerned about the treason that involves yourselves," echoing thereby sentiments voiced in perilous times by such worthies as Thomas More.

II

The education of Debs, it seems, was advanced by his 1895 jail term, during which he could do some "broad reading." This contributed to his development as a leader in the Socialist movement in this Country. As such, he must have been much more influential than Schenck or Abrams ever could have been.

Particularly troubling for the authorities, of course, was Debs's opposition to the war, and especially to any involvement by the United States in it. His fateful June 16, 1918, Canton speech included the observation (quoted by Geoffrey Stone), "The master class has always declared the wars; the subject class has always fought the battles." Justice Holmes, in his *Debs* Opinion, paraphrased as follows what had been said in the speech, "[T]he subject class has had nothing to gain and all to lose, including their lives; . . . the working class, who furnish the corpses, have never yet had a voice in declaring war."

What Debs said about the working class "furnish[ing] the corpses" may apply to our Vietnamese and Persian Gulf engagements, but it certainly did not apply to the First World War or, for that matter, to the Second World War. Indeed, the First World War probably would have been far less devastating for Western Civilization if the privileged classes in Europe *had* been able to shield their sons from combat, allowing *them* to revive their countries once the slaughter stopped. Instead, one "master class" after another, in various European countries, had been left in ruins by the war, all too often allowing the worst among the survivors to seize power.

III

There *was*, we have noticed, widespread evasion of the draft in this Country during the First World War. Primarily responsible for this, it seems, was *not* the agitation here and there of antiwar speakers but rather the apparent futility of that war. It must have been difficult for some in this Country to believe that the United States had been immediately threatened by the years of senseless carnage in Europe.

In fact, many citizens would come to believe instead that the great risk for the United States came from becoming involved in such a pointless war, not from avoiding it—and they evidently voted that way in reelecting President Woodrow Wilson in 1916. Therefore, the people primarily responsible for obstruction of recruitment in this Country were probably the thousands of reporters and editors who kept newspaper readers informed about what was going on in Europe. *Those* journalists were hardly likely to be indicted by anyone, whatever might be done with such marginal authors as Charles Schenck and Jacob Abrams.

The principal American actor in these matters *was* the President of the United States. After all, he had persuaded the large majority of his fellow citizens, during the first two years of the war, that it was not in the interest of this Country to become involved in the conflict. His high-minded passion to "make the world safe for democracy" contributed, however, to the cataclysm that put at jeopardy one decent regime after another in Europe and elsewhere.

IV

Photographs of Eugene Debs portray him as eminently respectable, with the one in the *Encyclopedia Britannica* resembling a quite reliable banker. Woodrow Wilson's legacy is compromised by the recollection that someone as decent as Debs could have been kept in federal prison long after the Armistice. We are told, by the *Encyclopedia of the American Constitution,* "President Wilson, in failing health and embittered by the war and its critics, refused to pardon Debs before leaving the White House in 1921."

Lincoln Steffens, who knew personally at least the American principals in the Versailles Treaty negotiations after the First World War, reports on the problems encountered by Wilson at that time. "When the Treaty of Versailles was printed and published," he remembers, "the world was shocked." It was evident that some of the victors were getting ready for "the next war."

Steffens himself, at a press conference in Paris, having heard Wilson say that he was satisfied with the peace he had made, asked him, "Mr. President, do you feel that you achieved here the peace that you expected to make?" Wilson answered, after a pause, "I think that we have made a better peace than I should have expected when I came here to Paris." We might well wonder whether Wilson ever came to suspect that his antiwar critics had been right in opposing armed American intervention in that senseless conflict.

V

However that may be, the *Encyclopedia of the American Constitution* recalls, it was left to Warren G. Harding, who was hardly an idealistic statesman, to "display greater compassion [than Woodrow Wilson] by granting [Eugene Debs] a pardon." Harding's fellow conservative Ohio Senator, Robert A. Taft, could (Geoffrey Stone reports) later attack the indictment, during the *Second* World War, of twenty-six American fascist leaders for conspiring to undermine the morale of the armed forces as "witch-hunting" that reminded him of the abuses of the First World War. Woodrow Wilson, it seems, never came to assess in this manner the prosecutions of the First World War for which he was primarily responsible.

Debs v. *United States* is perhaps the most serious free speech case in the history of the First Amendment. After all, the man jailed had, in his campaigns for the Presidency, polled almost 1 million votes in 1912 and again in 1920 (while in prison), equivalent to almost 3 million votes today. This should be compared to the 900,000 votes polled by George C. Wallace in 1968, the 1.2 million votes polled by Henry A. Wallace in 1948, and the 2.9 million votes polled by Ralph Nader in 2000.

All this means, therefore, that *Debs* v. *United States* may be the most disgraceful prosecution for unpopular political speech in the history of the Country. The imprisonment by the Wilson Administration of Eugene Debs was as if the Truman Administration had imprisoned Henry Wallace, or as if the Nixon Administration had imprisoned George Wallace, or as if a future Democratic Administration should imprison Ralph Nader. A distinguished student of freedom of speech in the United States, Zechariah Chafee, commented thus on the treatment of Eugene Debs: "Lincoln would not have allowed an old man, a Presidential opponent and the choice of nine hundred thousand American citizens to lie in prison for sincere and harmless, even though misguided, words, over a year after the last gun was fired."

VI

Of course, *we* can wonder, knowing the long-term effects of the First World War, whether Debs's words had indeed been "misguided." After all, the truly misguided and dreadfully mischievous words had been those of the Wilson Administration and the prosecutors who attempted to silence the most vigorous critics of the war. One consequence of this was to radicalize the American Left, probably making it less responsible politically than it might otherwise have been.

It should be remembered, that is, that one out of every twelve voters did support Debs in the 1912 Presidential election. It should also be remembered that "he served as city clerk of Terre Haute (1870–1883) and as a member of the Indiana legislature (1885)." Thus, it is likely that Debs, if he had been treated with respect, would have been able to keep the American Left more "relevant" politically than it became after the Communist Party inherited control of the radical movement from Debs and his associates.

Debs had, in 1905, helped found the Industrial Workers of the World (IWW), but he soon withdrew because of its extremism. His evident moderation was such that he could, as we have seen, attract significant support nationally both in 1912 and in 1920. He was the kind of sincere dissenting voice with whom the dominant parties in a community should consider themselves privileged to engage in serious debate about the Common Good.

VII

Benjamin Gitlow (born in New Jersey in 1891), who had been indicted with three others by the State of New York for the statutory crime of criminal anarchy, was a quite different kind of man from Eugene Debs. After having had his conviction confirmed in *Gitlow* v. *New York* and serving a term in prison, he eventually became (well before he died in 1965) a "professional" anti-Communist, providing (among other services) testimony before the House of Representatives Un-American Activities Committee. His 1925 case, the *Encyclopedia of the American Constitution* reports, "is most often cited today for the doctrine of 'incorporating' First Amendment free speech guarantees into the Due Process Clause of the Fourteenth Amendment, thus rendering the [First] Amendment applicable to the States as well as to the Congress."

"Criminal anarchy," according to the New York statutes of the day, "is the doctrine that organized government should be overthrown by force or violence, or by assassination of the executive head or of any of the executive officials of government, or by any unlawful means." The United States Supreme Court, in affirming the *Gitlow* convictions, paid particular attention (as had his indictment) to a document, "The Left Wing Manifesto," printed and distributed by a section of the Socialist Party in New York City. The Court, after conceding that "there was no evidence of any effect resulting from the publication and circulation of the Manifesto," devotes four pages of the *United States Reports* to reprinting extracts from the Manifesto, providing thereby a far greater distribution (and in a far more enduring form) for the Manifesto than Gitlow and his associates could ever have reasonably hoped for.

The Supreme Court "immortalized" the prose of the defendants in much the same way as had been done by the Illinois Supreme Court fifty years earlier for the defendants in the Haymarket bombing case, *Spies* v. *Illinois* (1887). That the "Red-baiting" Gitlow himself is remembered for the First Amendment–"incorporation" ruling can remind us of the chance elements in judicial developments. What was not accidental, however, was that the Bill of Rights would, one way or another, eventually be considered substantially applicable against the States as well as against the General Government.

VIII

This stage of the States-minded "incorporation" of the Bill of Rights took the form of this declaration by the *Gitlow* Court:

> For present purposes we may and do assume that freedom of speech and of the press—which are protected by the First Amendment from abridgment by Congress—was among the fundamental personal rights and "liberties" protected by the due process clause of the Fourteenth Amendment from impairment by the States.

It was probably inevitable, considering the traumas and consequences of the Civil War, that State governments would come to be obliged to respect those traditional rights of the English-speaking peoples that the General Government has always been bound to respect. Indeed, it had once been seriously argued, we recall, that the General Government itself would be thus bound whether or not a bill of rights was added to the Constitution—and if so, why not the States as well?

The odd feature of our States-minded incorporation during the twentieth century, which has thus been extended to most of the elements of the 1791 Bill of Rights, is that it was done by means of the Due Process Clause of the Fourteenth Amendment. This *is* odd because it means that "due process of law" in the Fourteenth Amendment is taken to mean something much more than, if not even quite different from, "due process of law" in, say, the Fifth Amendment. It is odd also because the Privileges and Immunities Clause of the Fourteenth Amendment would seem, on its face, a better way to provide for such a salutary incorporation.

But, it should be remembered, the Supreme Court, in the last quarter of the nineteenth century, had substantially limited the scope of the Privileges and Immunities Clause of the Fourteenth Amendment. And so it evidently came to be believed that something else, no matter how awkward it might seem, would have to be used to do what lawyers and judges, along with the People at large, regarded as fair and inevitable: the recognition that the States are pretty much bound by the same constitutional limitations as is the United States. Much the same adaptation to missteps by the Supreme Court in constitutional interpretation has been seen in the use of the Commerce Clause, thereby permitting the Congress to regulate State-abetted racial segregation in publicly patronized facilities, an adaptation made necessary by what the Court had done (also late in the nineteenth century) to the Equal Protection Clause of the Fourteenth Amendment.

IX

Such developments (discussed in my *Reflections on Constitutional Law*) can testify to that recognition of fundamental, perhaps even natural, rights which is promoted by a maturing national awareness and by an enlightened world opinion. Lawyers, legislators, and judges in these matters, reluctant to repudiate long-established readings of the Constitution, tend "to play it safe" by using either what has "worked" before (such as the Commerce Clause) or something (such as the Due Process Clause of the Fourteenth Amendment) which has *not* been already severely limited by the Court. The immediate practical consequences (such as desegregation) may be the same, whether or not constitutional terms are used as originally intended.

There is, however, the drawback, in proceeding thus, of making it harder to notice and to respect the remarkable coherence both of the Constitution and of its sources. Thus, in considering how State governments and the General Government are bound, "due process of law" should mean the same wherever it is found, just as do terms such as "ex post facto Law," "Bill of Attainder," and "Title of Nobility." It can become difficult to ascertain and to respect the "original intent" of the Constitution if its terms do not have stable (and hence rationally ascertainable) meanings.

We can be reminded of the pressures that can disturb the stability of language when we notice what happened in the *Gitlow Case* to *Schenck* and *Debs,* cases decided less than a decade before. One can hope that Eugene Debs, then in the last eighteen months of his life, was able to watch with a perhaps perverse pleasure the effort of Justice Holmes, in his *Gitlow* Dissenting Opinion, to explain away the reliance that had come to be placed by the Court on *Schenck.* It should have been evident, no matter what Justice Holmes said, that the language of the *Gitlow* Manifesto (which the Justice wanted to see protected) was much more inflammatory than what either Schenck or Debs had said and gone to jail for, with Justice Holmes's facile blessing.

4. Winston S. Churchill and the Cause of Freedom

I

Winston S. Churchill was perhaps the greatest hero of the Second World War. The heroic seems always to have appealed to him. He was particularly effective in dramatizing heroic exploits—his own, those of his illustrious family, those of comrades (such as the Royal Air Force), or those of his country and its allies.

Heroism was particularly to be enlisted in the cause of freedom, a cause which required the vigorous repudiation of enslavement. It is freedom that Churchill made so much of in his 1940 speech upon, at last, being entrusted with the office of Prime Minister. Particularly to be cherished, in efforts on behalf of freedom, is the honor to be won by the valiant.

The emphasis on freedom during the Second World War can be usefully compared with the emphasis on territorial integrity made much more of during the First World War. This is a difference that can be seen upon comparing the Fourteen Points developed by Woodrow Wilson (1918) with the Four Freedoms championed by Franklin D. Roosevelt (1941). Of those Four Freedoms, two of them, "freedom of speech and expression" and "freedom of . . . worship," are enshrined (in somewhat more rigorous language) in the First Amendment.

II

Churchill, abhorring slavery and sensitive to the demands of honor, can seem at his best when his back is up against a wall, fighting off the assaults of barbarism. Thus he recalls, as he brings a 1946 speech to its close, "Last time I saw it all coming and I cried aloud to my fellow-countrymen and to the world, but no one paid any attention." He explains:

116

Up till the year 1933 or even 1935 [the war began in 1939], Germany might have been saved from the awful fate which has overtaken her and we might all have been spared the miseries Hitler let loose upon mankind. There never was a war in all history easier to prevent by timely action than the one which has just desolated such great areas of the globe.

It can be granted that Churchill did see much that was coming in the early Thirties. But it can be wondered whether he indeed saw "it all coming" when he did not fully see what "*it*" came from. What it came from included, in large part, the incredible folly of the First World War, to which Churchill contributed his share, however more efficiently he would have conducted that war at times.

He could recall in 1946 that "no one [had] paid any attention" when he warned in the Thirties about a resurgent Germany. But he never seemed to recognize that the Allied leaders (including himself) who had longed (along with Germany) for the First World War had undermined their own authority, especially whenever they seemed to promote war. The folly of the First World War *had* been pointed out at that time, sometimes by upstarts who were (as we have seen) even jailed for presuming to question the glorious enterprise of 1914–1918.

III

In March 1946, Churchill traveled to Westminster College in Fulton, Missouri, to "cr[y] aloud" again. This time the whole world would "pa[y] attention," especially since the President of the United States introduced him to his audience. The "political" implications of this 1946 venture were underscored by the selection of the President's home State for its venue.

That the Ancient Westminister could be recalled in this New World Westminister should have reminded everyone of Churchill's career. He was, for half a century, preeminently a man of the House of Commons. The Parliament to which he devoted himself, it should also be remembered, is very much, as it is literally, a *talking* place.

Much had long been made by Churchill of "the English-speaking peoples," those peoples whose mutual attractions he hoped to reinforce by this speech. The emphasis upon *speaking* is neither accidental nor incidental. That language, grounded in significant part for him in Shakespeare and the King James Bible, was vital both to what he was and to what he longed for.

IV

Churchill, in his 1946 speech, celebrates the great alliance and the outcome of the Second World War. He does not mention, but he probably could never forget, that his mother had been an American. He could thus "relate" to the United States as perhaps no other British statesman (at least since Edmund Burke) has been able to do.

Respectful comments are made about the newly created United Nations Organization, with Churchill even suggesting that it should have a military capacity of its own. But he feels, almost in his bones, that it is ultimately the American connection upon which Great Britain should depend. He can even suggest, "Eventually there may come—I feel eventually there will come—the principle of common citizenship."

Such common citizenship can be said to be already implicit in the political and legal heritage that is shared, a heritage catalogued in this fashion:

> [W]e must never cease to proclaim in fearless tone the great principles of freedom and the rights of man which are the joint inheritance of the English-speaking world and which through Magna Carta, the Bill of Rights [that is, of 1689], the Habeas Corpus, trial by jury, and the English common law find their most famous expression in the American Declaration of Independence.

It is perhaps significant that Churchill does not emphasize, as an American might, the speech/press and religion provisions of the First Amendment. Those provisions may recognize the sovereignty of the People, which can be critically different from that sovereignty of Parliament (or of the Monarch-in-Parliament?) which British constitutionalism had long taken for granted.

V

Vital to Churchill's 1946 Fulton talk, and what makes it so memorable, is his description of "the present position in Europe." Here he even seems to take the stance he had had to assume in the early Thirties. He explains, before coming to the most ominous passage in the speech, "It is my duty . . . , for I am sure you would wish me to state the facts as I see them to you, to place before you certain facts about the present position in Europe."

Churchill, we should remember, was not in office when he made this speech, but the presence that day in Fulton of the President of the United States invested him with a remarkable authority. And so he could proclaim:

> From Stettin in the Baltic to Trieste in the Adriatic, an iron curtain has descended across the Continent. Behind that line lie all the capitals of the ancient states of Central and Eastern Europe. Warsaw, Berlin, Prague, Vienna, Budapest, Belgrade, Bucharest, and Sofia, all these famous cities and the populations around them lie in what I must call the Soviet sphere, and all are subject in one form or another, not only to Soviet influence but to a very high and, in many cases, increasing measure of control from Moscow.

Churchill says that he had given this address the title "The Sinews of Peace," but it was seen in some quarters virtually as a declaration of war (albeit a cold war), not least because the American President *was* very much present.

The inventory of "famous cities" in "the Soviet sphere" is followed by a noteworthy exception: "Athens alone—Greece with its immortal glories—is free to decide its future at an election under British, American and French observation." But, it should be added, outsiders (and especially the British) so conducted themselves in Greece in 1945–1946 that they contributed to that country's subjection to a ferocious (and probably unnecessary) civil war that lasted several years and that flared up again (in a different form) in the 1967–1974 military dictatorship. One continuing consequence of all this is the Cyprus issue, which still poisons relations between Greece and Turkey, if not also relations between Greece and the United States (which had foolishly supported the Greek Colonels responsible for the Cyprus debacle).

VI

It was far from clear that the Russians, after the first few postwar years, were truly strengthened by their "control" of Eastern Europe. Besides, the serious threat from the Soviets, worldwide, depended in large part upon economic and social conditions. We should recall here the third of Roosevelt's "four essential human freedoms": "freedom from want—which, translated into world terms, means economic understandings which will secure to every nation a healthy peacetime life for its inhabitants—everywhere in the world."

We should recall as well why Churchill was not still in office in 1946. The British electorate, as soon as Germany was defeated (and while the American-dominated war with Japan continued), turned to the Labour Party to guide the massive economic and social reconstruction and reforms that would be needed. Churchill, however innovative he could sometimes be in social programs, was evidently regarded as too much the warrior for the social revolution that was believed to be due and needed in Britain.

All this is *not* to say that Josef Stalin and his henchmen had not been ruthless and self-serving in taking advantage of the conditions they exploited in Eastern Europe and elsewhere, but it *is* to say that those conditions contributed significantly to their appeal in some countries and hardly at all in others (such as Great Britain and the United States). Much the same can be said about how it was that Adolf Hitler and his henchmen could do what they did in Germany. Much the same can be said as well about the basis for that religious fanaticism, in the Middle East and elsewhere, that we find so troubling today.

VII

Churchill's advice for his Fulton audience includes observations about the atomic bomb. This is a subject that he must have had to be careful in discussing, inasmuch as the American President who had introduced him had also introduced the world to the dropping of atomic bombs on an enemy, a decision that aroused early on serious misgivings in some quarters. Be that as it may, Churchill suggests that it would "be wrong and imprudent to entrust the secret knowledge or experience of the atomic bomb, which the United States, Great Britain and Canada [then] share[d], to [any] world organization."

He considered it reassuring that control of atomic bombs and bomb-making was "largely retained in American hands." "I do not believe," he recognized, "we should all have slept so soundly had the positions been reversed and if some Communist or neo-Fascist State monopolized for the time being these dread agencies." It is evident, with his talk of "at least a breathing space," that Churchill did not anticipate that the Russians would develop nuclear weapons as rapidly as they did.

This chance miscalculation in the West may have contributed significantly to American domestic apprehensiveness, especially when it was assumed that subversive activities in this Country must have permitted the Russians to move as fast as they did. Among the consequences of these miscalculations was the intensification of the loyalty/security programs that were established in 1947. In short, some of our most grievous wounds here have been self-inflicted.

VIII

The Russians, it should be remembered, were essential to the Allied victory during the Second World War. Their casualties were simply horrific in magnitude, which contributed to the atrocious way they conducted themselves when they entered Germany. And the Russians, it should also be remembered, accomplished what they did during that war *not* because of Stalin but, it can be said, in spite of Stalin and his blunders.

Be all this as it may, Churchill's 1946 speech was regarded as a hostile act by the intermittently insecure Russian leaders, however warmly the wartime alliance was spoken of by him. The presence of the American President on the occasion of the Fulton speech did accentuate the seriousness of the threat that the Russians associated with this maneuver. Also, it must have seemed to the Russians somewhat hypocritical for a longtime defender of the vast British Empire to speak as he did of the Russian Empire in Eastern Europe.

It was not only the Russians who came to consider themselves "marginalized" by the intimate Anglo-American alliance. The French, too, felt this way, something that was evident throughout the Second World War in the posture of Charles de Gaulle. One happy consequence of this, however, may have been the encouragement of that rapprochement between France and Germany which is so important for the enduring stability of Europe.

IX

We, upon considering the circumstances and consequences of Churchill's "Iron Curtain" speech, can be reminded of both the need for and the risks of freedom of speech. Among those risks is how those not schooled in the ways of freedom will take what is said among free men and women. It can be difficult for us to appreciate that others may not be as casual as we often are upon hearing provocative and even outlandish things among us.

Whatever reservations one might have about Churchill's 1946 speech, one cannot help but admire his 1940 speech upon becoming Prime Minister. It was then that he enlisted his countrymen in the campaign to liberate all mankind "from the foulest and most soul-destroying tyranny which has ever darkened and stained the pages of history." The spiritedness of the warrior may be seen in his speaking of the British "clawing down" enemy airplanes.

It is also the dedicated warrior who can say such things as this to his embattled people: "The interest of property, the hours of labor, are nothing compared with the struggle of life and honor, for right and freedom, to which we have vowed ourselves." So powerful an influence was Winston Churchill that many would, upon his death in 1965, be moved to visit British Consulates in Chicago and elsewhere in the United States to sign the condolence books made available to that generation of Americans who treasured memories of his inspiring gallantry during the Second World War. The enduring spirit of this remarkably self-conscious as well as self-confident man is evident in the opening sentence of his May 19, 1940, speech:

> I speak to you for the first time as Prime Minister in a solemn hour for the life of our country, of our Empire, of our Allies, and above all, of the cause of freedom.

5. *Dennis* v. *United States* (1951); the *Rosenberg Case* (1950–1953)

I

A dozen leaders of the Communist Party of the United States were indicted in July 1948 for violation of the conspiracy provisions of the Smith Act (the Alien Registration Act of 1940). "As the first federal peacetime sedition statute since 1798," the *Encyclopedia of the American Constitution* recalls, "the Smith Act in its most significant section made it a crime to 'knowingly, or willfully, advocate, abet, advise, or teach the duty, necessity, desirability, or propriety of overthrowing or destroying any government in the United States by force and violence." And, like the Sedition Act of 1798, this 1940 legislation was associated with measures designed to supervise the aliens among us, which seems to be a recurrent concern in this Country of immigrants, with the older immigrants and their descendants often being suspicious of the newer ones (whether "documented" or "undocumented").

Here is the Government's summary of its charges for the trial, which was to be conducted in New York City:

> The indictment charged that from April 1, 1945, to the date of the indictment [the defendants] unlawfully, wilfully, and knowingly conspired . . . (1) to organize as the Communist Party of the United States of America a society, group and assembly of persons who teach and advocate the overthrow and destruction of the United States by force and violence, and (2) knowingly and wilfully to advocate and teach the duty and necessity of overthrowing and destroying the Government of the United States by force and violence.

A verdict of guilty, as to all of the defendants, was returned by the jury on

October 14, 1949. The United States Court of Appeals, with an Opinion by Chief Judge Learned Hand, affirmed these convictions.

The tumultuous trial had extended over nine months. It had not helped the *Dennis* defendants that they drew the trial judge that they did, which helped bring out the worst in them, their lawyers, and the system itself. Nor did it help them, or the Country, that the United States Supreme Court reviewed their convictions, as well as the applicable statute, after the Korean War had begun.

II

It can be questioned (as is implicit in Justice Hugo L. Black's observation, "So long as this Court exercises the power of judicial review of legislation . . .") whether any Court of the United States should review, for constitutionality, any Act of Congress. Certainly, there is no indication in the Constitution itself that Congressional legislation should be subject to Judicial Review, whatever the Courts might have been expected to be able to do to protect their own prerogatives. Presumably appellate courts *had* been intended to provide authoritative interpretations, at least for Judicial purposes, of Congressional enactments, and intended as well to assess the records of trials both for the adequacy of the evidence relied upon and for the fairness of the process that had been used.

Whether or not Judicial Review is authorized, with respect to the constitutionality of Acts of Congress, Courts have long assumed that it is. In sedition cases, judges have, over the years, tended to side with the Government. That is, judges do tend to be moved by the patriotic passions that the Country at large is moved by.

It sometimes seems that it would be better if judges did not routinely address constitutionality issues explicitly, especially when the First Amendment is at issue. Their more or less automatic endorsement of the constitutionality of contested sedition measures tends to relieve legislators and other citizens (in government and out) of their own duty to think about the constitutionality of the measures that they deal with. That is, the Supreme Court, in the principal sedition cases in the twentieth century, tended to reassure, if not even to provide useful slogans and judgments for, those among us who have been determined to suppress any sedition that they have come to believe a threat to the Country.

III

How judges are routinely induced to go along with campaigns of suppression, however much they resist particular modes of expressing such acquiescence, may be seen in what happened to Learned Hand, who had earned the reputation of being somewhat skeptical about the reign of suppression which *preceded* him. This is how Justice William O. Douglas, in his 1969 *Brandenburg* v. *Ohio* Concurring Opinion, speaks of Judge Hand's involvement in *Dennis*:

> Judge Learned Hand, who wrote for the Court of Appeals in affirming the judgment in *Dennis,* coined the "not improbable" test, 183 F.2d 201, 214, which the [Supreme] Court adopted and which Judge Hand preferred over the "clear and present danger" test. Indeed, in his book, *The Bill of Rights* 59 (1958), in referring to Holmes's creation of the "clear and present danger" test, [Judge Hand] said, "I cannot help, thinking that for once Homer nodded."

Justice Douglas then says (with the support of Justice Black): "I see no place in the regime of the First Amendment for any 'clear and present danger' test, whether strict and tight as some [like Judge Hand?] would make it, or free-wheeling as the [Supreme] Court in *Dennis* rephrased it."

Justice Douglas continues thus in his *Brandenburg* Opinion (there were no dissents in this case, a State criminal syndicalism prosecution, *not* a national security proceeding)—a case with a ruling that would have been much more useful a generation earlier):

> When one reads the opinions closely and sees when and how the "clear and present danger" test has been applied, great misgivings are aroused. First, the threats were often loud but always puny and made serious only by judges so wedded to the *status quo* that critical analysis made them nervous. Second, the test was so twisted and perverted in *Dennis* as to make the trial of those teachers of Marxism an all-out political trial which was part and parcel of the Cold War that has eroded substantial parts of the First Amendment.

Thus, the Cold War is recognized by him as having helped weaken the Speech and Press guarantees recognized by the First Amendment. It should be recognized, on the other hand, that the Cold War may have contributed to the determination of the Government of the United States, including its Courts, to favor racial desegregation in the interest of an effective American foreign policy.

We can see, in how Judge Hand spoke of Justice Holmes and in how Justice Douglas spoke in turn of Judge Hand and others, that the fearfulness of one generation can readily be recognized in the next as unwarranted. Thus, Chief Justice Fred M. Vinson, in his *Dennis* Opinion *upholding* in 1951 the convictions of the Communist Party leaders, said of the fifteen thousand copies of the "objectionable" leaflet circulated by the defendants in *Schenck* v. *United States* (1919), with "its most inciting sentence" being "You must do your share to maintain, support and uphold the rights of the people of this country"—the Chief Justice said of all this: "This insubstantial gesture toward insubordination in 1917 during war was held to be a clear and present danger of bringing about the evil of military insubordination." He was similarly dismissive of "the puny efforts toward subversion" that had formed the basis of the convictions upheld not only in *Schenck* but also in *Debs* v. *United States* (1919) and *Abrams* v. *United States* (1919) (as well as in other cases, including, it seems, *Gitlow* v. *New York* [1925]).

IV

Chief Justice Vinson goes on, in his *Dennis* Opinion, to play down the seriousness of other actions which had gotten people jailed in the 1920s and 1930s. Judges in such cases, he argues, "were not confronted with any situation comparable to the instant one—the development of an apparatus designed and dedicated to the overthrow of the Government [of the United States], in the context of world crisis after crisis." Particularly threatening at that moment were probably the risks associated with the conflict in Korea, which had started a year earlier.

In these circumstances, the Chief Justice could endorse what Judge Hand had said, "writing for the majority below": "In each case [courts] must ask whether the gravity of the 'evil,' discounted by its improbability, justifies such invasion of free speech as is necessary to avoid the danger." The Chief Justice adds, "Likewise, we are in accord with the court below, which affirmed the trial court's finding that the requisite danger existed." It is then said, "The mere fact that from the period

1945 to 1948 [the defendants'] activities did not result in an attempt to overthrow the Government by force and violence is *of course* no answer to the fact that there was a group that was ready to make the attempt" (emphasis added).

The willingness of the *Dennis* Court to accept "the trial court's finding that the requisite danger existed" is questioned by both Justice Black and Justice Douglas in their Dissenting Opinions on that occasion, for "it sanctions the determination of a crucial issue of fact by the judge rather than by the jury." Even the dissenters, however, did not undertake to remind their colleagues and the bar that critical to the late eighteenth-century effort to secure the proper recognition of liberty of speech and of the press in England had been the insistence upon the prerogatives of the jury in such matters. One form this insistence took was the argument (respected, by the way, in the Sedition Act of 1798) that judges should *not* authoritatively identify any particular document as a seditious libel, leaving to the jury only the sworn duty of determining whether that document had indeed been published by the defendant in the case.

V

It is likely that a jury, in sedition cases, would not find otherwise than would a trial judge about such matters as the existence of "the requisite danger." But, at least, evidence would have to be systematically offered to the jury on the issue rather than having everyone involved obliged to consider the critical matter at issue to be something of which a judge might take judicial notice. We have here, in effect, a due process standard that is independent of, and indeed older than, the First Amendment.

Be that as it may, it was said to be held in *Dennis* that the applicable sections of the Smith Act "do not inherently, or as construed or applied in [this] case, violate the First Amendment and other provisions of the Bill of Rights . . . because of indefiniteness." It was then said, in bringing the "clear and present danger" test to bear on this matter, "[The defendants] intended to overthrow the Government of the United States as speedily as the circumstances would permit." This meant, in effect, that the "test" that had been three decades in the fashioning was left in shambles, with the defendants having in effect been convicted only because they were *both* unpopular *and* indicted.

The lack of seriousness, if not even the frivolity, of such an approach

to constitutional interpretation was anticipated by the Chief Justice's insistence, earlier in his *Dennis* Opinion:

> Nothing is more certain in modern society than the principle
> that there are no absolutes, that a name, a phrase, a standard has
> meaning only when associated with the considerations which gave
> birth to the nomenclature. . . . To those who would paralyze our
> Government in the face of impending threat by encasing it in a
> semantic straitjacket we must reply that all concepts are relative.

Shortly after this somewhat nihilistic observation, it was suggested by the
Chief Justice (in his *Dennis* Opinion) that self-preservation is "the ultimate
value of any society." Does this mean, in effect, that heroic self-sacrifice,
whether by a human being or by an association, is *not* to be encouraged?

VI

   The Chief Justice's Opinion, joined by three other Justices, was followed by a forty-page Concurring Opinion by another Justice. *His* pro-
lixity in civil liberties and other cases, as in his Opinion for the Court in
Communist Party of the United States v. *Subversive Activities Control Board*
(1961), made it unlikely that his "scholarly" expositions would be taken
seriously. Another Concurring Opinion, by Justice Robert H. Jackson,
made much of the law of conspiracy, reflecting the fact that he had devoted himself, as he had usefully done a few years before, to the Nuremberg
Trial, however irrelevant much of what he learned there about European
political turmoil was for American conditions.
   Justice Black singles out in his Dissenting Opinion the protection
provided by the First Amendment to "speech in the realm of public matters." He introduces his assessment of the *Dennis Case* with this recapitulation of the controversy:

> At the outset I want to emphasize what the crime involved in this
> case is, and what it is not. These [defendants] were not charged
> with an attempt to overthrow the Government. They were not
> charged with overt acts of any kind designed to overthrow the
> Government. They were not even charged with saying anything
> or writing anything designed to overthrow the Government. The

charge was that they agreed to assemble and to talk and publish certain ideas at a later date. The indictment is that they conspired to organize the Communist Party and to use speech or newspapers and other publications in the future to teach and advocate the forcible overthrow of the Government.

He concludes his three-page Dissenting Opinion with a prediction:

Public opinion being what it now is, few will protest the conviction of these Communist petitioners. There is hope, however, that in calmer times, when present pressures, passions and fears subside, this or some later Court will restore the First Amendment liberties to the high preferred place where they belong in a free society.

Justice Douglas, in his *Dennis* Dissenting Opinion, after insisting that "[n]ot a single seditious act is charged in the indictment," endorsed what seems to be John Stuart Mill's approach to such matters by suggesting:

Full and free discussion even of ideas we hate encourages the testing of our prejudices and preconceptions. Full and free discussion keeps a society from becoming stagnant and unprepared for the stresses and strains that work to tear all civilizations apart.

He endorsed, and quoted at length, what he considered the "classic statement" by Justice Louis D. Brandeis in *Whitney* v. *California* (1927), which begins, "Fear of serious injury cannot alone justify suppression of free speech and assembly; men feared witches and burnt women." Justice Douglas concludes his Dissenting Opinion with this observation:

[Andrei] Vishinksy wrote in 1939 in *The Law of the Soviet State*, "In our state [the Soviet Union], naturally, there is and can be no place for freedom of speech, press, and so on for the foes of socialism." Our concern should be that we accept no such standard for the United States. Our faith should be that our people will never give support to these advocates of revolution, so long as we remain loyal to the purposes for which our Nation was founded.

VII

Who was indicted and for what, in these matters, depended on chance. The timing of sedition prosecutors, since the Second World War, depended in large part upon how the Soviet Union was perceived to be conducting itself from time to time. Thus, foreign policy considerations could matter more than constitutional principles in both the development and the disposition of litigation.

A critical stage of the American campaign against domestic Communists during the Cold War can be seen in the trial and executions of Julius and Ethel Rosenberg for atomic espionage (and can be seen as well in the unfortunate companion espionage case touched upon in Appendix M of this volume). The Rosenbergs, whether guilty or innocent, were remarkably unlucky people, both in some of their associates and in their timing. If they had been detected and tried either five years earlier than they were (that is, while the Soviet Union was still regarded as a wartime ally) or five years later than they were (that is, when we had become accustomed to the Soviet Union as an adversary), they probably would never have been tried as they were *and then sentenced to death.*

The Rosenbergs were unlucky also in *their* trial judge, a peculiarly vindictive man who (curiously enough) later went on to become a decent Court of Appeals judge—a man who was somehow convinced that the Rosenbergs' atomic espionage contributed to the Korean War. They were also unlucky in that their executions came so early in the term of a new President, something that the outgoing President should have avoided by commuting their death sentences (if that *was* to be done). They were unlucky as well in that they were not detected and tried in Great Britain, where Klaus Fuchs, a much more serious atomic spy (also arrested in 1950), spent less than a decade in prison.

VIII

The ultimate stage of the American campaign against Communism was seen perhaps in our Vietnamese involvement. We at least had, in our Korean involvement, some plausible United Nations authority for what we did. But in Vietnam we were much more on our own, moved by a fear of Communism that was somewhat irrational (or, at least, nonrational).

This is not to suggest that the Russian tyrants always conducted themselves as they should have, either at home or abroad. Even so, one can wonder whether we could have been helped to think more clearly about the Russians, and about the challenges of worldwide Communism, if we had not succeeded in dismantling the Left in American politics. That is, we very much needed to hear arguments from vigorous champions of the Russians, arguments that challenged the prevailing anti-Communist orthodoxy in this Country.

We also needed, as a restraint upon the prevailing fear of the Soviet Union among us, a widespread recognition of the backward state of the Russian economy, not only compared to the United States but also compared to most of Europe. This was apparent to the American visitor at least as early as 1960—that is, well before we allowed ourselves to be frightened into our Vietnam involvement. It took many of the almost fifty thousand American battle deaths in Vietnam—roughly the same as American battle deaths during the First World War—before the way our foreign policy was being conducted could begin to be properly reconsidered.

IX

All this should remind us that freedom of speech and of the press, as protected by the First Amendment, is designed primarily for the benefit of the community as a whole, *not* primarily for the benefit of those who may want to say something. It should be obvious that when critical opinions are suppressed, the community is deprived of something that it may very much need to hear. And such opinions are apt to be suppressed if those holding them are routinely subjected to prosecution because of associations intimately linked to those opinions.

Of course, risks *are* run when associations can come and go as freely as they usually do in this Country. But even more risks may be run when a vigorous persecution of some associations makes it more difficult, if not practically impossible, to hear the sometimes crippling pieties of one's day questioned. In recent years, for example, we have not heard as much informed discussion as we need to hear about the objectives and methods of our extraordinarily burdensome (and yet largely ineffective, if not even mostly unnecessary) Homeland Security programs.

It need not be assumed that our leaders do not intend to do good at least as much as most of us do. But such leaders need the help of all who might have something to contribute to discussions of the issues of the day.

We, too, need the help of such discussions, especially if we are to judge usefully and fairly those who undertake to lead us, including those leaders who would spare us the trouble of judging the opinions of that minority among us who may even intend to do wicked things "as speedily as the circumstances would permit."

6. *Cohen* v. *California* (1971); *Texas* v. *Johnson* (1989)

A young man, Paul Richard Cohen was convicted during the Vietnam War of disturbing the peace and sentenced to thirty days' imprisonment for displaying on his jacket while in a corridor of a California courthouse a provocatively vulgar dismissal of the draft. The vulgarity employed by him was known to be offensive and, indeed, was likely chosen because of the effect it might create. A similar public expression directed against any other targets (including, say, *opponents* of the Vietnam War) might have been similarly resented by the policeman who arrested this young man.

A legal scholar has observed in the *Encyclopedia of the American Constitution* that, in overturning this 1968 conviction, "a 5–4 Supreme Court held that the *fighting words* exception to First Amendment protection did not apply where 'no individual . . . likely to be present could reasonably have regarded the words . . . as a direct personal insult,' and there was no showing that anyone who saw Cohen was in fact violently aroused or that . . . [he] . . . intended such a result." Even so, it should be noticed that the police officer who arrested this young man was very much aroused personally by the jacket. True, the officer was not violent in *his* response, but that may have been, at least in part, because he believed that legal means were available to punish this offender.

This scholarly recapitulation of the *Cohen Case* adds, "The State's assertion of other justifications [than the 'fighting words' doctrine] for punishing Cohen were similarly rejected: the jacket's message was not *obscenity*, because it was not erotic; the privacy interests of offended passers-by were insubstantial in this public place, and anyone offended might look away; there was no *captive audience*." This assessment ends thus:

133

Cohen's chief doctrinal importance lies in its rejection of the notion that speech can constitutionally be prohibited by the State because it is offensive. Because offensiveness is an "inherently boundless" category, any such prohibition would suffer from the vice of *vagueness*. And the First Amendment protects not only the cool expression of ideas but also "otherwise inexpressible emotions."

Another scholar, Harry Kalven Jr., has said (another instance of Homer nodding?) of the Court's Opinion in *Cohen,* with its review of various exceptions to the protection available for public speaking, that it "exemplifies the best of the judicial tradition as to the First Amendment."

II

Three dissenting Justices regarded "Cohen's absurd and immature antic" as "mainly conduct, and little speech." They considered the "Court's agonizing over First Amendment values [to be] misplaced and unnecessary." A fourth Justice would have remanded the case to the California Court of Appeals for reconsideration of a technical question (in effect) of judicial protocol.

Roger Newman reports that Justice Hugo L. Black, the most eminent judicial champion thus far of the First Amendment, at first "insisted that the Court summarily reverse the [Cohen] conviction without even holding oral argument." But, we are told:

Overnight he reversed his position. He was not deviating at all from his views, he told the justices at conference, but this was "conduct," not "speech." Picketing a courthouse was illegal conduct. People could not "tramp up and down the streets by the thousands" and threaten others.

Justice Black's position in *Cohen* is said to have surprised Justice William J. Brennan (who was one of the majority of five in this case).

But was not Justice Black's final position in *Cohen* anticipated in his Dissenting Opinion in *Tinker* v. *Des Moines Independent Community School District,* two years before, assessing the suspension of public school students for wearing (in defiance of a school regulation) black armbands to protest the government's policy in Vietnam? Justice Black observed in *Tinker* (1969),

> While I have always believed that under the First and Fourteenth Amendments neither the State nor the Federal Government has any authority to regulate or censor the content of speech, I have never believed that any person has a right to give speeches or engage in demonstrations where he pleases and when he pleases.

Further on in this *Tinker* Dissenting Opinion, he observed,

> [I]f the time has come when pupils of state-supported schools, kindergartens, grammar schools, or high schools, can defy and flout orders of school officials to keep their minds on their own schoolwork, it is the beginning of a new revolutionary era of permissiveness in this country fostered by the judiciary.

III

One can see in the disposition of the *Cohen Case* an instance of that approach to the First Amendment which regards it as protecting "the freedom of expression." The Court quotes a California Opinion in the case which reports, "The defendant testified that he wore the jacket knowing that the [offensive] words were on the jacket as a means of informing the public of the depth of his feelings against the Vietnam War and the draft." Even those of us who were severe critics of our Vietnam Intervention may well wonder what "depth" means here.

It should be remembered that vigorous criticisms of the draft *were* being voiced at that time in this Country without risk of arrest and prosecution. That is, however much *Schenck* v. *United States* (1919), with its "clear and present danger" test, continued to distort readings of the First Amendment, antidraft sentiments of the kind that had been voiced by Charles Schenck himself were no longer subject to prosecution in this Country. It was, it should be repeated, not the *argument* made by the defendant in *Cohen* that had been acted against, but rather the use of patently offensive language in public, however defensible the cause in which it was used.

The student of this case should consider what, if anything, may properly be done with the deliberate use in public of expressions known to be somewhat provocative, no matter what the cause in which they are thus used. Suppose someone, encountering such an exhibition, punches the provocateur. Surely we would not want to see honored, as a defense against an assault charge, an explanation that one's action had thereby informed the public of "the depth of [one's] feelings" upon encountering the deliberate provocation to which one had violently responded.

IV

Of course, there *is* in such matters the risk of selective enforcement of laws that do depend, for their effective use, upon the discretion of the authorities. This can be seen in how desecrations of the flag are responded to. Most flag desecrations (usually for commercial purposes) have always been ignored, often not even being recognized (by the general public) to be such.

It has been advocated by some who have been offended by judicially immunized flag desecrations that a constitutional amendment be provided which would permit prosecutions. This advocacy responds to the Supreme Court's invalidation, in *Texas* v. *Johnson* (1989), of convictions on First Amendment grounds. But is it not uncertain what the effect of such an amendment would be?

For one thing, First Amendment, as well as due process, questions might still be raised whenever it is obvious that only those flag desecrations are prosecuted which are in the service of an unpopular political opinion. That is, it is likely to be obvious that most desecrations—as on clothing or in advertising—are simply ignored by the authorities. On the other hand, it is also likely that desecration, as a means of political protest, would be more apt to be resorted to whenever it becomes known that the authorities can be provoked to respond to blatant desecration by arrests and trials.

V

Twenty years before *Cohen* (to the very week) there had been the Court's decision in *Dennis* v. *United States* (1951). The Chief Justice had disclosed, on that 1951 occasion, "Nothing is more certain in modern society than the principle that there are no absolutes." It could be disclosed at the same time, as we have seen, "that all concepts are relative."

The Opinion of the Court in *Cohen* is, curiously enough, in the same spirit as that of the far more repressive Court in *Dennis*, insisting, "Surely the State has no right to cleanse public debate to the point where it is grammatically palatable to the most squeamish among us." The Court then explains, "For, while the particular four-letter word being litigated here is perhaps more distasteful than most others of its genre, it is nevertheless often true that one man's vulgarity is another's lyric." "Indeed," the Opinion continues, "we think it is largely because governmental officials cannot make principled distinctions in this area that the Constitution leaves matters of taste and style so largely to the individual."

The concern here in *Cohen,* however, is *not,* as the Court indicates, lest "the most squeamish among us" dictate the taste of the community. Rather, the concern is, or at least should be, lest the most vulgar among us should determine the level of public discourse. Leaving such matters "largely to the individual" can mean, in practice, that the community at large is held hostage by the most reckless and the least squeamish—by those who, figuratively, slap the unwary people they encounter.

VI

We are left to wonder, after cases such as *Cohen* v. *California,* what the community may properly do to reduce vulgarity and to elevate sensibilities. We recall the direction laid down by the Articles of Confederation Congress in the Northwest Ordinance of 1787: "Religion, morality and knowledge, being necessary to good government and the happiness of mankind, schools and the means of education shall forever be encouraged [in the Northwest Territory]." The framers of this directive no doubt assumed that the discouragement of deliberate vulgarity should be routinely aimed at by any community that takes itself seriously.

Consider, for example, what we have come to accept in the form of regulating the placing of billboards along our highways. It is not merely "the most squeamish" who would like to see the beauty of our landscapes preserved. Much the same can be said about regulations with respect to, say, noise levels in a neighborhood.

And what is communal support of the arts but an effort, in part, to suppress vulgarity? Even more critical here is what deliberately ministering to sensibilities does to the level of public discourse. On the other hand, systematic indulgence of citizens with vulgar tastes makes it less likely that serious thinking will be done by either a speaker or his audience.

VII

The Opinion of the *Cohen* Court attempts to appear modernist and otherwise sophisticated in its orientation. Thus it can speak of "constitutional values," of "enduring values," and of "fundamental societal values." Thus, also, it can speak of permitting persons to "ventilate their dissident views."

But it is not truly sophisticated—that is, it is not thoughtful—to consider the public discourse protected by the First Amendment to be "ventilation," as if only a kind of emoting is involved. Nor is it thoughtful to *seem* to suggest that the community cannot be trusted to distinguish between an "unseemly expletive"and "Keats' poems or Donne's sermons." This is, in short, silly (if not even irresponsible) talk by the Court.

How silly all this is may be seen upon noticing again this suggestion: "Those in the Los Angeles courthouse could effectively avoid further bombardment of their sensibilities simply by averting their eyes." This means, in effect, that an aggressive young man gets in one slap at every unsuspecting bystander he chances to encounter as he walks through a public place. *He,* it seems, should not be obliged to control *him*self at all, but only those he indiscriminately attacks.

VIII

We should be reminded that people have long felt deeply about critical issues of the day without "having" to resort to patently offensive language in response. This may be seen, for example, in how so dedicated an opponent of slavery as Frederick Douglass could make the case he did against its atrocities. Paul Cohen's language, by contrast, revealed a lack of elementary self-discipline.

Such displays of one's passions cannot be taken seriously, except perhaps by one's therapist. One suggests thereby that one does not have any argument of consequence. In any event, it is hard to respect anyone who cavalierly shows a lack of respect toward those before whom he deliberately exposes himself.

The ability of citizens to think properly about the most critical issues of the day can be impaired when passionate outbursts are routinely relied upon. It is his "personality" that the dissenter thereby submits as an "argument," not serious reasoning. Those bombarded by such displays are often inclined to "avert" their minds, assessing thereby not the message but rather the messenger.

IX

Perhaps the most troubling aspect of the Opinion of the Court in *Cohen* is that its dubious display of "sophistication" should have been authored by a Justice whose grandfather had truly distinguished himself as a thoughtful Member of the Supreme Court almost a century before. *That* Justice's Dissenting Opinions in controversial race-related cases had *not* relied upon any suggestion that differences about the issues of one's day could be explained away as mere differences in taste. To make much, in judicial pronouncements, of the inconsequentiality of differences in taste is to license more and more tastelessness in public discourse.

This, in turn, tends to undermine that respect for moderation and prudence upon which sound public policy depends. It is odd that the *Cohen* Court can present itself as a champion of "individual dignity and choice." Certainly, those gratuitously and unexpectedly "assaulted" by a young man they encountered in a public place could not have felt that *their* "individual dignity and choice" had been respected.

Critical to the Court's pronouncements in *Cohen* is its identification of the First Amendment as protective of the "constitutional right of free *expression*" (emphasis added). To see matters thus *is* to place the emphasis upon an individual's desire to exhibit "the depth of his feelings" about whatever might move him. It is *not* to recognize what the community is accustomed and entitled to expect from those who, sometimes at great personal risk, challenge the wrongheaded policies of the day.

7. The *Pentagon Papers Case* (1971)

I

The publication of substantial excerpts from a forty-seven-volume "Top Secret" Vietnam War–related report began in the *New York Times* on June 13, 1971, and continued for two more daily installments before being enjoined in the Courts of the United States until June 30, at which time it resumed for seven more installments. In the meantime, similar publication started in the *Washington Post,* the *Boston Globe,* and the *St. Louis Post-Dispatch,* all of which evidently drew extensively on other copies of the thousands of pages originally made available to the *New York Times.* Each newspaper was similarly enjoined as it appeared in print with excerpts from these materials.

The United States Supreme Court decision of June 30, 1971, permitted all newspapers with access to these "Pentagon Papers" archives to publish what they chose. Those archives dealt with the history of American involvement in the Vietnam War. It has been said that nothing prepared subsequent to 1968 was in this particular collection.

The legal and political controversy about the publication of these documents took place while American involvement in Vietnam was being bitterly contested in this Country. The immensity of this 1971 assault upon official policies, distributed by the National press, should be compared with the triviality of the leaflets prepared by Charles Schenck, Jacob Abrams, and their like during the First World War. Thus, Abrams was sentenced to ten years imprisonment for leaflets questioning the draft, some of which were distributed (it should be remembered) by being thrown out of a New York City office window.

II

No one was ever imprisoned either for releasing the Pentagon Papers archives to the press or for publishing thereafter substantial portions of those "Top Secret" documents. These facts testify to the disillusionment in the United States, by 1971, with American involvement in the Vietnam War. Indeed, the Pentagon Papers controversy can perhaps be seen as marking the beginning of the end of the Cold War.

The extent of American disillusionment with our Vietnam effort is suggested by the April 16, 2005, revelation that the Secretary of Defense who had originally commissioned the Pentagon Papers study had "even offered to testify for the *New York Times* in the event of a criminal prosecution." This former Secretary of Defense is said to have been "steeped in depression and despair over the failure of his Vietnam policies." During the Cuban Missile Crisis, almost two decades before, that remarkably impressionable official had believed the United States was on the brink of nuclear devastation, something which seemed to me at the time highly unlikely.

There was no prosecution of any newspaper for the Pentagon Papers publication. There *was* a trial, but no conviction, of the man who had distributed to the press in 1971 copies of the "Top Secret" materials with which he had been entrusted. A further indication of how the Cold War was unraveling was the dramatic visit to China in 1972 by a Cold War–oriented President of the United States.

III

To identify the Pentagon Papers controversy as perhaps marking the beginning of the end of the Cold War is not to suggest that this was generally recognized at that time. The collapse of the Soviet Union was still almost two decades off. The causes of that collapse, almost a generation ago, have yet to be reliably assessed.

Much is made of the parts played in that collapse both by a President in Washington and by a Bishop in Rome. But as I have already indicated in these *Reflections,* it was evident to the American visitor in Russia as early as 1960 (and probably well before) that the Soviet Union was not only weak economically and politically, but that it was steadily falling further and further behind its competitors in the West. It was also evident that ordinary Russians were well aware of this disparity, something that could disturb them even more as they recalled the great sacrifices they had made almost a generation before during the Second World War.

I had occasion in a November 1983 talk (published in my *American*

Moralist collection) to comment in this fashion on the Good (something which is discussed at greater length in the *Reflections* I have prepared on life, death, and the Constitution):

> All men, we have been taught by Aristotle, aim at the good in all that they do. . . . One must wonder about the morale of [the tyrants depicted in George Orwell's *1984*]. Do they not need some sincere belief, aside from [the] mere self-interest [made so much of in this novel], if they are to consider their own lives meaningful and worthwhile? Otherwise, would there not be a void that they or their successors, the youth of the following generation, will fall into and be engulfed by?

I then added, "This is, it has long seemed to me, one of the serious problems faced by Russian leaders since at least the Second World War." A challenge to this kind of assessment is posed when the tyrants involved are as mad as those who "led" the Khmer Rouge in Cambodia.

IV

What the Supreme Court *did* in the 1971 *Pentagon Papers Case* was far more important than what it *said.* It simply refused to keep newspapers from publishing a number of "Top Secret" documents related to the continuing hostilities in Vietnam. That is, the Court refused to allow itself to be used as an enforcer for the military security practices of the Administration.

We can be reminded by this controversy of how difficult it is for governments in this Country either to retrieve or to suppress materials that become available to the press. Certainly, there has never been any requirement of routine review by officials of whatever is prepared for publication. When there *is* such a system, the mere fact of publication without explicit approval can itself constitute an offense, without any need to describe or assess the material published.

The argument *against* routine review in advance of publication is an argument against a system of censorship, or previous restraint (also known as prior restraint). This is an argument, in effect, *for* due process of law. It is this traditional position (celebrated in John Milton's *Areopagitica* and drawn on, for example, in *Near* v. *Minnesota* [1931]) that the Supreme Court affirmed by what it refused to do in the *Pentagon Papers Case.*

V

What the Supreme Court did do in this case depended upon two propositions which even the three dissenting Justices can be understood to have accepted. First, there has always been a presumption in American constitutional law against any restraint upon a publisher prior to publication, except perhaps in the case of immediately impending irreparable harm to the security of the United States. Second, the Government did not (perhaps could not?) show in the *Pentagon Papers Case* that there *was* "irreparable harm" threatening the Country as a result of the intended publication.

Justice Hugo L. Black, in his Concurring Opinion in this case, observed that "paramount among the responsibilities of a free press is the duty to prevent any part of the government from deceiving the people and sending them off to distant lands to die of foreign fevers and foreign shot and shell." There is something archaic, and perhaps therefore reassuring, about his "foreign fevers and foreign shot and shell." That is, it was appropriate, in the course of unprecedented litigation that touched upon questions about the very nature of our regime, that one of the oldest Justices ever to sit on the United States Supreme Court should have, in his last official pronouncement before retiring, instinctively reached back in language as well as in thought to the very foundations of the Republic.

It should be recognized in the kind of "situation" considered in the *Pentagon Papers Case* that much, perhaps most if not all, of the critical information under consideration is already likely to be known to the Country's adversaries. The primary concern of the Government, therefore, is not apt to be to keep other governments from learning what the United States Government has been saying and doing, but rather to keep the People of the United States in ignorance about these matters. Any potential publisher, whether or not enjoined from publishing *here* and whether or not publishing, could often quietly distribute controversial material abroad (where it could be legally published by others) without ever exposing himself to the risks of publication in the United States.

VI

The three Justices who dissented in the *Pentagon Papers Case* did not argue that the Government had made the required showing with respect to immediately impending "irreparable harm" to the Country. But complaints *were* registered by the dissenters about the lack of sufficient time to make and to study the kind of record needed for proper consideration of the issues in the case. There *is* something to the complaints that this litigation had been "conducted in unseemingly haste," a haste which may even remind some of the closing days in 1953 of the *Rosenberg Case.*

It was pointed out in one Dissenting Opinion that the *New York Times* was pressing for an immediate disposition of the case in the name of its readers' "right to know," when it had itself held back the documents and its story for months. On the other hand, is it relevant how long a publisher has been contemplating and preparing any publication? When he does move, he is constitutionally (although, perhaps, not always morally) entitled to be able to publish immediately unless there is a clear legal prohibition.

One of the dissenting Justices reminded his colleagues that "First Amendment absolutism ha[d] never commanded a majority of this Court." This reminder is reinforced with a quotation taken by him from Justice Oliver W. Holmes in *Schenck* (1919): "When a nation is at war [even an undeclared war, we may wonder?] many things that might be said in time of peace are such a hindrance to its effort that their utterance will not be endured so long as men fight and that no Court could regard them as protected by any constitutional right." Such sentiments, as well as the talk about "unseemly haste," stand in dramatic opposition to the declaration of faith found in the opening paragraph of Justice Black's Concurring Opinion in the *Pentagon Papers* litigation (and quoted, in part, earlier in these *Reflections*):

> I adhere to the view that the Government's case against the *Washington Post* should have been dismissed and that the injunction against the *New York Times* should have been vacated without oral argument when the cases were first presented to this Court. I believe that every moment's continuance of the injunctions against these newspapers amounts to a flagrant, indefensible, and continuing violation of the First Amendment. . . . In my view it is unfortunate that some of my Brethren are apparently willing to hold that the publication of news may sometimes be enjoined. Such a holding would make a shambles of the First Amendment.

VII

It should not be forgotten, in any event, how chance-ridden the *Pentagon Papers* litigation was. After all, there would have been no injunction-related case at all—and no haste, unseemly or otherwise—if the *New York Times* had published in one issue everything it had, foregoing thereby (despite the extraordinary prepublication costs that it had incurred) the considerable commercial advantages of serial publication. Nor would there have been a case requiring desperate appeals to the Supreme Court, after accelerated hearings in the trial and intermediate appellate courts, if the government had limited itself to what it clearly had a legal right to try at leisure (assuming the existence of a relevant statute): a criminal prosecution of those persons improperly distributing, possessing, or communicating classified documents.

All such litigation as the *Pentagon Papers Case* is highly likely to be accidental in any regime where there is no systematic pre-publication governmental review of materials. This assessment is supported by what happened in 1979 when the *Progressive Magazine* was judicially enjoined from publishing an article describing the information publicly available about "how to build a hydrogen bomb." The Government of the United States would not have had any opportunity to secure an injunction against this publication, however, if the *Progressive* editors had not consulted others about its impending publication.

It can be argued that the *Progressive* either should have published whatever it considered fit to publish or, *if* it believed that it had the duty to secure (directly or indirectly) a governmental opinion, it should have been more respectful than it evidently was of the government's concern. On the other hand, the government, by conducting itself as it did, probably discouraged future consultation by any publisher sitting on a "hot story." However this may be, the difficulties confronting governmental attempts to suppress publications in *this* Country are evident when it is recalled that another journal published on its own (and legally) the enjoined *Progressive Magazine* article, thereby effectively mooting the *Progressive Magazine* litigation.

VIII

Of course, the editors of the *Progressive* had no doubt been directed by a judge not to supply their hydrogen bomb article to others, pending disposition of their litigation. But the copies of the article, floating around in the magazine's offices and elsewhere (including in homes where adventurous students might be lurking), must have been hard, if not impossible, to keep track of. This is still another way of saying that this *is,* for good as for ill, a free Country.

In practice, therefore, the only effective control of sensitive materials (which were evidently *not* drawn on by the *Progressive*) depends upon the reliability of the people entrusted with such things. Their patriotism has to be relied upon, something that can be bolstered by considerations of self-interest. Such self-interest can include concerns about prosecution for unauthorized release of documents, even if done for high-minded reasons.

The man who distributed the Pentagon Papers to the press in 1971 *had* been a zealous advocate of American involvement in Vietnam. He evidently expected that he would be imprisoned for what he did after he became a zealous critic of that involvement. He was surprised to hear from me the prediction, during our televised conversation in Chicago, that he would never spend a night in prison because of what he had done, a prediction which turned out to be sound (and on the basis of which he still owes me a dinner).

IX

The *Pentagon Papers Case* can be said to have been anticipated by another case involving one of the newspapers, *New York Times* v. *Sullivan* (1964). Attempts had been made in Alabama to use private libel suits to penalize a newspaper for criticism of local officials and their segregation policies. When the *Sullivan Case,* with its $500,000 verdict against the *Times,* reached the Supreme Court in 1964, the *Encyclopedia of the American Constitution* recalls,

> it was one of eleven libel claims, totaling $5,600,000 pending against the *Times* in Alabama. It was obvious that libel suits were being used to discourage the press from supporting the Civil Rights movement in the South.

It was also obvious that this kind of campaign against the press would not be tolerated by the Supreme Court, being in effect an adaptation (in the Civil Rights struggle) of the centuries-old charge of seditious libel. The only serious question was whether any kind of libel suit, involving public policy controversies, could thereafter be maintained, a question that was answered by *Gertz* v. *Robert Welch, Inc.* (1974). Elmer Gertz, a feisty Chicago lawyer, collected substantial damages from the John Birch Society, damages which were spent on a well-publicized voyage around the world by him and his wife.

New York Times v. *Sullivan* can be understood as but one of many judicial pronouncements designed to show that the Supreme Court had meant what it had said in *Brown* v. *Board of Education* (1954). The vocabulary used in the Concurring Opinion by Justice Black is indicative of the steady movement in this Country away from Civil War stances and rhetoric, with this native Alabaman speaking easily of "[t]his Nation of ours." Although the Supreme Court did not go as far as Justice Black did when he insisted that "[a]n unconditional right to say what one pleases about public affairs is . . . the minimum guarantee of the First Amendment," his colleagues must have all recognized the common sense evident in the following observation by him:

> Montgomery [Alabama] is one of the localities in which widespread hostility to desegregation has been manifested. This hostility has somehow extended itself to persons who favor desegregation, particularly to so-called "outside agitators," a term which can be made to fit papers like the *Times,* which is published in New York. The scarcity of testimony to show that [Montgomery City] Commissioner [L. B.] Sullivan suffered any actual damage at all suggests that these feelings of hostility had at least as much to do with rendition of this half-million-dollar verdict as did an appraisal of damages. Viewed realistically, this record lends support to an inference that instead of being damaged Commissioner Sullivan's political, social, and financial prestige has likely been enhanced by the *Times'* publication [about an official "wave of terror" against Civil Rights advocates].

8. Obscenity and the Law

I

It is obvious, at least to citizens accustomed to a republican regime, that freedom of speech and freedom of the press are essential to effective self-government. These are freedoms (we have seen) that can usefully be traced back, in the Anglo-American tradition, to the parliamentary immunity needed by legislators if they are to be able to do what is expected of them. This is the argument made by Thomas More in 1521, justifying thereby a practice (or, at least, an expectation) already familiar to parliamentarians.

Such immunity means that discussion of public issues should, in the normal course of things, be completely unfettered, free of threats of official reprisal. This also means that it usually should not matter what the medium is in which such issues are discussed. This means as well that improper, even crippling, repression by the authorities, with respect to the discussion of public issues, can take many forms.

Parliamentary immunity is recognized in Article I, Section 6, of the Constitution of 1787, where Senators and Representatives are assured that "for any Speech or Debate in either House, they shall not be questioned in any other Place." But however Members of Congress are protected from being "questioned [that is, officially acted against] in any other Place" for what they say in Congress, they *are* subject to supervision by their colleagues (as well as by their relevant constituencies). Thus, it is provided in Section 5 of Article I of the Constitution, "Each House may determine the Rules of its Proceedings, punish its Members for disorderly Behaviour, and, with the Concurrence of two thirds, expel a Member."

II

In the Country at large, too, distinctions have been drawn between, on the one hand, that discussion of public issues which should be left unregulated and, on the other hand, various forms of expression subject to official supervision. Thus, a "liberal" Chief Justice of the United States argued (in *Jacobellis* v. *Ohio* [1964]) that there is a "right of the Nation and of the States to maintain a decent society." And his successor, a "conservative" Chief Justice, argued (in *Miller* v. *California* [1973]) that "to equate the free and robust exchange of ideas and political debate with commercial exploitation of obscene materials demeans the grand conception of the First Amendment."

Obscenity has traditionally been regarded as one of several forms of expression that are subject to official sanctions. Other forms thus regarded include pornography, slander and libel, routine criminal solicitation, fraud, and misleading commercial advertising. Still other forms of expression, related to sedition, treason, and incitement of political violence, have been more controversial, inasmuch as it can sometimes be suspected that attempts are being made, by the use of sanctions here, to stifle unwelcome criticism of the government of the day.

That it was fitting and proper that governments should be able to suppress obscenity was long widely accepted even in regimes that protected virtually unlimited political discourse. An 1868 legal formulation by Lord Cockburn indicates (in *Regina* v. *Hicklin*) how obscenity has been long regarded: "I think the test of obscenity is this, whether the tendency of the matter charged as obscenity is to deprave and corrupt those whose minds are open to such immoral influences, and into whose hands a publication of this sort may fall." This formulation could, when used as a basis for prosecutions, be modified in one respect, by providing explicitly for what may have been implied: "into whose hands a publication of this sort is *intended* or is *likely* to fall."

III

The test of "deprave and corrupt," which may be limited to materials dealing with specified bodily functions or perhaps even extended to some portrayals of violence, does draw upon contemporary standards. It takes for granted that the difference between good and bad character can generally be recognized. It also takes for granted that the character of citizens is a vital concern of the entire community.

Thus, it has been pointed out (by Patrick Devlin) that a "nation of debauchees would not in 1940 have responded satisfactorily to Winston Churchill's call to blood and toil and sweat and tears." It is evident, that is, that heroic responses to grave threats do depend upon the character of those challenged. But in ordinary times, too, the character of citizens at large can matter.

That is, an effective freedom of speech may well depend upon the moral, as well as upon the intellectual, competence both of the speaker and of those addressed. An enlightened citizen-body senses what it needs if it is to be able to do what only it can do. It also senses what kind of community is worth preserving—what the character and the aspirations of its members should be, and how such traits can be developed and maintained.

IV

It is the healthy self-governing political community that fosters and depends upon freedom of speech, properly understood. The primary emphasis of the First Amendment, in its Speech and Press provision, is upon free and open discussion of public affairs. This should be distinguished, as we have seen, from what is now celebrated as "freedom of expression."

"Freedom of expression" implicitly looks more to one's desires as an individual than to one's duties as a citizen. An aspect of freedom of expression may be implicit in the "free exercise [of religion]" provision of the First Amendment. Guidance for the person drawing upon *that* right is provided, if at all, not by the citizen-body and its governments but by "authorities" of a more or less spiritual character.

An unregulated freedom of expression can, in some circumstances, undermine the character and education needed for sustained self-government. Freedom of expression, such as in artistic activity, is something that a people should want to see protected to a considerable extent. But there cannot be for all forms of expression the absolute protection that seems to be confirmed by the First Amendment for "freedom of speech [and] of the press"—that is, for completely unfettered (even "subversive," if not "treasonous") public discussion of public affairs.

V

Freedom of expression is protected primarily by those rights to property, liberty, and privacy that can be taken away or regulated only by due process of law. The constitutional provisions that protect property and liberty, such as the Fifth Amendment, are more individualistic (or personal) and less civic-minded (or public-spirited) in their primary orientation than the Speech and Press Clauses of the First Amendment were traditionally understood to be. Everyone, it can be hoped, would agree with the observation of Justice William O. Douglas (dissenting in *Miller v. California*), however much its application in the circumstances it was made may be disputed, "To send men to jail for violating standards they cannot understand, construe, and apply is a monstrous thing to do in a Nation dedicated to fair trials and due process."

Critical, then, to the regulation of any form of expression (at least so long as the writ of *habeas corpus* does not have to be suspended) is an insistence that due process of law be respected. *All* forms of expression are not protected by the First Amendment, but what *is* protected includes the vigorous challenges that may be posed as to whether there should be any particular regulation. These challenges can take such a form as that exhibited in Justice William J. Brennan's Dissenting Opinion in *Paris Adult Theater I* v. *Slaton* (1973):

> I am forced to conclude that the concept of 'obscenity' cannot be defined with sufficient specificity and clarity to provide fair notice to persons who create and distribute sexually oriented materials, to prevent substantial erosion of protected speech as a byproduct of the attempt to suppress unprotected speech, and to avoid very costly institutional harms.

Such requirements as "fair notice" are vital to that due process of law upon which the administration of justice does depend (and not only among us?)—and as such they can be respected by even the most zealous critic of improper publications. It should be recalled here that the traditional arguments against any system of "previous restraint" (or censorship) of publications do depend in large part upon a respect for due process and the rule of law. A serious due process question can arise, for example, from that deliberate harassment of purveyors resulting from governmental shopping among jurisdictions in which to bring prosecutions most inconvenient for defendants.

VI

The American dedication to liberty contributes to the insistence in our constitutions (State as well as National) that the People, as the ultimate source of all governmental authority in this Country, are entitled to discuss public affairs as much as they wish (but not necessarily whenever and wherever they wish). Such republicanism includes unfettered discussion not only in the selecting and assessing of officers of government but also in the framing and amending of forms of government. These and like prerogatives are regarded as essential for any people that is to be truly self-governing.

On the other hand, the American dedication to *equality* has come to have, as a particularly dramatic manifestation, that emphasis upon "freedom of expression" with which we have become familiar in recent decades. This means, among other things, that the *self* or the *individual* has become more important in modernity, even in public discourse, than the *citizen*, with special respect now shown for personal privacy. The "quarrel between the ancients and the moderns," it has been noticed by Leo Strauss, "concerns eventually, and perhaps even from the beginning, the status of 'individuality.'"

When individuality does become more important, there is apt to be less of that sense of duty and of self-sacrifice which is traditionally associated with citizenship. An ever greater emphasis on personal gratification and on a right to privacy can be expected among us, with minimal awareness of or concern about what is happening in the community at large. Symbolic of this development may be the cell phone conversations that people routinely have in public these days, people who are largely oblivious of those among whom they move and upon whom they may nevertheless very much depend.

VII

Such developments depend in large part upon our remarkable technology, including that medical technology which has made our lives both much longer and more comfortable. Chronic disease and starvation in many parts of the world should remind us, however, that the remarkable progress in the West has depended upon well-ordered communities. And these, in turn, have seemed to depend, at least thus far, upon a sturdy moral character among citizens at large in one country after another.

It remains to be seen how much even the technology we find so attractive depends upon a conscientious workforce shaped, in part, by the sense of discipline instilled by the community in its schools and otherwise.

However this may be, it should be evident (as Francis Bacon anticipated in his *New Atlantis*) that risks are run when technological innovations are permitted on the basis primarily of personal choices, without much regard for long-term consequences. This is beginning to become evident as a serious problem for us as we contemplate what "we" are to do (for centuries to come) with the insidious nuclear waste that we are steadily generating along with our beneficent electricity.

Even more insidious may be the spiritual waste we are generating by developing, and thereafter by catering to, all kinds of lascivious tastes. Technological developments have been such that it will soon be, if it is not already, impossible for any sizable community to exercise effective control over the corrupting influences to which its members are apt to be exposed. It can then become largely a matter of chance who does what to whom.

VIII

What should not be a surprise is the coarsening of the finer passions, especially as people become so jaded that they desperately experiment with one innovation after another. Much of this experimentation may be done in the name either of liberty or of love, but it tends toward that lowering of standards which debases not only those immediately corrupted but also all those who are likely to be associated with the debased. This is, therefore, not true liberation, but rather virtual enslavement, a development that is considered in the 1989 memoranda found in Appendix N of this volume.

It is highly likely, in these circumstances, that the obscenity cases considered by Courts from time to time can do little more than remind us of how steady the decline has been in the "literature" to which we have become accustomed. One can be sympathetic to the outrage of those who very much resent what has happened to popular "culture." But even most of *those* people would not want to have televison (including cable transmissions) in this Country shut down altogether, however salutary that would be.

We should, in considering useful remedies in our predicament, be reminded of the folly of the Prohibition Amendment of 1919, not a good year for constitutional vintages. For 1919 *was* the year of that decision in *Schenck* v. *United States* which ratified the efforts of the Government of the United States to suppress much-needed criticism of its disastrous foreign policy. That folly was even worse than that of the Prohibition Amendment, which not only contributed considerably to the development of organized crime in the United States but also gave governmental promotion of morality a bad name.

IX

American liberals tend to endorse unfettered discussion of the issues of the day. Otherwise, they fear, a Republican Form of Government is subverted. Thus, even we liberals are, in such civic-mindedness, essentially conservatives.

On the other hand, American conservatives tend to be aware of the limits that the community is entitled to place on the desire for self-expression, especially when such expression takes the form of unseemly public exhibitions. But most conservatives do not like to dwell upon the fact that the question of obscenity is intimately related to the question of property, to the question of what one may legitimately do with one's own. Even more disturbing for them can be questions about what is truly one's own.

That property issues are critical here is suggested by the fact that the American pornography industry now grosses more than $10 billion a year, with the advent of video and the VCR having moved most viewing of pornography from "adult" theaters and bookstores into the home. It seems that this Country's most "successful" purveyors of pornography—among whose "clients" are 20 percent of our households with cable-access service—are far more likely (à la Al Capone) to be jailed for tax evasion than for corrupting their fellow citizens. The extent of corruption in these matters is suggested by the fact that a well-known pornography industry leader in this Country can be acclaimed as a philanthropist in his hometown, rather than being shunned as a systematic corruptor on a large scale of his fellow citizens.

9. Private Property and Public Freedom

I

A challenging discussion of the relations between economic freedom and political freedom (especially freedom of speech) is provided in the opening essay of Milton Friedman's *Capitalism and Freedom*. Particularly challenged by him, almost half a century ago, were "intellectuals" who are socialist, or at least somewhat anticapitalist, in their inclinations. Both he and those whom he challenges are assumed to be in favor of personal freedom.

The author is a noted economist, one of the dozen most influential in the twentieth century. As a quite decent partisan of the free market, he continues a tradition in which Adam Smith particularly stands out. But Smith, it should be remembered, was also the author of an important treatise on Moral Sentiments.

Smith's successors today, however, tend to be narrower in their interests. For one thing, they are not apt to be sensitive to the language they employ, often being unaware of the problems implicit in their terms. These terms include *freedom, goodness,* and of course *property.*

II

Economic freedom is, for Milton Friedman, very much a good. It is not only "an indispensable means toward the achievement of political freedom." It is even "an end in itself."

"Intellectuals," he emphasizes, "have a strong bias against regarding this aspect of freedom as important." His own bias against the inclinations of intellectuals, or at least contemporary intellectuals, is evident throughout his essay. This may be seen, early on, in his complaint that "[t]hey tend to express contempt for what they regard as the material aspects of life, and to regard their own pursuit of allegedly higher values as on a different plane of significance and as deserving of special attention."

Critical to the Friedman assessment of the social organizations, both the economic and the political systems, are assumptions about the nature of private property. It sometimes seems to be assumed, for example, that one somehow *has* property virtually independent of any political order. It would be denied upon reflection, of course, that any such assumption is made, considering, for example, the role of governments in the supply and maintenance of money—but the feeling is still there, that there is such an entity as the "individual" who possesses property apart from meddlesome governments.

III

Thus, it can be argued, "The citizen of Great Britain, who after World War II was not permitted to spend his vacation in the United States because of exchange control, was being deprived of an essential freedom no less than the citizen of the United States, who was denied the opportunity to spend his vacation in Russia because of his political views." Whether or not the British "exchange control" ever made sense, it did seem to be a rule of general application. The American restriction referred to, on the other hand, was clearly designed (as described) to affect only a handful of citizens, not all Americans who might have wanted to visit Russia.

The Friedman passage just quoted continues, "The [British restriction] was ostensibly an economic limitation on freedom, and the [American restriction was] a political limitation, yet there is no essential difference between them." It need not be disputed that economic policy may sometimes be foolish and even harmful. But can it be seriously maintained that there is *no* "essential difference" between an "economic limitation on freedom" and a "political limitation"?

What is being assumed, by such a denial of any "essential difference," about the relative importance for the human soul of economic causes, on the one hand, and political causes, on the other? Have those men been simply foolish who, for the sake of political freedom, have been willing to "pledge to each other [their] Lives, [their] Fortunes, and [their] sacred Honor"? In short, does the modern economist deny any essential, or practically relevant, distinction between the High and the Low, thereby making much more of the Material Causes than of the Final Causes of human things?

IV

All this is *not* to deny that there is merit in the Friedman insistence that economic arrangements can contribute to political freedom "because of their effect on the concentration or dispersion of power." Thus, it is pointed out, "The kind of economic organization that provides economic freedom directly, namely, competitive capitalism, also promotes political freedom because it separates economic power from political power and in this way enables the one to offset the other." The contributions of "competitive capitalism" to political freedom and a decent life are inventoried both in the remainder of this Friedman essay and in the book from which it is taken.

Particularly significant is the observation, "I know of no example in time or place of a society that has been marked by a large measure of political freedom, and that has not also used something comparable to a free market to organize the bulk of economic activity." It is recognized, further on, that "capitalism is [only] a necessary condition for political freedom," that it is not a sufficient condition (as seen at times, during the past century and a half, in Italy, Spain, Germany, Japan, and Tsarist Russia). But should it not be wondered, when political freedom and economic freedom coexist, which is prior, especially when it is said that political freedom is always accompanied by economic freedom, but not vice versa?

Also to be wondered about is the report that "the typical state of mankind is tyranny, servitude, and misery." Is this kind of assessment, dismissing as it does those multitudes across millennia who had considered their regimes to be decent and their lives very much worth having, to be expected from those economists who consider "the free market and the development of capitalist institutions" absolutely necessary for the emergence and perpetuation of the truly human? Of course, all this obliges the observer to consider what is truly human, how it can be known, *and* how it can be known that it *is* known.

V

A reliable investigation into the nature of things presupposes an informed awareness of the terms one is using. Prominent among these terms in the Friedman essay is "value(s)," a term that seems to be grounded in the science of economics. It is a term which assumes that there is no intrinsic worth to things, that much (if not virtually all) depends on an ever-changing supply and demand.

Consider also the implications of this observation by an author who had, in the preceding paragraph, identified himself as a liberal:

> The liberal conceives of men as imperfect beings. He regards the problem of social organization to be as much a negative problem of preventing "bad" people from doing harm as of enabling "good" people to do good, and, of course, "bad" people and "good" people may be the same people, depending on who is judging them.

Good and *bad* are both put in quotation marks here in such a way as to suggest (as it is often fashionable for contemporary intellectuals to do) that what is good or bad, whether for a liberal or for a conservative, is arbitrary, or dependent primarily on one's circumstances. Had it been a quite limited view of what was truly good which had led that author to identify, as we have seen, almost all of known human existence across millennia as really miserable?

Also revealing in this Friedman essay are the dozen or so uses of "individual(s)." Individuals, it seems, have opportunities to be happy in ways that citizens as citizens do not, in that individuals are better able to take advantage of markets, while citizens are regulated by governments who believe they know what people "ought to want." In short, a market economy promotes freedom more often, and more reliably, than any benevolent government is likely to do.

VI

We are obliged to wonder, of course, about who is truly free. It is, considering how deluded human beings can be, not enough to regard as free those among us who *consider* themselves to be free. Related to this problem is the identification of freedom primarily with the absence of controls.

An old-fashioned opinion is that only those human beings are truly free who want to do, and can indeed do, what they should. A corollary to this opinion has been the assumption that, unless a people is vouchsafed divine revelation, guidance toward freedom has to be provided to most human beings by a community that knows what it is doing. The truly free, thus developed, are not only free, but know that they are so.

One consequence of genuine freedom is that a reliable grasp of *excellence* can be developed. Thus, freedom can be properly desired not only for its own sake but also for its consequences. The excellence that results can be recognized across millennia by all who understand human beings and their ever-varying communities and circumstances.

VII

The truly free human being, therefore, is not bound by the desires that happen to be fashionable from time to time. Circumstances may limit how long, if at all, excellence (either personal or social) may be secured. But an aspect of the excellent, seen in one's understanding of things, may be available (if only to a few) even in miserable circumstances.

Tyranny and poverty can (as Aristotle observed) blight the excellence, and hence the happiness, that one might otherwise enjoy. But license and abundance can also be destructive here, perhaps more so because people, when both allowed and equipped to enjoy themselves as they chance to want to do, may believe that they are indeed free and happy. If much is made of individualism, an insistence upon enduring standards may even come to seem tyrannical.

Much *is* made, in the Friedman thesis, of the contributions that wealthy patrons (in a market economy) can make even to radical causes. If this approach (very much dependent on chance) is extended to the development of cultural influences, it would mean that we should be suspicious of official allocations of resources for education and the arts. All this is to assume, in still another way, that the truly good is not to be regarded as knowable enough to justify entrusting any government with the power to attempt to shape its citizen-body.

VIII

Whatever reservations one may have about Milton Friedman's understanding of the matters touched upon thus far in this discussion of his essay, his heart, so to speak, does seem to be in the right place. Thus he can speak of "our experience with McCarthyism," tacitly recognizing thereby that there had been something questionable about the methods, if not also about the objectives, of the now-notorious former Senator from Wisconsin. And so he can observe:

> Entirely aside from the substantive issues involved, and the merits of the charges made, what protection did individuals, and in particular government employees, have against irresponsible accusations and probings into matters that it went against their conscience to reveal? Their appeal to the Fifth Amendment would have been a hollow mockery without an alternative to governmental employment.

This observation is introduced as an illustration of "the role of the market in preserving political freedom." This discussion followed upon a recollection of the "Hollywood Ten" blacklist in the 1950s, a much-publicized proscription which had attempted to bar "suspected Communists or fellow travelers" from preparing scripts for movies. But, it was reported, at least 15 percent of Hollywood movies at that time came to be written by blacklisted writers.

Thus, the desire of film producers to compete effectively in the entertainment market led them, blacklist or no blacklist, to buy the best movie scripts they could find. That is, what they did was to make the best financial deals they could for themselves, without discussing publicly either the alleged threats to the Country of "subversives" or the possible harm being done to the Country if the campaign against "subversives" (and not only in the movie industry) was ill-conceived. One can be reminded here of the determined efforts of quite respectable tobacco industry executives to maximize their profits, without serious consideration (at least in public) of the considerable damage that their products might be causing.

IX

Thus, although material self-interest can lead to the promotion of freedom, it can also lead to the neglect of that public character upon which an enduring freedom depends. Critical to these developments is the possibility that the capitalist as capitalist may not truly care about the Common Good. That is to say, does not systematic selfishness, which can no doubt often be productive and socially useful, need to be supervised by a decent community that somehow knows what is needed and how to get it?

It is perhaps an awareness of such systematic selfishness, which may have found its most devastating political expression in the First World War, that contributes to the anomaly lamented in the concluding paragraph of the Friedman essay discussed here. It is argued in that essay that "the groups in our society that have the most at stake in the preservation and strengthening of competitive capitalism are those minority groups which can most easily become the object of the distrust and enmity of the majority—the Negroes, the Jews, the foreign-born." "Yet, paradoxically enough," it is then argued,

> the enemies of the free market—the Socialists and Communists—have been recruited in disproportionate measure from these groups. Instead of recognizing that the existence of the market has protected them from the attitudes of their fellow countrymen, they mistakenly attribute the residual discrimination to the market.

Is enough credit given, by Milton Friedman and those of like mind, to the sensibilities and intuition of those who come to suspect capitalists of being insufficiently sensitive not only to the plight of the poor but also to the demands of patriotism? When we are reminded of what can be posited about a market economy being necessary for societies that have been "marked by a large measure of political freedom," we can wonder about a theory which in effect makes honorary capitalists out of those in antiquity who, from time to time, enjoyed decent regimes, as in China, India, Egypt, Greece, Mesopotamia, Israel, and Rome. Be all this as it may—for it *is* difficult to be certain about the workings of ancient economies—are those quite talented people among us truly free who devote the only lives they will ever have primarily to making money?

10. *Buckley* v. *Valeo* (1976)

I

The Federal Election Campaign Act of 1971, as amended in 1974, was reviewed in 1975–1976 by the United States Supreme Court in *Buckley* v. *Valeo*. The Court produced a remarkable document, featuring a 230-page Per Curiam Opinion. This "book" looks like a Congressional study, if not even like a part of the voluminous federal budget.

The Per Curiam Opinion, which very much bears on the Milton Friedman essay just discussed, includes this preliminary description of those parts of the Act which are of particular interest for us:

> The intricate statutory scheme adopted by Congress to regulate federal election campaigns includes restrictions on political contributions and expenditures that apply broadly to all phases of and all participants in the election process. The major contribution and expenditure limitations in the Act prohibit individuals from contributing more than $25,000 in a single year or more than $1,000 to any single candidate for an election campaign and from spending more than $1,000 a year "relative to a clearly identified candidate." Other provisions restrict a candidate's use of personal and family resources in his campaign and limit the overall amount that can be spent by a candidate in campaigning for federal office.

An indication is provided further on by the Court of the concerns that prompted this legislation:

> Under a system of private financing of elections, a candidate lacking immense personal or family wealth must depend on financial contributions from others to provide the resources necessary to con-

duct a successful campaign. The increasing importance of the communications media and sophisticated mass-mailing and polling operations to effective campaigning make the raising of large sums of money an ever more essential ingredient of an effective candidacy. To the extent that large contributions are given to secure a political *quid pro quo* from current and potential office holders, the integrity of our system of representative democracy is undermined.

The Court continues: "Although the scope of such pernicious practices [just described] can never be reliably ascertained, the deeply disturbing examples surfacing after the 1972 election demonstrate that the problem is not an illusory one."

The Court, further on, can speak of "Congress' valid interest in encouraging citizen participation in political campaigns while continuing to guard against the corrupting potential of large financial contributions to candidates." All this is not a new concern for Members of Congress: in 1884, for example, the Supreme Court had noticed (in *Ex parte Yarbrough*) the corruption feared from "the free use of money in elections, arising from the vast growth of recent wealth." And, as recently as June 2006, the Supreme Court more or less confirmed (in *Randall* v. *Sorrell*) the position it had taken in *Buckley.*

II

The *Buckley* v. *Valeo* Court, in its 1976 Per Curiam Opinion, expressed again and again a competing concern about how Congressional regulations of these matters affected First Amendment interests. Thus it observed:

> The First Amendment denies government the power to determine that spending to promote one's political views is wasteful, excessive, or unwise. In the free society ordained by our Constitution it is not the government, but the people—individually as citizens and candidates and collectively as associations and political communities—who must retain control over the quantity and range of debate on public issues in a political campaign.

It is noted here, however, that "Congress may engage in public financing of election campaigns and may condition acceptance of public funds on an agreement by the candidate to abide by specified expenditure limitations."

The Court had opened its Per Curiam Opinion with this indication of what it would be considering: "These appeals present constitutional challenges to the key provisions of the Federal Election Campaign Act of 1971, and related provisions of the Internal Revenue Code of 1954, all as amended in 1974." The pertinent parts of the Federal Election Campaign Act are set forth in the Appendix to that Opinion. It is noticed, early on in the Opinion, "The constitutional power of Congress to regulate federal elections is well established and is not questioned by any of the [many] parties in this case."

The Court begins in this way its summary of that portion of its Opinion that we are primarily concerned with here, its review of contribution and expenditure limitations:

> [T]he provisions of the Act that imposes a $1,000 limitation on contributions to a single candidate, §608(b)(1), a $5,000 limitation on contributions by a political committee to a single candidate, §608(b)(2), and a $25,000 limitation on total contributions by an individual during any calendar year, §608(b)(3), are constitutionally valid. These limitations, along with the disclosure provisions, constitute the Act's primary weapons against the reality or appearance of improper influence stemming from the dependence of candidates on large campaign contributions. The contribution ceilings thus serve the basic governmental interest in safeguarding the integrity of the electoral process without directly impinging upon the rights of individual citizens and candidates to engage in political debate and discussion.

But, the Court's summary continues, "By contrast, the First Amendment requires the invalidation of the Act's independent expenditure ceiling, §608(e)(1), its limitation on a candidate's expenditures from his own personal funds, §608(a), and its ceilings on overall campaign expenditures, §608(c)." "These provisions," the Court argues, "place substantial and direct restrictions on the ability of candidates, citizens, and associations to engage in protected political expression, restrictions that the First Amendment cannot tolerate."

III

What *has* come to be tolerated, it seems, is the Court's determined involvement in these matters. Indeed, it seems to be acting here as a third branch of the National Legislature. One can even be reminded of its ill-conceived twentieth-century efforts to regulate State "burdens on interstate commerce," something else (I have argued in my *Reflections on Constitutional Law*) that Congress is far better equipped to attempt to deal with.

All this can serve to remind us as well of the reservations we should have about the Court's claim of a comprehensive power to review Acts of Congress for their constitutionality. Our freedom of speech entitles us to question this claim, however much we should usually acquiesce in what the Court does from time to time. Particularly disturbing, we have noticed, can be the development of the habit in Congress of depending on the Court to make the constitutional judgments that Congress, for one reason or another, would rather not make.

In short, we can wonder what business the Court had to produce its own treatise on campaign expenditures in this Country. Certainly, the Court's members have had far less experience with these matters than have the five hundred and thirty-five Members of Congress. We can also wonder, of course, whether there was any First Amendment question of consequence in what Congress had provided in attempting to regulate campaign expenditures as it did.

IV

"It is clear," the Court said in *Buckley* v. *Valeo,* "that a primary effect of [certain] expenditure limitations [in the Federal Election Campaign Act] is to restrict the quantity of campaign speech by individuals, groups, and candidates." It is then said, "[While neutral] as to the ideas expressed, [these restrictions] limit political expression 'at the core of our electoral process and of the First Amendment freedoms.'" Of course, just the opposite may be true if curbs on expenditures should, say, discourage reliance on television advertising, perhaps encouraging thereby more serious political discourse during political campaigns.

One can begin to assess the contending claims here by studying what happens wherever strict limits on campaign expenditures are found. Tyrannical governments can display the risks of such limitations, which of course are not applied as well to the propaganda of such governments. On the other hand, it can be useful to consider what happens in Great Britain, where severe limitations are placed upon expenditures on behalf of particular candidates (but not on political parties) during that country's brief parliamentary campaigns.

Is it not obvious that the British have, year in and year out, a considerable freedom of speech? It may well be that the quality of their political discourse is often, if not even usually, superior to ours. Certainly, their political discourse is far less likely to be cluttered up with the kind of television advertising originally developed to sell merchandise.

V

An excellent model for proper political discourse is provided us by the Lincoln-Douglas debates held in Illinois in 1858. No doubt, political organizing, for which money is needed, helped determine the outcome of that Senatorial race. But the public could be confident that it had gotten from the candidates, in their half dozen three-hour encounters, reliable notions of what they stood for and why.

Indeed, it is the confidence of the public in their institutions that such measures as campaign expenditure restrictions tend to bolster, even when they are somewhat ineffective. Justice Thurgood Marshall, in taking issue with the *Buckley* Court's invalidation of a curb upon one's use of one's personal fortune in support of one's own candidacy, observed:

> One of the points on which all Members of the Court agree is that money is essential for effective communication in a political campaign. It would appear to follow that the candidate with a substantial personal fortune at his disposal is off to a significant "headstart." . . . [A] wealthy candidate's immediate access to a substantial personal fortune may give him an initial advantage that his less wealthy opponent can never overcome. And even if the advantage can be overcome, the perception that personal wealth wins elections may not only discourage potential candidates without significant personal wealth from entering the political arena, but [may] also undermine public confidence in the integrity of the electoral process.

This argument, with its emphasis upon how the appearance of things may undermine faith in the system, is reinforced (in Justice Marshall's opinion) by a 1971 quotation from a Member of the House of Representatives: "In the Nation's seven largest States in 1970, 11 of the 15 major Senatorial candidates were millionaires; the four who were not millionaires lost their bid for election."

Of course, we know that millionaires do sometimes lose their bids for election in this Country. And it *is* likely, at least in this Country, that those citizens who can become and remain wealthy are people of talent. Even so, is it not a legitimate concern of Congress that the wealthy not *appear* to be buying an election—or at least buying an opportunity to make a real race of it?

VI

Justice Byron R. White, in his own separate Opinion in *Buckley* v. *Valeo,* found it strange that the Court, in striking down some of the provisions of the Act, had claimed "more insight as to what may improperly influence candidates than is possessed by the majority of Congress that passed this bill and the President who signed it." This was done despite the Court's acceptance of "the Congressional judgment that the evils of unlimited contributions are sufficiently threatening" to warrant some restrictions. Should not the decision as to where lines are to be drawn here depend more upon political than upon judicial judgment?

It seemed to be generally recognized at the time of the *Buckley* decision that there *was* a need to "insulat[e] candidates from the time-consuming and entangling task of raising huge sums of money." It was this need that was referred to by the late Paul Simon, in 1995, when he announced that he would not seek reelection to the Senate. Even so, one would have thought that someone of his stature in Illinois would not need much money for a successful reelection campaign.

It would seem, in any event, that the critical concerns here are not those grounded in the First Amendment but rather those that draw on standards of fairness and of efficiency. The British experience does suggest that an effective freedom of political speech survives severe restrictions upon campaign expenditures. And parliamentary experience generally suggests that a legislator's freedom of speech is not improperly abridged when he is restricted in the resources available to him in debates (the principal resources there being the speaking opportunities and the time allocated to each member).

VII

However all this may be, money is not everything in politics. Even billionaires (as well as millionaires) are known to have failed in their public efforts. And people who started quite poor have risen to the very top.

That one chances to be identified and hence generally known one way rather than another can make all the difference in the world in politics, as often elsewhere in life. Of course, incumbency can matter, so much so that some can protest (as noted in *Buckley*) that limits on campaign expenditures may "discriminate against candidates opposing incumbent office holders." But, then, it is not suggested that incumbents be given special protection when circumstances make incumbency a liability—that is, when sentiment is strong for "voting the rascals out."

It should be recognized, no matter what rules *are* permitted and adopted with respect to campaign expenditures, that there will be substantial efforts to circumvent them. The *Buckley* Court recognized, for example, "It would naively underestimate the ingenuity and resourcefulness of persons and groups desiring to buy influence to believe that they would have much difficulty devising expenditures that skirted the restrictions" that are in place. But then, do we not want people involved in politics to be both determined and ingenious in pursuing what they happen to regard as good?

VIII

It is not the determination or the ingenuity of ambitious people that we should strive to correct, but rather what they regard as good. Particularly in need of correction here may be the opinion that one's wealth *entitles* one to have more political influences than do the poor. After all, it is often the efforts and sacrifices of the poor, say in the form of police and military services, that permit their privileged fellow citizens to be secure in their wealth.

The *Buckley* Court insisted, "The primary governmental interest served by the [Federal Election Campaign] Act—the prevention of actual and apparent corruption of the political process—does not support

the limitation on the candidate's expenditure of his own personal funds."
"Indeed," the Court went on to argue, "the use of personal funds reduces
the candidate's dependence on outside contributions and thereby coun-
teracts the coercive pressures and attendant risks of abuse to which the
Act's contribution limitations are directed." But the wealthy have another
advantage, in that they, unlike opponents who have to raise considerable
money, can devote all of their time and energy to campaigning.

There is, as *is* usually the case in any sustained controversy, something
to be said on both sides here. One measure that could somewhat relieve
difficulties here would be to limit how much television each candidate
could use, and at no cost to himself. Still another measure, which I presume to offer here for the first time, would be that any candidate who uses
his own funds (above a specified maximum) would have to supply each of
his certified opponents an equal amount of money for campaign purposes,
a requirement that public opinion might effectively insist upon even if no
legislature would ever do so.

IX

The ingenuity of candidates, already referred to, means that repeated
efforts have to be made to keep campaign funding laws relevant to the
ever-shifting practices of the day. It can even be doubted whether such
laws ever really make much difference. Or put otherwise, can they make
much difference in a country such as ours, whatever they may really do in
a country such as Great Britain?

Perhaps the serious problem here is not with the laws we do, or do
not, have regulating campaign finances. Rather, the underlying problem
may be with the character of the American electorate. Should that electorate be encouraged to believe that it is being bought by those who pour
fortunes, however secured, into their campaigns?

It does not seem, no matter what the Supreme Court says, that freedom of speech is seriously threatened by laws that attempt to limit and
regulate campaign spending, at least in this Country. Certainly, freedom
of speech is vigorously used by those among us who consider such laws
to be threats to our freedoms. It remains to be seen how much one's right
to use one's property pretty much as one wishes, including that property
which the community makes possible, threatens the right of a community
both to govern itself and (perhaps more critical here) to appear to do so.

11. The Regulation of Commercial Speech

I

The extent to which commercial speech can claim First Amendment protection is suggested by what the United States Supreme Court has done to official efforts (by State courts, State bars, and others) to restrict severely the advertising that lawyers might do. What the Court has now done about legal advertising was anticipated by what it had done in *Virginia State Board of Pharmacy* v. *Virginia Citizens Consumer Council* (1976). The *Virginia Pharmacy Case* has been described thus in the *Encyclopedia of the American Constitution*:

> Traditionally commercial speech was assumed to be outside the First Amendment's protection. This decision made clear that this assumption was obsolete. Virginia's rules governing professional pharmacists forbade the advertising of prices of prescription drugs. The Supreme Court, 7–1, held this rule invalid at the behest of a consumers' group, thus prompting the notion of a "right to receive" in the freedom of speech.

The state of affairs prior to *Virginia Pharmacy* has been described thus in the *Encyclopedia*: "Until 1976 'commercial speech'—a vague category encompassing advertisements, invitations to deal, credit or financial reports, prospectuses, and the like—was subject to broad regulatory authority, with little or no protection from the First Amendment." In the *Virginia Pharmacy Case,* we are further told, "The Court rejected the State's 'highly paternalistic approach,' preferring a system in which 'people will perceive their own best interests if only they are well enough informed, and that the best means to that end is to open the channels of communication rather than to close them.'" But, it has also been noticed, "where regulation of commercial expression is not directed at potential deception but intended to advance other interests such as aesthetics or conservation, the Supreme Court has followed a relatively permissive approach to State regulatory interests."

The revolutionary step with respect to advertising by lawyers was taken by the Supreme Court in *Bates* v. *State Bar of Arizona* (1977). That case has been described thus in the *Encyclopedia of the American Constitution*:

> In 1976 two Phoenix lawyers ran newspaper advertisements offering "routine" legal services for "very reasonable" prices. A 5–4 Supreme Court declared here that the First Amendment protected this form of commercial speech. The majority rejected a number of "countervailing State interests" urged against the freedom of speech protection, relying on [the *Virginia Pharmacy Case*].

The dissenting Justices "strenuously objected to the majority's equating intangible services—which they found impossible to standardize and rarely 'routine'—with 'prepackaged' prescription drugs.'"

II

Judicial invalidation of traditional restraints upon advertising by lawyers indicates how much commercial speech has come to be protected by the First Amendment against regulation. If the half-million lawyers in this Country can no longer be regulated as they had once been, that indicates how far the "reach" of the First Amendment has been extended. Does not the extension of considerable First Amendment protection to advertising tend to reinforce the notion that the desire to make money is somehow vital, if not primary, even among the learned professions?

Of course, advertising of legal services can be explained, with some plausibility, as efforts to help laymen understand what services are available. But, the response is made, such useful information can be provided by bar associations and other public interest groups. Concerned lawyers and others can urge such groups to supply what the public needs to know.

Of course, also, freedom of speech, as traditionally understood, protected the right of citizens, including lawyers, to question the need for and the effectiveness of all restrictions upon what lawyers may say or do. Such restrictions are always subject to reconsideration, just as are restrictions upon obscenity, libel, and various other forms of expression that have traditionally been subject to regulation. If even the Constitution may be questioned by critics proposing amendments to it, so may all kinds of State regulations, no matter how long established.

III

Perhaps more critical to State regulations of commercial speech than invocations of the First Amendment have been invocations of the market. Restrictions upon advertising of services as well as of goods keep both suppliers and consumers from being able to make the most efficient use of their resources. Such interference can be condemned as an invasion of the rights of property.

The critique here by the champions of a market economy extends to reservations about the regulation of various professions, including law and medicine. Indeed, even licensing requirements can be called into question as interfering with the salutary operation of market forces. Such an operation, it is sometimes argued, should be depended upon to expose and eliminate incompetent practitioners.

Faith healers and astrologers are not routinely licensed by the State, nor does there seem to be much of an effort to change this state of affairs. Why, it is asked by the more dedicated champions of a market economy, should not doctors and lawyers be treated the same way? Publicity and damage suits would (it is argued) be counted on to accomplish, and usually more efficiently, what is now attempted by licensing and professional regulation.

IV

What, it must be wondered, does it mean to say that even the workings of the traditional professions should be governed by the market? The concern is expressed, by the dissenters in *Bates,* about the profound changes in the practice of law to be expected because of the ruling in that case. It is a ruling that can be said to be grounded in a sense of realism as to how people live and what they need.

"It is not difficult to show," Fisher Ames said in 1801, "that stable liberty is the best condition of nations for the advancement of [their] commercial interest." But should it also be said that "commercial interest," in the form of a market economy, is "the best condition" for the advancement of liberty? The free market advocate would add, as we have seen, that a substantial part of one's liberty includes being left alone to do pretty much as one wishes with one's property.

However this may be, participants in a market economy do seem to be substantially, if not even primarily, concerned to make money. Or, at least, how well they do—how they are regarded by others, if not also by themselves—tends to be dependent upon how much money they do make. Or, perhaps more precisely, how they are generally regarded depends, in large part, upon how much money they are believed to make and to have—with advertising being useful not only for making money but also for displaying it.

V

At the heart of the issues touched upon in cases such as *Bates* is the question of what it should mean for one to be a member of a *profession*. It is sensed by traditionalists that advertising by professionals tends to look more to money-making than to service. What is aimed at, ultimately, by the businessman as businessman (that is, as money-maker) is likely to be his own good, not that of his customer.

Service to others, then, is not an end in itself, but merely a way of advancing one's own interests. The patron saint of such self-seeking could be the Thrasymachus of Book I of Plato's *Republic*. He makes explicit what others are ashamed to admit about the selfishness that we all exhibit and naturally depend upon in our dealings with one another.

It is not only professionalism that is, in effect, called into question by a dedication to the market economy. Patriotism, too, is put at risk. That is, both political associations and religious allegiances tend to be weakened by the kind of economic organization from which we benefit so much.

VI

What, in these matters, is *cause* and what is *effect* can be hard to determine. The commercialization of the law is evident in what has happened in the past half-century to the size of the major law firms among us. A related development has been the opening by some law firms of substantial offices all over this Country as well as abroad.

One consequence of this development has been the transitory character of any lawyer's association with a law firm. My University of Chicago Law School classmates generally assumed, a half-century ago, that the big-city firms which first took them on were likely to be the firms with which they would spend their careers. But these days (one hears) relatively few of those taken on ever become full partners in the firms that first hire them.

This is said to be due, at least in part, to the "need" to have a large cadre of young lawyers to handle the traffic which generates the substantial profits that the full partners divide. Indeed, the younger lawyers tend to be regarded as employees, even if they should be called "junior partners." The Marxist, with his theories about the use and abuse of "surplus value," should find illuminating a study of the typical large American law firm.

VII

All this may simply be recognizing that the modern law firm is primarily a business. This means, among other things, that the younger lawyer cannot be subsidized through an extended apprenticeship. It may even be largely a matter of chance who is eventually admitted to the ranks of the most privileged.

A recourse to systematic advertising is, in these circumstances, more or less "natural." This simply recognizes still another way that lawyering is now becoming, if it is not already, primarily a commercial enterprise. Serious reform here could well begin with a severe limitation, by the organized bar, upon the number of partners and associates permitted in a firm.

This is hardly likely to happen without once again regarding the lawyer as primarily a minister of justice, if not even as a secular priest. If it is only "realistic" to recognize the law as a business, then advertising is very much in order. To attempt to restrict the size of law firms might even come to be seen as an unlawful restraint of trade.

VIII

Of course, we might still wonder why the typical youngster goes to law school. A desire to make a comfortable living can usually be assumed. But is there not often something more, perhaps even a calling to the cause of justice?

This kind of dedication depends upon how the law itself is regarded. Consider how old-fashioned (that is, unrealistic) William Blackstone can sound when, in the lecture ("On the Study of the Law") with which he inaugurated in 1758 his *Commentaries on the Laws of England,* he speaks of his country:

> A land, perhaps the only one in the universe, in which political or civil liberty is the very end and scope of the constitution. This liberty, rightly understood, consists in the power of doing whatever the laws permit; which is only to be effected by a general conformity of all orders and degrees to those equitable rules of action, by which the meanest individual is protected from the insults and oppression of the greatest.

The high-mindedness of this approach is suggested by the coupling of "whatever the laws permit" with "a general conformity . . . to . . . equitable rules of action."

Further on in this inaugural lecture, Blackstone can speak of the law as "a science, which distinguishes the criterions of right and wrong; which teaches to establish the one, and prevent, punish, or redress the other, which employs in it's theory the noblest faculties of the soul, and exerts in it's practice the cardinal virtues of the heart." To speak of law thus is indeed to consider the calling to the bar as a form of initiation into a secular priesthood. Would not those who regard any profession in this way be reluctant to have it treated as a business for which everyday advertising is appropriate?

IX

Whether lawyering should be regarded as a business will continue to be debated. Also subject to debate is the issue of what kind of advertising is appropriate for such a "business." It can be expected that regulations of any business, including its advertising, should be subject to scrutiny for their conformity to the due process, equal protection, and any like standards upon which the healthy community depends.

But it is quite a different matter when it is assumed that the regulation of *any* kind of commercial speech is subject, in the ordinary course of things, to First Amendment standards. It can be indicated, as the Court did in the *Virginia Pharmacy Case,* that the regulation for falsity in commercial advertising cases would never be applied to political speech. Yet precedents are now available which permit speech supposedly protected somewhat by the First Amendment (such as commercial advertising) to be officially tested for its truth.

This does seem to be a repudiation, however partial, of the "absolutism" traditionally associated, at least by "purists," with the First Amendment protection of "freedom of speech [and] of the press." One consequence of these developments is to provide commercial speech with more constitutional immunity than it is entitled to. The far more ominous, perhaps related, consequence is to provide political speech with less constitutional immunity than is necessary for a Republican Form of Government.

12. The Universal Declaration
of Human Rights (1948)

I

The Universal Declaration of Human Rights was promulgated by a 1948 resolution of the United Nations General Assembly. Its Preamble opens with the observation that "recognition of the inherent dignity and of the equal and inalienable rights of all members of the human family is the foundation of freedom, justice and peace in the world." No particular country or people is provided for by name, but rather all of humanity.

Thus, the United Nations General Assembly proclaims this Universal Declaration "as a common standard of achievement for all peoples and all nations." Unlike, say, the English Magna Carta or the American Bill of Rights, this Declaration does not purport to reaffirm and extend rights already exercised. Rather, it provides the standard it does "to the end that every individual and every organ of society . . . shall strive by teaching and education to promote respect for [the] rights and freedoms" enumerated in the thirty articles of the Declaration.

There is, in the Universal Declaration (set forth in Appendix L of this volume), little accommodation to the history and the circumstances of various peoples and states. Although the privileges of citizenship are referred to here and there, the emphasis is on the overarching prerogatives of human beings. Thus, Article 1 of the Declaration provides:

All human beings are born free and equal in dignity and rights. They are endowed with reason and conscience and should act towards one another in a spirit of brotherhood.

II

It is evident, again and again in the Universal Declaration, that there are human rights abuses worldwide that are known to be ongoing. Such abuses are alluded to in the hope that they can be curtailed. Thus, in Article 5, it is said, "No one shall be subjected to torture or to cruel, inhuman or degrading treatment or punishment."

Particularly startling is the apparent recognition, in Article 4, of the existence (down to our day) of "slavery and the slave trade." Related to this concern is the repeated recognition of the difficulties people have in establishing themselves anywhere as self-governing. Worldwide turmoil is recognized in various ways.

Thus, it is asserted, in Article 13, "Everyone has the right to freedom of movement and residence within the borders of each State." This is supplemented by the assertion, "Everyone has the right to leave any country, including his own, and to return to his country." This is immediately followed by the assertion, in Article 14, "Everyone has the right to seek and to enjoy in other countries asylum from persecution."

III

One can see again and again in the Universal Declaration vestiges of the traumas of the Second World War. The systematic atrocities, on an unprecedented scale by tyrannical regimes in Europe and Asia, had been only a few years before. And so it is recognized, in the Preamble, that "disregard for human rights have resulted in barbarous acts which have outraged the conscience of mankind."

The hopes as well as the horrors of the Second World War are remembered. It is recalled in the Preamble that "the advent of a world in which human beings shall enjoy freedom of speech and belief and freedom from fear and want has been proclaimed as the highest aspiration of the common people." It must be wondered, however, whether the rights collected in the Declaration are the highest aspirations *of* the common people or rather the highest aspirations *for* the common people.

To ask this question is once again to distinguish this Declaration from those great charters which, for the most part, reaffirm and extend rights already established at particular times and in particular places. Various of the rights proclaimed in the Declaration came out of the experience of particular states and peoples, mostly in the West. Other rights are those developed by intellectuals who are Westernized in their perspective.

IV

The experience and hard-won compromises of one Western country after another may be seen throughout the Universal Declaration. Thus, it is said in Article 18: "Everyone has the rights to freedom of thought, conscience and religion; this right includes freedom to change his religion or belief, and freedom either alone or in community with others and in public or private, to manifest his religion or belief in teaching, practice, worship and observance." Even the term *conscience* (used here as well as in the Preamble, in Article 1 of the Declaration, and elsewhere) presupposes a (debatable) moral perspective that is distinctively Western.

Be that as it may, an insistence upon the right to change one's "religion or belief" can seem highly improper to some. Questions can be raised here as to what the source is for the religious affiliations of any particular people and what duties are thereby recognized. Does the Declaration assume that all "religions" are equal—and does either principle or experience support that assumption?

It might even be argued, in response to the assertion of "the *right* to change [one's] religion," that there may be, in some instances, a *duty* to change one's religion—or at least to repudiate the religion which one has inherited. After all, there have been (indeed, there may still be) religions with monstrous practices. Others may have doctrines that are, to say the least, highly questionable, raising the issue of whether one has the "right" either to be or to do wrong.

V

In various ways, therefore, the primary perspective evident in the Universal Declaration seems to be that of modern individualism. This may be seen not only in what is said about one's right to choose one's religion but also in what is said about one's right to choose one's education, one's spouse, and one's culture. Limits are thereby placed, at least implicitly, upon the community's power to develop and regulate these matters.

The Declaration, in promoting as it does the prerogatives of individualism, recalls (in its Preamble) that "the United Nations have in [their] Charter reaffirmed their faith in fundamental human rights, in the dignity and worth of the human person and in the equal rights of men and women." And it is recognized, in the Preamble, that human beings "have recourse, as a last resort, to rebellion against tyranny and oppression." We hear in this recognition an echo of that right of revolution invoked in the Declaration of Independence, but not with the political emphasis evident throughout that 1776 document.

Central to the 1948 Declaration (in Articles 15 and 16 of its thirty articles) is the emphasis placed both on "the right to a nationality" and on the family as "the natural and fundamental group unit of society." But the ultimate dependence of both one's nationality and one's family on political determinations is neither recognized nor developed. Or rather, there is far more concern expressed, throughout this Universal Declaration, about political improprieties than about political accomplishments.

VI

Political improprieties are to be minimized, if not altogether eliminated, by the establishment worldwide of democratic regimes. "The will of the people," it is proclaimed in Article 21 of the Universal Declaration, "shall be the basis of the authority of government." This will of the people, it is added, "shall be expressed in periodic and genuine elections which shall be by universal and equal suffrage and shall be held by secret vote or by equivalent free voting procedures."

It is evident throughout (as in Article 29) that "a democratic society" is (in the spirit of Jean-Jacques Rousseau?) alone regarded as legitimate among the available forms of government. One can wonder about the propriety of any standard which calls into question most governments that have ever existed. It is unlikely that even half of the countries represented in the United Nations General Assembly which promulgated this Declaration were "democratic" in the sense indicated therein.

The rule of law is properly insisted upon (in the Preamble), including (as in Article 11) immunity from *ex post facto* impositions. And it is several times recognized that one is entitled to a proper trial when detained. But it is evident throughout the Declaration that the countries subscribing to it do not have "in their bones" any "feel" for the power of the writ of *habeas corpus* in the hands of a substantially independent judiciary.

VII

The principal influences evident in the Universal Declaration do seem much more the work of intellectuals than the results of political processes. There is assumed, as in Article 29, the working of "a democratic society." The orientation assumed throughout the document is primarily that of the West.

The Western orientation is anticipated by the use in the Preamble of "barbarous." This term, like others such as "conscience," can remind us of the moral and political sensibilities that chanced to be developed in the West. Thus, it can be said, a deeply Greek (that is, not-barbarian) orientation is prescribed for peoples everywhere.

The limited effectiveness of noble proclamations, when not grounded in a people's character and experience, was evident in the noble rhetoric of the Soviet Constitution. The wide-ranging rights guaranteed there, imported for the most part from the West, were mocked by the routine political and legal oppressiveness of the Soviet regime. The dependence of the development of truly free, or at least decent, institutions does depend considerably upon the circumstances of a people.

VIII

Consider, however, what is said in Article 19 of the Universal Declaration about how what Americans know as "freedom of speech, [and] of the press" can be spoken of: "Everyone has the right to freedom of opinion and expression; this right includes freedom to hold opinions without interference and to seek, receive and impart information and ideas through any media and regardless of frontiers." The apolitical orientation of this approach is indicated by the reliance upon the modern "freedom . . . of expression" formulation, instead of (as in the Preamble of the Declaration) the traditional "freedom of speech." It is further indicated by the deliberate depreciation here of "frontiers."

This is related to what we have noticed about that "freedom to change [one's] religion" insisted upon in Article 18. Once again modern individualism is, in effect, endorsed. This is consistent with the implication, again and again in the Universal Declaration, that one owns property somehow independent of what any political order provides.

The subordination of *the political* seems to be assumed in the insistence in Article 16 "[t]hat the family is the natural and fundamental group unit of society and is entitled to protection by society and the state." The family—not the tribe or the political order—is identified here as "the natural and fundamental group unit of society." Thus, the *family* is talked about somewhat as *property* is, however loosely "the human family" is spoken of in the Preamble of the Declaration.

IX

And yet, does not the *family* depend, as does *property,* upon some political order for its definition (as well as for its protection)? In this sense, the political order can seem (as Aristotle teaches in his *Politics*) fundamental, prior in principle if not always in time. And what constitutes a good and useful political order can very much depend upon circumstances.

The importance here of circumstances suggests the utopian character of any "universal declaration." The particular "human rights" that are proclaimed are likely to be taken out of various traditions. If the traditions drawn on are diverse, the rights enumerated are apt to conflict with one another; if the traditions drawn on are substantially the same, the rights proclaimed are apt to be meaningless for much of the world which is rooted in other traditions.

However useful a "universal declaration" may sometimes be as a statement of aspirations, it may not have the solid effects of a system of international law developed and applied across centuries (including that "Law of Nations" recognized in the Constitution of 1787). Such a system does make much of established political orders, depending on an approach that respects—much more than an emphasis on human and social rights is likely to do—the prerogatives and duties of citizenship. Indeed, it is the citizen, in a particular kind of regime, who both needs and knows what to do with our traditional "freedom of speech [and] of the press."

13. The Future of the First Amendment?

I

I ventured three decades ago to advocate the abolition of broadcast television in the United States. There were no "takers" in response to this proposal, even though it was published in several places (besides in my *American Moralist*). And yet, would this not have been an eminently prudent measure on behalf of the Common Good?

It was already evident in the 1970s that the then relatively new television industry was having a *mostly* adverse effect on our way of life. Particularly distressing was what was happening to the character of our people. Various institutions, ranging from our religious organizations to our political parties to our sports, were being steadily demeaned even as their progress was proclaimed.

One side effect, or set of unanticipated consequences, has been the ever-growing costs of political campaigning on television. It was already apparent, in the 1970s, that it would be salutary, even if television could not be shut down completely, to keep our political processes off television. In short, the argument I was making was that we, as citizens, should once again take charge of our lives, an objective drawn upon in the 1989 memoranda (endorsing municipal regulations of "sexually-oriented businesses") collected in Appendix N of this volume.

II

There was, I argued in my television proposal, no First Amendment problem in curtailing, if not even in shutting down altogether, television broadcasting in this Country. Nor would there have been much of a technical problem in "throwing the shut-down switch." But the relevant circumstances today are more complicated.

We have now a much more complex network of electronic communications than was available three decades ago. The Internet, for example, is evidently becoming worldwide in scope. That scope is even reflected in the steadily increasing amount of advertising devoted to that operation.

Of course, worldwide "talk" does not take into account local conditions and hence local problems and risks. Not even the most conscientious of "authors" can anticipate today the likely effect of what he is saying. This is a far cry from the rather prosaic eight-page-or-so weekly newspaper published in the Southern Illinois town in which I grew up.

III

It is difficult for any community to control steadily and competently what is distributed on the Internet. This is so even for a political tyranny, unless it is willing (in the fashion of North Korea) to shut off for its people most access as well to the commercial, technical, and other communications upon which the modern industrial state very much depends. There is even likely to come a time (as satellites are developed) when access to electricity alone can mean, no matter what a government may try to do, unsupervised access also to whatever "everyone" elsewhere is saying and doing.

Thus, political tyranny *is* apt to be undermined, or at least threatened, by the Internet and its successors. But also apt to be undermined are the sense of community and the character of a people. This can amount to another, even more insidious, form of tyranny.

All this means as well that although the Internet and other electronic marvels can be acclaimed as "empowering," they may also be crippling. After all, people can be so connected to each other (as through the ubiquitous cell phone) that one is never alone. To be thus perpetually tied to (if not even enslaved by) "everyone" can mean that the intimacy of a couple or of a family is always, at best, tentative.

IV

Rampant individualism is promoted even as one is more and more entangled. The unprecedented anonymity now available in what one says publicly can permit one to be irresponsible. At the same time, one can become, as the target of the irresponsible utterances of others, ever more vulnerable.

Thus, although cascades of information are available on the Internet, it can become difficult to assess the reliability of what is presented as "the gospel truth." Nor should the sloppiness of much that *is* presented these days inspire confidence. We can be reminded, by way of contrast, of the assurances evidently provided by an established publisher's imprint.

Anonymity, as well as distance, can promote acrimony in the exchanges found on the Internet. One can see there what power without responsibility may do, much as what happens in one's dreams. Symptomatic of this state of affairs are the assaults of malicious, or at least of irresponsible, "hacking" that decent Internet users must fend off from time to time.

V

At the heart of the problem here is the question of whether the community *should* be able to shape the character of its members. To the extent that this *is* a question, to that extent the need of proper character-formation for a good life has been forgotten. Certainly, one is not made better or happier if one is permitted to be irresponsible either in the development or in the exercise of one's passions.

One consequence of current conditions is the proliferation of conspiracy theories, which means that questionable passions are promoted and reinforced. Those among us with undisciplined fancies are less likely today than heretofore to feel restrained (if not even disciplined) by their obvious differences from all the others with whom they routinely associate. That is, they too can now find on the Internet dozens, if not hundreds and perhaps even thousands, of others who "think" as they do, thereby being reinforced in their delusions by a like-minded "community."

Thus, instead of the tyranny of public opinion that novelists (such as Gustave Flaubert and Sinclair Lewis) have railed against from time to time, there is the tyranny of an undisciplined imagination. Such liberation of ordinary people does not recognize, for example, even how much discipline has been required to develop and maintain the electronic and other marvels upon which we so much rely. This is still another way of saying that it is useful, if not even essential, to know oneself.

VI

When one truly knows oneself, one is better equipped to recognize what aspects of one's self should best be kept to oneself. A healthy sense of shame is essential for mature development. But much in our way of life can make a proper reticence seem unduly timid if not even unhealthy.

Anonymity can encourage, as well as empower, shamelessness. It can, however, be surprising also to encounter what is now available from many who are not even shielded by anonymity. This may routinely be seen on television screens and heard in casual conversation.

It may be seen as well in print—that is, in a form that does not yet have the relaxed feel of flitting images seen on a screen. It is likely, however, that the uninhibited effusions of the Internet have begun to influence editors of print media. This is comparable to what the informality of e-mail is evidently doing to the traditional letter, reinforcing thereby the somewhat adverse effects of the development of inexpensive long-distance telephone service.

VII

Whether innovations such as the Internet are, overall, liberating or enslaving may depend, in part, on chance. Critical to such developments can be opinions about what one is entitled to do with one's property. Even more critical, and less likely to be examined, are (we have seen) questions about what should be regarded as simply, or as completely, one's property.

Threats to the liberty of a people can come in two forms. One form is that of repression, either political or religious (which may be the political spiritualized). A stouthearted people is apt to recognize and to oppose repression when they see it.

The other form that threats to liberty can take is more insidious, in that it is apt to be sought for and treasured as liberation. This is the form seen in the collapse of the character of a people, especially as its baser passions are built up and catered to. Such a collapse is apt to be hastened, and intensified, wherever it becomes fashionable to insist that the "legislation of morality" is not at all the business of any political community.

VIII

It should be recalled, again and again, what the Speech and Press provisions of the First Amendment were primarily intended to do. It should be recalled, that is, that such provisions in the Anglo-American constitutional tradition go back to the kind of parliamentary immunity championed by Speaker Thomas More in his 1521 petition to Henry VIII. Protection of political discourse has to be wide-ranging, if not even absolute, if there is to be responsible and effective self-government.

But immunity from official sanctions is not enough. Those exercising the freedom thus protected have to be competent if they are to be effective. Such competence must be reinforced by the character of those addressed as well as by the integrity of those speaking.

Thus, people should feel free to speak their minds. But the immunity properly provided by the First Amendment should not be expected to shield the adventurous speaker from the moral judgments and the social sanctions exhibited by his audience. The sounder the character of the People at large, the more instructive and in other ways useful such judgments and sanctions should be.

IX

It remains to be seen whether the constitutional pieties appropriate for a Country of 3 to 4 million can continue to shape and guide a Country that is now almost a third of a billion. It is likely to become evident that modern government, in a thriving industrial state, cannot effectively curtail what people all over the world say to that state's people. The key issue here, then, may be whether a people can be so trained that it thinks and acts as it should, even when government cannot effectively regulate the terms of the ongoing debate.

Fundamental to an appropriate training here is an insistence, by the shapers of opinion, that effective citizenship depends upon good character. It should be recognized, as well, that the community at large, through its governments and otherwise, must promote and sustain the required character. Otherwise, the First Amendment can become politically irrelevant, doing little more than assuring us of our "freedom of expression," which *is* likely to be more attractive to self-seeking individuals than it is to public-spirited citizens.

We have seen that the personal gratification that the "freedom of expression" caters to very much depends upon the passions and inclinations that an individual happens to have. This is hardly the spirit of that Republican Form of Government that the First Amendment was intended to serve. It is in this spirit that Publius, in the first number of *The Federalist*

(October 27, 1787), identified a challenge which continues to inspire the
true (properly disciplined) citizens among us:

> It has been frequently remarked, that it seems to have been re-
> served to the people of [the United States], by their conduct and
> example, to decide the important question, whether societies of
> men are really capable or not, of establishing good government
> from reflection and choice . . .

Appendix A

The Declaration of Independence (1776)

In CONGRESS, July 4, 1776.
A DECLARATION
By the REPRESENTATIVES of the
UNITED STATES OF AMERICA,
In GENERAL CONGRESS ASSEMBLED.

When in the Course of human Events, it becomes necessary for one People to dissolve the Political Bands which have connected them with another, and to assume among the Powers of the Earth, the separate and equal Station to which the Laws of Nature and of Nature's God entitle them, a decent Respect to the Opinions of Mankind requires that they should declare the causes which impel them to the Separation.

We hold these Truths to be self-evident, that all Men are created equal, that they are endowed by their Creator with certain unalienable Rights, that among these are Life, Liberty, and the Pursuit of Happiness—That to secure these Rights, Governments are instituted among Men, deriving their just Powers from the Consent of the Governed, that whenever any Form of Government becomes destructive of these Ends, it is the Right of the People to alter or to abolish it, and to institute new Government, laying its Foundation on such Principles, and organizing its Powers in such Form, as to them shall seem most likely to effect their Safety and Happiness. Prudence, indeed, will dictate that Governments long established should not be changed for light and transient Causes; and accordingly all Experience hath shewn, that Mankind are more dis-

Sources: See *The Declaration of Independence and the Constitution of the United States,* 96th Cong., 1st sess., House Document No. 96-143 (Washington, D.C.: Government Printing Office, 1979). See also, George Anastaplo, *The Constitution of 1787: A Commentary* (Baltimore: Johns Hopkins University Press, 1989), 235, 239–44. See, as well, George Anastaplo, *Abraham Lincoln: A Constitutional Biography* [preferred title, *Thoughts on Abraham Lincoln*] (Lanham, Md.: Rowman & Littlefield, 1999), 1–38.

posed to suffer, while Evils are sufferable, than to right themselves by abolishing the Forms to which they are accustomed. But when a long Train of Abuses and Usurpations, pursuing invariably the same Object, evinces a Design to reduce them under absolute Despotism, it is their Right, it is their Duty, to throw off such Government, and to provide new Guards for their future Security. Such has been the patient Sufferance of these Colonies; and such is now the Necessity which constrains them to alter their former Systems of Government. The History of the present King of Great-Britain is a History of repeated Injuries and Usurpations, all having in direct Object the Establishment of an absolute Tyranny over these States. To prove this, let facts be submitted to a candid World:

He has refused his Assent to Laws, the most wholesome and necessary for the public Good.

He has forbidden his Governors to pass Laws of immediate and pressing Importance, unless suspended in their Operation till his Assent should be obtained; and when so suspended, he has utterly neglected to attend to them.

He has refused to pass other Laws for the Accommodation of large Districts of People, unless those People would relinquish the Right of Representation in the Legislature, a Right inestimable to them, and formidable to Tyrants only.

He has called together Legislative Bodies at Places unusual, uncomfortable, and distant from the Depository of their public Records, for the sole Purpose of fatiguing them into Compliance with his Measures.

He has dissolved Representative Houses repeatedly, for opposing with manly Firmness his Invasions on the Rights of the People.

He has refused for a long Time, after such Dissolutions, to cause others to be elected; whereby the Legislative Powers, incapable of Annihilation, have returned to the People at large for their exercise; the State remaining in the mean time exposed to all the Dangers of Invasion from without, and Convulsions within.

He has endeavoured to prevent the Population of these States; for that Purpose obstructing the Laws for Naturalization of Foreigners; refusing to pass others to encourage their Migrations hither, and raising the Conditions of new Appropriations of Lands.

He has obstructed the Administration of Justice, by refusing his Assent to Laws for establishing Judiciary Powers.

He has made Judges dependent on his Will alone, for the Tenure of their Offices, and the Amount and Payment of their Salaries.

He has erected a Multitude of new Offices, and sent hither Swarms of Officers to harass our People, and eat out their Substance.

He has kept among us, in Times of Peace, Standing Armies, without the consent of our Legislatures.

He has affected to render the Military independent of and superior to the Civil Power.

He has combined with others to subject us to a Jurisdiction foreign to our Constitution, and unacknowledged by our Laws; giving his Assent to their Acts of pretended Legislation:

For quartering large Bodies of Armed Troops among us:

For protecting them, by a mock Trial, from Punishment for any Murders which they should commit on the Inhabitants of these States:

For cutting off our Trade with all Parts of the World:

For imposing Taxes on us without our Consent:

For depriving us, in many Cases, of the Benefits of Trial by Jury:

For transporting us beyond Seas to be tried for pretended Offences:

For abolishing the free System of English Laws in a neighbouring Province, establishing therein an arbitrary Government, and engaging its Boundaries, so as to render it at once an Example and fit Instrument for introducing the same absolute Rule into these Colonies:

For taking away our Charters, abolishing our most valuable Laws, and altering fundamentally the Forms of our Governments:

For suspending our own Legislatures, and declaring themselves invested with Power to legislate for us in all Cases whatsoever.

He has abdicated Government here, by declaring us out of his Protection and waging War against us.

He has plundered our Seas, ravaged our Coasts, burnt our Towns, and destroyed the Lives of our People.

He is, at this Time, transporting large Armies of foreign Mercenaries to compleat the Works of Death, Desolation, and Tyranny, already begun with circumstances of Cruelty and Perfidy, scarcely paralleled in the most barbarous Ages, and totally unworthy the Head of a civilized Nation.

He has constrained our fellow Citizens taken Captive on the high Seas to bear Arms against their Country, to become the Executioners of their Friends and Brethren, or to fall themselves by their Hands.

He has excited domestic Insurrections amongst us, and has endeavoured to bring on the Inhabitants of our Frontiers, the merciless Indian

Savages, whose known Rule of Warfare, is an undistinguished Destruction, of all Ages, Sexes, and Conditions.

In every stage of these Oppressions we have Petitioned for Redress in the most humble Terms: Our repeated Petitions have been answered only by repeated Injury. A Prince, whose Character is thus marked by every act which may define a Tyrant, is unfit to be the Ruler of a free People.

Nor have we been wanting in Attentions to our British Brethren. We have warned them from Time to Time of Attempts by their Legislature to extend an unwarrantable Jurisdiction over us. We have reminded them of the Circumstances of our Emigration and Settlement here. We have appealed to their native Justice and Magnanimity, and we have conjured them by the Ties of our common Kindred to disavow these Usurpations, which, would inevitably interrupt our Connections and Correspondence. They too have been deaf to the Voice of Justice and of Consanguinity. We must, therefore, acquiesce in the Necessity, which denounces our Separation, and hold them, as we hold the rest of Mankind, Enemies in War, in Peace, Friends.

We, therefore, the Representatives of the UNITED STATES OF AMERICA, in General Congress, Assembled, appealing to the Supreme Judge of the World for the Rectitude of our Intentions, do, in the Name, and by Authority of the good People of these Colonies, solemnly Publish and Declare, That these United Colonies are, and of Right ought to be, Free and Independent States; that they are absolved from all Allegiance to the British Crown, and that all political Connection between them and the State of Great-Britain, is and ought to be totally dissolved; and that as Free and Independent States, they have full Power to levy War, conclude Peace, contract Alliances, establish Commerce, and to do all other Acts and Things which Independent States may of right do. And for the support of this Declaration, with a firm Reliance on the Protection of divine Providence, we mutually pledge to each other our Lives, our Fortunes, and our sacred Honor.*

[Signatures omitted.]

*Richard Henry Lee, of Virginia, had introduced in the Continental Congress, on June 7, 1776, the following resolution proposing the issuance of a declaration of independence and thereafter the adoption of articles of confederation:

"*Resolved*, That these United Colonies are, and of right ought to be, free and independent States, that they are absolved from all allegiance to the British Crown, and that all political connection between them and the State of Great Britain is, and ought to be, totally dissolved.

"That it is expedient forthwith to take the most effectual measures for forming foreign Alliances.

"That a plan of confederation be prepared and transmitted to the respective Colonies for their consideration and approbation."

Appendix B

The United States Constitution (1787)

The Constitution of the United States

We the People of the United States, in Order to form a more perfect Union, establish Justice, insure domestic Tranquility, provide for the common defence, promote the general Welfare, and secure the Blessings of Liberty to ourselves and our Posterity, do ordain and establish this Constitution for the United States of America.

Article. I.

Section. 1. All legislative Powers herein granted shall be vested in a Congress of the United States, which shall consist of a Senate and a House of Representatives.

Section. 2. The House of Representatives shall be composed of Members chosen every second Year by the People of the several States, and the Electors in each State shall have the Qualifications requisite for Electors of the most numerous Branch of the State Legislature.

No person shall be a Representative who shall not have attained to the Age of twenty five Years, and been seven Years a Citizen of the United States, and who shall not, when elected, be an Inhabitant of that State in which he shall be chosen.

Representatives and direct Taxes shall be apportioned among the several States which may be included within this Union, according to their respective Numbers, which shall be determined by adding to the whole Number of free Persons, including those bound to Service for a Term of

Sources: See *Documents Illustrative of the Formation of the Union of the American States,* 69th Cong., 1st sess., House Document No. 398 (Washington, D.C.: Government Printing Office, 1927). See also, George Anastaplo, *The Constitution of 1787: A Commentary* (Baltimore: Johns Hopkins University Press, 1989), 236, 266–79. See, on constitutionalism, George Anastaplo, *The Constitutionalist: Notes on the First Amendment* (Dallas: Southern Methodist University Press, 1971; Lanham, Md.: Lexington Books, 2005).

Years, and excluding Indians not taxed, three fifths of all other Persons. The actual Enumeration shall be made within three Years after the first Meeting of the Congress of the United States, and within every subsequent Term of ten Years, in such Manner as they shall by Law direct. The Number of Representatives shall not exceed one for every thirty Thousand, but each State shall have at Least one Representative; and until such enumeration shall be made, the State of New Hampshire shall be entitled to chuse three, Massachusetts eight, Rhode-Island and Providence Plantations one, Connecticut five, New-York six, New Jersey four, Pennsylvania eight, Delaware one, Maryland six, Virginia ten, North Carolina five, South Carolina five, and Georgia three.

When vacancies happen in the Representation from any State, the Executive Authority thereof shall issue Writs of Election to fill such Vacancies.

The House of Representatives shall chuse their Speaker and other Officers; and shall have the sole Power of Impeachment.

Section. 3. The Senate of the United States shall be composed of two Senators from each State, chosen by the Legislature thereof, for six Years; and each Senator shall have one Vote.

Immediately after they shall be assembled in Consequence of the first Election, they shall be divided as equally as may be into three Classes. The Seats of the Senators of the first Class shall be vacated at the Expiration of the second Year, of the second Class at the Expiration of the fourth Year, and of the third Class at the Expiration of the sixth Year, so that one third may be chosen every second Year; and if Vacancies happen by Resignation, or otherwise, during the Recess of the Legislature of any State, the Executive thereof may make temporary Appointments until the next Meeting of the Legislature, which shall then fill such Vacancies.

No Person shall be a Senator who shall not have attained to the Age of thirty Years, and been nine Years a Citizen of the United States, and who shall not, when elected, be an Inhabitant of that State for which he shall be chosen.

The Vice President of the United States shall be President of the Senate, but shall have no Vote, unless they be equally divided.

The Senate shall chuse their other Officers, and also a President pro tempore, in the Absence of the Vice President, or when he shall exercise the Office of President of the United States.

The Senate shall have the sole Power to try all Impeachments. When sitting for that Purpose, they shall be on Oath or Affirmation. When the

President of the United States is tried, the Chief Justice shall preside: And no Person shall be convicted without the Concurrence of two thirds of the Members present.

Judgment in Cases of Impeachment shall not extend further than to removal from Office, and disqualification to hold and enjoy any Office of honor, Trust or Profit under the United States: but the Party convicted shall nevertheless be liable and subject to Indictment, Trial, Judgment and Punishment, according to Law.

Section. 4. The Times, Places and Manner of holding Elections for Senators and Representatives, shall be prescribed in each State by the Legislature thereof; but the Congress may at any time by Law make or alter such Regulations, except as to the Places of chusing Senators.

The Congress shall assemble at least once in every Year, and such Meeting shall be on the first Monday in December, unless they shall by Law appoint a different Day.

Section. 5. Each House shall be the Judge of the Elections, Returns and Qualifications of its own Members, and a Majority of each shall constitute a Quorum to do Business; but a smaller Number may adjourn from day to day, and may be authorized to compel the Attendance of absent Members, in such Manner, and under such Penalties as each House may provide.

Each House may determine the Rules of its Proceedings, punish its Members for disorderly Behaviour, and, with the Concurrence of two thirds, expel a Member.

Each House shall keep a Journal of its Proceedings, and from time to time publish the same, excepting such Parts as may in their Judgment require Secrecy; and the Yeas and Nays of the Members of either House on any question shall, at the Desire of one fifth of those Present, be entered on the Journal.

Neither House, during the Session of Congress, shall, without the Consent of the other, adjourn for more than three days, nor to any other Place than that in which the two Houses shall be sitting.

Section. 6. The Senators and Representatives shall receive a Compensation for their Services, to be ascertained by Law, and paid out of the Treasury of the United States. They shall in all Cases, except Treason, Felony and Breach of the Peace, be privileged from Arrest during their Attendance at the Session of their respective Houses, and in going to and returning from the same; and for any Speech or Debate in either House, they shall not be questioned in any other Place.

No Senator or Representative shall, during the Time for which he was elected, be appointed to any civil Office under the Authority of the United States, which shall have been created, or the Emoluments whereof shall have been encreased during such time; and no Person holding any Office under the United States, shall be a Member of either House during his Continuance in Office.

Section. 7. All Bills for raising Revenue shall originate in the House of Representatives; but the Senate may propose or concur with Amendments as on other Bills.

Every Bill which shall have passed the House of Representatives and the Senate, shall, before it become a Law, be presented to the President of the United States; If he approve he shall sign it, but if not he shall return it, with his Objections to that House in which it shall have originated, who shall enter the Objections at large on their Journal, and proceed to reconsider it. If after such Reconsideration two thirds of that House shall agree to pass the Bill, it shall be sent, together with the Objections, to the other House, by which it shall likewise be reconsidered, and if approved by two thirds of that House, it shall become a Law. But in all such Cases the Votes of both Houses shall be determined by Yeas and Nays, and the Names of the Persons voting for and against the Bill shall be entered on the Journal of each House respectively. If any Bill shall not be returned by the President within ten Days (Sundays excepted) after it shall have been presented to him, the Same shall be a Law, in like Manner as if he had signed it, unless the Congress by their Adjournment prevent its Return, in which Case it shall not be a Law.

Every Order, Resolution, or Vote to which the Concurrence of the Senate and House of Representatives may be necessary (except on a question of Adjournment) shall be presented to the President of the United States; and before the Same shall take Effect, shall be approved by him, or being disapproved by him, shall be repassed by two thirds of the Senate and House of Representatives, according to the Rules and Limitations prescribed in the Case of a Bill.

Section. 8. The Congress shall have Power

To lay and collect Taxes, Duties, Imposts and Excises, to pay the Debts and provide for the common Defence and general Welfare of the United States; but all Duties, Imposts and Excises shall be uniform throughout the United States;

To borrow Money on the credit of the United States;

To regulate Commerce with foreign Nations, and among the several States, and with the Indian Tribes;

To establish an uniform Rule of Naturalization, and uniform Laws on the subject of Bankruptcies throughout the United States;

To coin Money, regulate the Value thereof, and of foreign Coin, and fix the Standard of Weights and Measures;

To provide for the Punishment of counterfeiting the Securities and current Coin of the United States;

To establish Post Offices and post Roads;

To promote the Progress of Science and useful Arts, by securing for limited Times to Authors and Inventors the exclusive Right to their respective Writings and Discoveries;

To constitute Tribunals inferior to the supreme Court;

To define and punish Piracies and Felonies committed on the high Seas, and Offences against the Law of Nations;

To declare War, grant Letters of Marque and Reprisal, and make Rules concerning Captures on Land and Water;

To raise and support Armies, but no Appropriation of Money to that Use shall be for a longer Term than two Years;

To provide and maintain a Navy;

To make Rules for the Government and Regulation of the land and naval Forces;

To provide for calling forth the Militia to execute the Laws of the Union, suppress Insurrections and repel Invasions;

To provide for organizing, arming, and disciplining, the Militia, and for governing such Part of them as may be employed in the Service of the United States, reserving to the States respectively, the Appointment of the Officers, and the Authority of training the Militia according to the discipline prescribed by Congress;

To exercise exclusive Legislation in all Cases whatsoever, over such District (not exceeding ten Miles square) as may, by Cession of particular States, and the Acceptance of Congress, become the Seat of the Government of the United States, and to exercise like Authority over all Places purchased by the Consent of the Legislature of the State in which the Same shall be, for the Erection of Forts, Magazines, Arsenals, dock-Yards, and other needful Buildings;—And

To make all Laws which shall be necessary and proper for carrying into Execution the foregoing Powers, and all other Powers vested by this

Constitution in the Government of the United States, or in any Department or Officer thereof.

Section. 9. The Migration or Importation of such Persons as any of the States now existing shall think proper to admit, shall not be prohibited by the Congress prior to the Year one thousand eight hundred and eight, but a Tax or duty may be imposed on such Importation, not exceeding ten dollars for each Person.

The Privilege of the Writ of Habeas Corpus shall not be suspended, unless when in Cases of Rebellion or Invasion the public Safety may require it.

No Bill of Attainder or ex post facto Law shall be passed.

No Capitation, or other direct, Tax shall be laid, unless in Proportion to the Census or Enumeration herein before directed to be taken.

No Tax or Duty shall be laid on Articles exported from any State.

No Preference shall be given by any Regulation of Commerce or Revenue to the Ports of one State over those of another: nor shall Vessels bound to, or from, one State, be obliged to enter, clear, or pay Duties in another.

No Money shall be drawn from the Treasury, but in Consequence of Appropriations made by Law; and a regular Statement and Account of the Receipts and Expenditures of all public Money shall be published from time to time.

No Title of Nobility shall be granted by the United States: And no Person holding any Office of Profit or Trust under them, shall, without the Consent of the Congress, accept of any present, Emolument, Office, or Title, of any kind whatever, from any King, Prince, or foreign State.

Section. 10. No State shall enter into any Treaty, Alliance, or Confederation; grant Letters of Marque and Reprisal; coin Money; emit Bills of Credit; make any Thing but gold and silver Coin a Tender in Payment of Debts; pass any Bill of Attainder, ex post facto Law, or Law impairing the Obligation of Contracts, or grant any Title of Nobility.

No State shall, without the Consent of the Congress, lay any Imposts or Duties on Imports or Exports, except what may be absolutely necessary for executing it's inspection Laws: and the net Produce of all Duties and Imposts, laid by any State on Imports or Exports, shall be for the Use of the Treasury of the United States; and all such Laws shall be subject to the Revision and Controul of the Congress.

No State shall, without the Consent of Congress, lay any Duty of

Tonnage, keep Troops, or Ships of War in time of Peace, enter into any Agreement or Compact with another State, or with a foreign Power, or engage in War, unless actually invaded, or in such imminent Danger as will not admit of delay.

Article. II.

Section. 1. The executive Power shall be vested in a President of the United States of America. He shall hold his Office during the Term of four Years, and, together with the Vice President, chosen for the same Term, be elected, as follows

Each State shall appoint, in such Manner as the Legislature thereof may direct, a Number of Electors, equal to the whole Number of Senators and Representatives to which the State may be entitled in the Congress: but no Senator or Representative, or Person holding an Office of Trust or Profit under the United States, shall be appointed an Elector.

The Electors shall meet in their respective States, and vote by Ballot for two Persons, of whom one at least shall not be an Inhabitant of the same State with themselves. And they shall make a List of all the Persons voted for, and of the Number of Votes for each; which List they shall sign and certify, and transmit sealed to the Seat of the Government of the United States, directed to the President of the Senate. The President of the Senate shall, in the Presence of the Senate and House of Representatives, open all the Certificates, and the Votes shall then be counted. The Person having the greatest Number of Votes shall be the President, if such Number be a Majority of the whole Number of Electors appointed; and if there be more than one who have such Majority, and have an equal Number of Votes, then the House of Representatives shall immediately chuse by Ballot one of them for President; and if no Person have a Majority, then from the five highest on the List the said House shall in like Manner chuse the President. But in chusing the President, the Votes shall be taken by States, the Representation from each State having one Vote; A quorum for this Purpose shall consist of a Member or Members from two thirds of the States, and a Majority of all the States shall be necessary to a Choice. In every Case, after the Choice of the President, the Person having the greatest Number of Votes of the Electors shall be the Vice President. But if there should remain two or more who have equal Votes, the Senate shall chuse from them by Ballot the Vice President.

The Congress may determine the Time of chusing the Electors, and the Day on which they shall give their Votes; which Day shall be the same throughout the United States.

No Person except a natural born Citizen, or a Citizen of the United States, at the time of the Adoption of this Constitution, shall be eligible to the Office of President; neither shall any Person be eligible to that Office who shall not have attained to the Age of thirty five Years, and been fourteen Years a Resident within the United States.

In Case of the Removal of the President from Office, or of his Death, Resignation, or Inability to discharge the Powers and Duties of the said Office, the Same shall devolve on the Vice President, and the Congress may by Law provide for the Case of Removal, Death, Resignation or Inability, both of the President and Vice President, declaring what Officer shall then act as President, and such Officer shall act accordingly, until the Disability be removed, or a President shall be elected.

The President shall, at stated Times, receive for his Services, a Compensation, which shall neither be encreased nor diminished during the Period for which he shall have been elected, and he shall not receive within that Period any other Emolument from the United States, or any of them.

Before he enter on the Execution of his Office, he shall take the following Oath or Affirmation:—"I do solemnly swear (or affirm) that I will faithfully execute the Office of President of the United States, and will to the best of my Ability, preserve, protect and defend the Constitution of the United States."

Section. 2. The President shall be Commander in Chief of the Army and Navy of the United States, and of the Militia of the several States, when called into the actual Service of the United States; he may require the Opinion, in writing, of the principal Officer in each of the executive Departments, upon any Subject relating to the Duties of their respective Offices, and he shall have Power to grant Reprieves and Pardons for Offences against the United States, except in Cases of Impeachment.

He shall have Power, by and with the Advice and Consent of the Senate, to make Treaties, provided two thirds of the Senators present concur; and he shall nominate, and by and with the Advice and Consent of the Senate, shall appoint Ambassadors, other public Ministers and Consuls, Judges of the supreme Court, and all other Officers of the United States, whose Appointments are not herein otherwise provided for, and which shall be established by Law: but the Congress may by Law vest the Appointment of such inferior Officers, as they think proper, in the President alone, in the Courts of Law, or in the Heads of Departments.

The President shall have Power to fill up all Vacancies that may happen during the Recess of the Senate, by granting Commissions which shall expire at the End of their next Session.

Section. 3. He shall from time to time give to the Congress Information of the State of the Union, and recommend to their Consideration such Measures as he shall judge necessary and expedient; he may, on extraordinary Occasions, convene both Houses, or either of them, and in Case of Disagreement between them, with Respect to the Time of Adjournment, he may adjourn them to such Time as he shall think proper; he shall receive Ambassadors and other public Ministers; he shall take Care that the Laws be faithfully executed, and shall Commission all the Officers of the United States.

Section. 4. The President, Vice President and all civil Officers of the United States, shall be removed from Office on Impeachment for, and Conviction of, Treason, Bribery, or other high Crimes and Misdemeanors.

Article. III.

Section. 1. The judicial Power of the United States, shall be vested in one supreme Court, and in such inferior Courts as the Congress may from time to time ordain and establish. The Judges, both of the supreme and inferior Courts, shall hold their Offices during good Behaviour, and shall, at stated Times, receive for their Services, a Compensation, which shall not be diminished during their Continuance in Office.

Section. 2. The judicial Power shall extend to all Cases, in Law and Equity, arising under this Constitution, the Laws of the United States, and Treaties made, or which shall be made, under their Authority;—to all Cases affecting Ambassadors, other public Ministers and Consuls;—to all Cases of admiralty and maritime Jurisdiction;—to Controversies to which the United States shall be a Party;—to Controversies between two or more States;—between a State and Citizens of another State;—between Citizens of different States,—between Citizens of the same State claiming Lands under Grants of different States, and between a State, or the Citizens thereof, and foreign States, Citizens or Subjects.

In all Cases affecting Ambassadors, other public Ministers and Consuls, and those in which a State shall be a Party, the supreme Court shall have original Jurisdiction. In all the other Cases before mentioned, the supreme Court shall have appellate Jurisdiction, both as to Law and Fact, with such Exceptions, and under such Regulations as the Congress shall make.

The Trial of all Crimes, except in Cases of Impeachment, shall be by Jury; and such Trial shall be held in the State where the said Crimes shall have been committed; but when not committed within any State, the Trial shall be at such Place or Places as the Congress may by Law have directed.

Section. 3. Treason against the United States, shall consist only in levying War against them, or in adhering to their Enemies, giving them Aid and Comfort. No Person shall be convicted of Treason unless on the Testimony of two Witnesses to the same overt Act, or on Confession in open Court.

The Congress shall have Power to declare the Punishment of Treason, but no Attainder of Treason shall work Corruption of Blood, or Forfeiture except during the Life of the Person attainted.

Article. IV.

Section. 1. Full Faith and Credit shall be given in each State to the public Acts, Records, and judicial Proceedings of every other State. And the Congress may by general Laws prescribe the Manner in which such Acts, Records and Proceedings shall be proved, and the Effect thereof.

Section. 2. The Citizens of each State shall be entitled to all Privileges and Immunities of Citizens in the several States.

A Person charged in any State with Treason, Felony, or other Crime, who shall flee from Justice, and be found in another State, shall on Demand of the executive Authority of the State from which he fled, be delivered up, to be removed to the State having Jurisdiction of the Crime.

No Person held to Service or Labour in one State, under the Laws thereof, escaping into another, shall, in Consequence of any Law or Regulation therein, be discharged from such Service or Labour, but shall be delivered up on Claim of the Party to whom such Service or Labour may be due.

Section. 3. New States may be admitted by the Congress into this Union; but no new State shall be formed or erected within the Jurisdiction of any other State; nor any State be formed by the Junction of two or more States, or Parts of States, without the Consent of the Legislatures of the States concerned as well as of the Congress.

The Congress shall have Power to dispose of and make all needful Rules and Regulations respecting the Territory or other Property belonging to the United States; and nothing in this Constitution shall be so construed as to Prejudice any Claims of the United States, or of any particular State.

Section. 4. The United States shall guarantee to every State in this Union a Republican Form of Government, and shall protect each of them against Invasion; and on Application of the Legislature, or of the Executive (when the Legislature cannot be convened) against domestic Violence.

Article. V.

The Congress, whenever two thirds of both Houses shall deem it necessary, shall propose Amendments to this Constitution, or, on the Application of the Legislatures of two thirds of the several States, shall call a Convention for proposing Amendments, which, in either Case, shall be valid to all Intents and Purposes, as Part of this Constitution, when ratified by the Legislatures of three fourths of the several States, or by Conventions in three fourths thereof, as the one or the other Mode of Ratification may be proposed by the Congress; Provided that no Amendment which may be made prior to the Year One thousand eight hundred and eight shall in any Manner affect the first and fourth Clauses in the Ninth Section of the first Article; and that no State, without its Consent, shall be deprived of it's equal Suffrage in the Senate.

Article. VI.

All Debts contracted and Engagements entered into, before the Adoption of this Constitution, shall be as valid against the United States under this Constitution, as under the Confederation.

This Constitution, and the Laws of the United States which shall be made in Pursuance thereof; and all Treaties made, or which shall be made, under the Authority of the United States, shall be the supreme Law of the Land; and the Judges in every State shall be bound thereby, any Thing in the Constitution or Laws of any State to the Contrary notwithstanding.

The Senators and Representatives before mentioned, and the Members of the several State Legislatures, and all executive and judicial Officers, both of the United States and of the several States, shall be bound by Oath or Affirmation, to support this Constitution; but no religious Test shall ever be required as a Qualification to any Office or public Trust under the United States.

Article. VII.

The Ratification of the Conventions of nine States, shall be sufficient for the Establishment of this Constitution between the States so ratifying the Same.

DONE in Convention by the Unanimous Consent of the States present the Seventeenth Day of September in the Year of our Lord one thousand seven hundred and Eighty seven and of the Independence of the United States of America the Twelfth. In witness whereof We have hereunto subscribed our Names,

[signatures omitted].

Appendix C

The Amendments to the
United States Constitution (1791–1992)

Articles in Addition to, and Amendment of, the Constitution of the United States, Proposed by Congress and Ratified by the Several States, Pursuant to the Fifth Article of the Original Constitution

Amendment I [1791]

Congress shall make no law respecting an establishment of religion, or prohibiting the free exercise thereof; or abridging the freedom of speech, or of the press; or the right of the people peaceably to assemble, and to petition the Government for a redress of grievances.

Amendment II [1791]

A well regulated Militia, being necessary to the security of a free State, the right of the people to keep and bear Arms, shall not be infringed.

Amendment III [1791]

No Soldier shall, in time of peace be quartered in any house, without the consent of the Owner, nor in time of war, but in a manner to be prescribed by law.

Sources: See *The Declaration of Independence and the Constitution of the United States,* 96th Cong., 1st sess., House Document No. 96-143 (Washington, D.C.: Government Printing Office, 1979). See also, George Anastaplo, *The Constitution of 1787: A Commentary* (Baltimore: Johns Hopkins University Press, 1989), 237, 288–97; George Anastaplo, *The Amendments to the Constitution: A Commentary* (Baltimore: Johns Hopkins University Press, 1996), 243, 375–84. The dates of ratification of the Amendments are provided in brackets. "Sec." is written here as "Section" in all Amendments.

Amendment IV [1791]

The right of the people to be secure in their persons, houses, papers, and effects, against unreasonable searches and seizures, shall not be violated, and no Warrants shall issue, but upon probable cause, supported by Oath or affirmation, and particularly describing the place to be searched, and the persons or things to be seized.

Amendment V [1791]

No person shall be held to answer for a capital, or otherwise infamous crime, unless on a presentment or indictment of a Grand Jury, except in cases arising in the land or naval forces, or in the Militia, when in actual service in time of War or public danger; nor shall any person be subject for the same offence to be twice put in jeopardy of life or limb; nor shall be compelled in any criminal case to be a witness against himself, nor be deprived of life, liberty, or property, without due process of law; nor shall private property be taken for public use, without just compensation.

Amendment VI [1791]

In all criminal prosecutions, the accused shall enjoy the right to a speedy and public trial, by an impartial jury of the State and district wherein the crime shall have been committed, which district shall have been previously ascertained by law, and to be informed of the nature and cause of the accusation; to be confronted with the witnesses against him; to have compulsory process for obtaining witnesses in his favor, and to have the Assistance of Counsel for his defence.

Amendment VII [1791]

In Suits at common law, where the value in controversy shall exceed twenty dollars, the right of trial by jury shall be preserved, and no fact tried by a jury, shall be otherwise re-examined in any Court of the United States, than according to the rules of the common law.

Amendment VIII [1791]

Excessive bail shall not be required, nor excessive fines imposed, nor cruel and unusual punishments inflicted.

Amendment IX [1791]

The enumeration in the Constitution, of certain rights, shall not be construed to deny or disparage others retained by the people.

Amendment X [1791]

The powers not delegated to the United States by the Constitution, nor prohibited by it to the States, are reserved to the States respectively, or to the people.

Amendment XI [1798]

The Judicial power of the United States shall not be construed to extend to any suit in law or equity, commenced or prosecuted against one of the United States by Citizens of another State, or by Citizens or Subjects of any Foreign State.

Amendment XII [1804]

The Electors shall meet in their respective states, and vote by ballot for President and Vice-President, one of whom, at least, shall not be an inhabitant of the same state with themselves; they shall name in their ballots the person voted for as President, and in distinct ballots the person voted for as Vice-President, and they shall make distinct lists of all persons voted for as President, and of all persons voted for as Vice-President, and of the number of votes for each, which lists they shall sign and certify, and transmit sealed to the seat of the government of the United States, directed to the President of the Senate;—The President of the Senate shall, in the presence of the Senate and House of Representatives, open all the certificates and the votes shall then be counted;—The person having the greatest number of votes for President, shall be the President, if such number be a majority of the whole number of Electors appointed; and if no person have such majority, then from the persons having the highest numbers not exceeding three on the list of those voted for as President, the House of Representatives shall choose immediately, by ballot, the President. But in choosing the President, the votes shall be taken by states, the representation from each state having one vote; a quorum for this purpose shall consist of a member or members from two-thirds of the states, and a majority of all the states shall be necessary to a choice. And if the House of Representatives shall not choose a President whenever the right of choice shall devolve upon them, before the fourth day of March next following, then the Vice-President shall act as President, as in the case of the death or other constitutional disability of the President.—The person having the greatest number of votes as Vice-President, shall be the Vice-President, if such number be a majority of the whole number of Electors appointed, and if no person have a majority, then from the two highest numbers on the list, the Senate shall choose the Vice-President; a quorum for the purpose shall consist of two-thirds of the whole number of Senators, and a majority of the whole number shall be necessary to a choice. But no person constitutionally ineligible to the office of President shall be eligible to that of Vice-President of the United States.

Amendment XIII [1865]

Section 1. Neither slavery nor involuntary servitude, except as a punishment for crime whereof the party shall have been duly convicted, shall exist within the United States, or any place subject to their jurisdiction.

Section 2. Congress shall have power to enforce this article by appropriate legislation.

Amendment XIV [1868]

Section 1. All persons born or naturalized in the United States, and subject to the jurisdiction thereof, are citizens of the United States and of the State wherein they reside. No State shall make or enforce any law which shall abridge the privileges or immunities of citizens of the United States; nor shall any State deprive any person of life, liberty, or property, without due process of law; nor deny to any person within its jurisdiction the equal protection of the laws.

Section 2. Representatives shall be apportioned among the several States according to their respective numbers, counting the whole number of persons in each State, excluding Indians not taxed. But when the right to vote at any election for the choice of electors for President and Vice President of the United States, Representatives in Congress, the Executive and Judicial officers of a State, or the members of the Legislature thereof, is denied to any of the male inhabitants of such State, being twenty-one years of age, and citizens of the United States, or in any way abridged, except for participation in rebellion, or other crime, the basis of representation therein shall be reduced in the proportion which the number of such male citizens shall bear to the whole number of male citizens twenty-one years of age in such State.

Section 3. No person shall be a Senator or Representative in Congress, or elector of President and Vice President, or hold any office, civil or military, under the United States, or under any State, who, having previously taken an oath, as a member of Congress, or as an officer of the United States, or as a member of any State legislature, or as an executive or judicial officer of any State, to support the Constitution of the United States, shall have engaged in insurrection or rebellion against the same, or given aid or comfort to the enemies thereof. But Congress may by a vote of two-thirds of each House, remove such disability.

Section 4. The validity of the public debt of the United States, authorized by law, including debts incurred for payment of pensions and bounties for services in suppressing insurrection or rebellion, shall not be questioned. But neither the United States nor any State shall assume or pay any debt or obligation incurred in aid of insurrection or rebellion against the United States, or any claim for the loss or emancipation of any slave; but all such debts, obligations and claims shall be held illegal and void.

Section 5. The Congress shall have power to enforce, by appropriate legislation, the provisions of this article.

Amendment XV [1870]

Section 1. The right of citizens of the United States to vote shall not be denied or abridged by the United States or by any State on account of race, color, or previous condition of servitude.

Section 2. The Congress shall have power to enforce this article by appropriate legislation.

Amendment XVI [1913]

The Congress shall have power to lay and collect taxes on incomes, from whatever source derived, without apportionment among the several States, and without regard to any census or enumeration.

Amendment XVII [1913]

The Senate of the United States shall be composed of two Senators from each State, elected by the people thereof, for six years; and each Senator shall have one vote. The electors in each State shall have the qualifications requisite for electors of the most numerous branch of the State legislatures.

When vacancies happen in the representation of any State in the Senate, the executive authority of such State shall issue writs of election to fill such vacancies: *Provided,* That the legislature of any State may empower the executive thereof to make temporary appointments until the people fill the vacancies by election as the legislature may direct.

This amendment shall not be so construed as to affect the election or term of any Senator chosen before it becomes valid as part of the Constitution.

Amendment XVIII [1919]

Section 1. After one year from the ratification of this article the manufacture, sale, or transportation of intoxicating liquors within, the importation thereof into, or the exportation thereof from the United States and all territory subject to the jurisdiction thereof for beverage purposes is hereby prohibited.

Section 2. The Congress and the several States shall have concurrent power to enforce this article by appropriate legislation.

Section 3. This article shall be inoperative unless it shall have been ratified as an amendment to the Constitution by the legislatures of the several States, as provided in the Constitution, within seven years from the date of the submission hereof to the States by the Congress.

Amendment XIX [1920]

The right of citizens of the United States to vote shall not be denied or abridged by the United States or by any State on account of sex.

Congress shall have power to enforce this article by appropriate legislation.

Amendment XX [1933]

Section 1. The terms of the President and Vice President shall end at noon on the 20th day of January, and the terms of Senators and Representatives at noon on the 3d day of January, of the years in which such terms would have ended if this article had not been ratified; and the terms of their successors shall then begin.

Section 2. The Congress shall assemble at least once in every year, and such meeting shall begin at noon on the 3d day of January, unless they shall by law appoint a different day.

Section 3. If, at the time fixed for the beginning of the term of the President, the President elect shall have died, the Vice President elect shall become President. If a President shall not have been chosen before the time fixed for the beginning of his term, or if the President elect shall have failed to qualify, then the Vice President elect shall act as President until a President shall have qualified; and the Congress may by law provide for the case wherein neither a President elect nor a Vice President elect shall have qualified, declaring who shall then act as President, or the manner in which one who is to act shall be selected, and such person shall act accordingly until a President or Vice President shall have qualified.

Section 4. The Congress may by law provide for the case of the death of any of the persons from whom the House of Representatives may choose a President whenever the right of choice shall have devolved upon them, and for the case of the death of any of the persons from whom the Senate may choose a Vice President whenever the right of choice shall have devolved upon them.

Section 5. Sections 1 and 2 shall take effect on the 15th day of October following the ratification of this article.

Section 6. This article shall be inoperative unless it shall have been ratified as an amendment to the Constitution by the legislatures of three-fourths of the several States within seven years from the date of its submission.

Amendment XXI [1933]

Section 1. The eighteenth article of amendment to the Constitution of the United States is hereby repealed.

Section 2. The transportation or importation into any State, Territory, or possession of the United States for delivery or use therein of intoxicating liquors, in violation of the laws thereof, is hereby prohibited.

Section 3. This article shall be inoperative unless it shall have been ratified as an amendment to the Constitution by conventions in the several States, as provided in the Constitution, within seven years from the date of the submission hereof to the States by the Congress.

Amendment XXII [1951]

Section 1. No person shall be elected to the office of the President more than twice, and no person who has held the office of President, or acted as President, for more than two years of a term to which some other person was elected President shall be elected to the office of the President more than once. But this Article shall not apply to any person holding the office of President when this Article was proposed by the Congress, and shall not prevent any person who may be holding the office of President, or acting as President, during the term within which this Article becomes operative from holding the office of President or acting as President during the remainder of such term.

Section 2. This article shall be inoperative unless it shall have been ratified as an amendment to the Constitution by the legislatures of three-fourths of the several States within seven years from the date of its submission to the States by the Congress.

Amendment XXIII [1961]

Section 1. The District constituting the seat of Government of the United States shall appoint in such manner as the Congress may direct:

A number of electors of President and Vice President equal to the whole number of Senators and Representatives in Congress to which the District would be entitled if it were a State, but in no event more than the least populous State; they shall be in addition to those appointed by the States, but they shall be considered, for the purposes of the election of President and Vice President, to be electors appointed by a State; and they shall meet in the District and perform such duties as provided by the twelfth article of amendment.

Section 2. The Congress shall have power to enforce this article by appropriate legislation.

Amendment XXIV [1964]

Section 1. The right of citizens of the United States to vote in any primary or other election for President or Vice President, for electors for President or Vice President, or for Senator or Representative in Congress, shall not be denied or abridged by the United States or any State by reason of failure to pay any poll tax or other tax.

Section 2. The Congress shall have power to enforce this article by appropriate legislation.

Amendment XXV [1967]

Section 1. In case of the removal of the President from office or of his death or resignation, the Vice President shall become President.

Section 2. Whenever there is a vacancy in the office of the Vice President, the President shall nominate a Vice President who shall take office upon confirmation by a majority vote of both Houses of Congress.

Section 3. Whenever the President transmits to the President pro tempore of the Senate and the Speaker of the House of Representatives his written declaration that he is unable to discharge the powers and duties of his office, and until he transmits to them a written declaration to the contrary, such powers and duties shall be discharged by the Vice President as Acting President.

Section 4. Whenever the Vice President and a majority of either the principal officers of the executive departments or of such other body as Congress may by law provide, transmit to the President pro tempore of the Senate and the Speaker of the House of Representatives their written declaration that the President is unable to discharge the powers and duties of his office, the Vice President shall immediately assume the powers and duties of the office as Acting President.

Thereafter, when the President transmits to the President pro tempore of the Senate and the Speaker of the House of Representatives his written declaration that no inability exists, he shall resume the powers and duties of his office unless the Vice President and a majority of either the principal officers of the executive department or of such other body as Congress may by law provide, transmit within four days to the President pro tempore of the Senate and the Speaker of the House of Representatives their written declaration that the President is unable to discharge the powers and duties of his office. Thereupon Congress shall decide the issue, assembling within forty-eight hours for that purpose if not in session. If the Congress, within twenty-one days after receipt of the latter written declaration, or, if Congress is not in session, within twenty-one days after Congress is required to assemble, determines by two-thirds vote of both Houses that the President is unable to discharge the powers and duties of his office, the Vice President shall continue to discharge the same as Acting President; otherwise, the President shall resume the powers and duties of his office.

Amendment XXVI [1971]

Section 1. The right of citizens of the United States, who are eighteen years of age or older, to vote shall not be denied or abridged by the United States or by any State on account of age.

Section 2. The Congress shall have power to enforce this article by appropriate legislation.

Amendment XXVII [1992]

No law varying the compensation for the services of the Senators and Representatives shall take effect until an election of Representatives shall have intervened.

Appendix D

Thomas More, Petition to Henry VIII on Parliamentary Freedom of Speech (1521)

Sythe I perceive, most redoubted soveraigne, that it standethe not with your highe pleasure to reforme this election [of Thomas More as Speaker of the House of Commons] and cause it to be changed, but have by the mouth of the most reverend father in god, the legate, your highnes Chauncellor [i.e., Cardinal Wolsey], therunto geven your most royal assent, and have of your benignity determyned, farre above that I may beare, to enhable me and for this office to repute me meete, rather then ye should seeme to impute unto your comons [i.e., the House of Commons] that they had unmeetely chosen, I am therefore, and alway shalbe, ready obediently to conforme my self to thaccomplishment of your highe commandement, In my most humble wise beseeching your most noble maiestie that I may with your graces favour, before I farther enter therunto, make mine humble intercession unto your highnes for two lowly petitions: The one privately concerning my self, the other the whole assembly of your comon house.

For my self, gratioius Soveraigne, that if it misshapp me in anye thinge hereafter that is on the behalf of your comons in your highe presence to be declared, to mistake my message, and in the lack of good utteraunce, by my misrehersall, to perverte or impaire their prudent instructions, It may

Sources: This is based upon William Roper, *The Lyfe of Sir Thomas Moore, Knighte,* edited by Elsie Vaughan Hitchcock (London: Oxford University Press, 1935), 12–16. The author is identified on the title page as "William Roper, Esquire, whiche married Margreat, daughter of the sayed Thomas Moore." This document displays sixteenth-century spelling, which is used in this appendix for the most part. See, for another version of this document, George Anastaplo, *The Constitutionalist: Notes on the First Amendment* (Dallas: Southern Methodist University Press, 1971; Lanham, Md.: Lexington Books, 2005), 538–39.

then like your most noble maiestie, of your aboundant grace, with the eye of your accostomed pitye, to pardon my simplenes, geving me leave to repaire againe to the comen house, and there to conferre with them, and to take their substancial advise what thing and in what wise I shall on their behalf utter and speak before your noble grace, To thentente their prudent devises and affaires be not my simplenes and Folly hindered or impaired: which thing, if it should so mishappe, as it were well likely to mishappe in me, if your gratious benignity releaved not my oversight, It could not faile to be during my life a perpetuall grudge and hevines to my harte, The helpe and remedy whereof, in manner aforesaid remembred, is, most gracious soveraigne, my first lowly suit and humble petition unto your most noble grace.

Mine other humble request, moste excellent Prince, is this: Forasmuche as there be of your comons, heare by your highe commandment assembled for your parliament, a greate number which are, after thaccustomed manner, appointed in the comen house to treate and advise of the comon affaires among themselfes aparte; And albeit, most deere leige Lord, that according to your prudent advise, by your honorable writes every wheare declared, there hath bine as due diligens used in sending upp to your highnes courte of parliament the most discreete persons out of every quarter that men could esteeme meete thereunto, Wherby it is not to be doubted but that there is a very substanciall assembly of right wise and polliticke persons; yeat, most victorious Prince, sith among so many wise men neyther is every man wise alike, nor among so many men, like well witted, every man like well spoken, And it often happeneth that, likewise as much folly is uttered with painted polished speache, so many, boystyous and rude in language, see deepe indeed, and give right substanciall councell; And sithe also in matters of great inportaunce, the mynd is often so occupied in the matter that a man rather studieth what to say then howe, By reson whereof the wisest man and the best spoken in a whole country fortuneth among, while his mynd is fervent in the matter, somewhat to speake in such wise as he wold afterward wishe to have bine uttered otherwise, and yeat no wors will had when he spake it, then he hath when he wold so gladly chaunge it; Therefore, most gracious soveraigne, considering that in your highe court of parliament is nothing intreated but matter of weight and importance concerning your realme and your own roiall estate, It could not faile to let and put to silence from the geving of their advice and councell many of your discreete comons, to the greate hinderaunce of the comon affaires, excepte that every of your comons were utterly discharged of all doubte and feare howe any thing that it should happen them to speake, should happen of your highnes to be taken. And in this point, though your well knowen and proved benignity puttethe every man in ryght good hope, yeat such is the waight of the matter, such is the reverend dread that the tymorous hartes of your naturall subiectes conceave toward your highe maiestie, our most redoubted king and undoubted soveraigne, that they cannot in this point finde themselfes satisfied, except your gracious bounty therein declared put away the scruple of their timorous myndes, and animate and incourage them, and put them out of doubte. It may therefore like your most aboundant grace, our most benigne and godly kinge, to give to all your comons heare assembled your most gracious licens and pardon, freely, without doubte of your dreadfull displeasure, every man to discharge his consciens, and boldlye in every thinge incident among us to declare his advise; and whatsoever happen any man to say, that it may like your noble maiestye, of your inestimable goodnes, to take all in good parte, interpreting every mans wordes, howe unconingly soever they be couched, to proceed yeat of good zeale towardes the profit of your realme and honor of your royall person, the prosperous estate and preservation whereof, most excellent soveraigne, is the thinge which we all, your most humble loving subiectes, according to the most bounden duty of our naturall alleageans, moste highlye desire and pray for.

Appendix E

The Virginia Statute of Religious Liberty (1786)

An Act for Establishing Religious Freedom

I. Whereas Almighty God hath created the mind free; that all attempts to influence it by temporal punishments or burthens, or by civil incapacitations, tend only to beget habits of hypocrisy and meanness, and are a departure from the plan of the Holy author of our religion, who being Lord both of body and mind, yet chose not to propagate it by coercions on either, as was his Almighty power to do; that the impious presumption of legislators and rulers, civil as well as ecclesiastical, who being themselves but fallible and uninspired men, have assumed dominion over the faith of others, setting up their own opinions and modes of thinking as the only true and infallible, and as such endeavouring to impose them on others, hath established and maintained false religions over the greatest part of the world, and through all time; that to compel a man to furnish contributions of money for the propagation of opinions which he disbelieves, is sinful and tyrannical; that even the forcing him to support this or that teacher of his own religious persuasion, is depriving him of the comfortable liberty of giving his contributions to the particular pastor, whose morals he would make his pattern, and whose powers he feels most persuasive to righteousness, and is withdrawing from the ministry

Sources: This is based upon *Statutes at Large of Virginia,* vol. 12, edited by William Waller Hening (Richmond, Va., 1823), 84–86. In the spirit of this statute is President George Washington's 1790 letter to the Hebrew Congregation of Newport, Rhode Island. See *Papers of George Washington,* vol. 335, Library of Congress, 19–20. See also, George Anastaplo, *The Amendments to the Constitution: A Commentary* (Baltimore: Johns Hopkins University Press, 1995), 407.

those temporary rewards, which proceeding from an approbation of their personal conduct, are an additional incitement to earnest and unremitting labours for the instruction of mankind; that our civil rights have no dependence on our religious opinions, any more than our opinions in physics or geometry; that therefore the proscribing any citizen as unworthy the public confidence by laying upon him an incapacity of being called to offices of trust and emolument, unless he profess or renounce this or that religious opinion, is depriving him injuriously of those privileges and advantages to which in common with his fellow-citizens he has a natural right; that it tends only to corrupt the principles of that religion it is meant to encourage, by bribing with a monopoly of worldly honours and emoluments, those who will externally profess and conform to it; that though indeed these are criminal who do not withstand such temptation, yet neither are those innocent who lay the bait in their way; that to suffer the civil magistrate to intrude his powers into the field of opinion, and to restrain the profession or propagation of principles on supposition of their ill tendency, is a dangerous fallacy, which at once destroys all religious liberty, because he being of course judge of that tendency will make his opinions the rule of judgment, and approve or condemn the sentiments of others only as they shall square with or differ from his own; that it is time enough for the rightful purposes of civil government, for its officers to interfere when principles break out into overt acts against peace and good order; and finally, that truth is great and will prevail if left to herself, that she is the proper and sufficient antagonist to error, and has nothing to fear from the conflict, unless by human interposition disarmed of her natural weapons, free argument and debate, errors ceasing to be dangerous when it is permitted freely to contradict them:

II. *Be it enacted by the General Assembly,* That no man shall be compelled to frequent or support any religious worship, place, or ministry whatsoever, nor shall be enforced, restrained, molested, or burthened in his body or goods, nor shall otherwise suffer on account of his religious opinions or belief; but that all men shall be free to profess, and by argument to maintain, their opinion in matters of religion, and that the same shall in no wise diminish, enlarge, or affect their civil capacities.

III. And though we well know that this assembly, elected by the people for the ordinary purposes of legislation only, have no power to restrain the acts of succeeding assemblies, constituted with powers equal to our own, and that therefore to declare this act to be irrevocable would be of no effect in law; yet we are free to declare, and do declare, that the rights hereby asserted are of the natural rights of mankind, and that if any act shall be hereafter passed to repeal the present, or to narrow its operation, such act will be an infringement of natural right.

Appendix F

Some Stages of the Religion/Speech/Press/Assembly/Petition Provisions in the First Congress (1789)

I. James Madison's Proposals in the House of Representatives (June 8, 1789)

. . . Fourthly. That in article 1st, section 9 [of the Constitution], between clauses 3 and 4, be inserted these clauses, to wit: The civil rights of none shall be abridged on account of religious belief or worship, nor shall any national religion be established, nor shall the full and equal rights of conscience be in any manner, or on any pretext, infringed.

The people shall not be deprived or abridged of their right to speak, to write, or to publish their sentiments; and the freedom of the press, as one of the great bulwarks of liberty, shall be inviolable.

The people shall not be restrained from peaceably assembling and consulting for their common good; nor from applying to the Legislature by petitions, or remonstrances, for redress of their grievances. . . .

Fifthly. That in article 1st, section 10, between clauses 1 and 2, be inserted this clause, to wit: No State shall violate the equal rights of conscience, or the freedom of the press, or the trial by jury in criminal cases.

II. Amendment Proposals Reported by a House of Representatives Committee (August 15 and 17, 1789)

[4] Article 1. Section 9 [of the Constitution]. Between paragraphs

Sources: See George Anastaplo, *The Constitutionalist: Notes on the First Amendment* (Dallas: Southern Methodist University Press, 1971; Lanham, Md.: Lexington Books, 2005), 289–93.

two and three insert, "No religion shall be established by law, nor shall the equal rights of conscience be infringed." . . .

[5] "The freedom of speech, and of the press, and the right of the people peaceably to assemble and consult for their common good, and to apply to the Government for redress of grievances, shall not be infringed." . . .

[12] Article 1. Section 10 [of the Constitution], between the first and second paragraphs, insert, "No State shall infringe the equal rights of conscience, nor the freedom of speech, or of the press, nor of the right of trial by jury in criminal cases."

III. Amendment Proposals Passed by the House of Representatives (August 24, 1789)

Article the Third. Congress shall make no law establishing Religion or prohibiting the free exercise thereof, nor shall the rights of conscience be infringed.

Article the Fourth. The freedom of speech, and of the press, and the right of the people peaceably to assemble, and consult for their common good, and to apply to the government for a redress of grievances, shall not be infringed. . . .

Article the Fourteenth. No State shall infringe the right of trial by Jury in criminal cases, nor the rights of conscience, nor the freedom of speech, or of the press.

IV. Amendment Proposals Passed by the Senate (September 9, 1789)

The third article . . . Congress shall make no law establishing articles of faith, or a mode of worship, or prohibiting the free exercise of religion, or abridging the freedom of speech, or of the press, or the right of the people peaceably to assemble, and petition to the government for a redress of grievances.

V. Amendments Proposed by Congress for Ratification by the States (September 25, 1789)

Article the Third. Congress shall make no law respecting an establishment of religion, or prohibiting the free exercise thereof; or abridging the freedom of speech, or of the press, or the right of the people peaceably to assemble, and to petition the Government for a redress of grievances.

Appendix G

The Sedition Act (1798)

Section 1. *Be it enacted by the Senate and House of Representatives of the United States of America, in Congress assembled,* That if any persons shall unlawfully combine or conspire together, with intent to oppose any measure or measures of the government of the United States, which are or shall be directed by proper authority, or to impede the operation of any law of the United States, or to intimidate or prevent any person holding a place or office in or under the government of the United States, from undertaking, performing or executing his trust or duty; and if any person or persons, with intent as aforesaid, shall counsel, advise or attempt to procure any insurrection riot, unlawful assembly, or combination, whether such conspiracy, threatening, counsel, advice, or attempt shall have the proposed effect or not, he or they shall be deemed guilty of a high misdemeanor, and on conviction, before any court of the United States having jurisdiction thereof, shall be punished by a fine not exceeding five thousand dollars, and by imprisonment during a term not less than six months nor exceeding five years; and further, at the discretion of the court may be holden to find sureties for his good behaviour in such sum, and for such time, as the said court may direct.

Sec. 2. *And be it further enacted,* That if any person shall write, print, utter or publish, or shall cause or procure to be written, printed, uttered or published, or shall knowingly and willingly assist or aid in writing, print-

Sources: This is based upon *An Act in addition to the Act, entitled "An Act for the punishment of certain crimes against the United States,"* 5th Congress, 2nd Session, Chapter 74, July 14, 1798. See 1 Stat. 596 (1798). See also, George Anastaplo, ed., *Liberty, Equality & Modern Constitutionalism: A Source Book,* vol. 2 (Newburyport, Mass.: Focus Publishing Company, 1999), 26–36.

ing, uttering or publishing any false, scandalous and malicious writing or writings against the government of the United States, or either house of the Congress of the United States, or the President of the United States, with intent to defame the said government, or either house of the said Congress, or the said President, or to bring them, or either of them, into contempt or disrepute; or to excite against them, or either or any of them, the hatred of the good people of the United States, or to stir up sedition within the United States or to excite any unlawful combinations therein, for opposing or resisting any law of the United States, or any act of the President of the United States, done in pursuance of any such law, or of the powers in him vested by the Constitution of the United States, or to resist, oppose, or defeat any such law or act, or to aid, encourage or abet any hostile designs of any foreign nation against the United States, their people or government, then such person, being thereof convicted before any court of the United States having jurisdiction thereof, shall be punished by a fine not exceeding two thousand dollars, and by imprisonment not exceeding two years.

Sec. 3. *And be it further enacted and declared,* That if any person shall be prosecuted under this act, for the writing or publishing any libel aforesaid, it shall be lawful for the defendant, upon the trial of the cause, to give in evidence in his defence, the truth of the matter contained in the publication charged as a libel. And the jury who shall try the cause, shall have a right to determine the law and the fact, under the direction of the court, as in other cases.

Sec. 4. *And be it further enacted,* That this act shall continue and be in force until the third day of March, one thousand eight hundred and one, and no longer: *Provided,* that the expiration of the act shall not prevent or defeat a prosecution and punishment of any offence against the law, during the time it shall be in force.

Appendix H

The Virginia Resolutions (1798)

RESOLVED, that the General Assembly of Virginia doth unequivocally express a firm resolution to maintain and defend the Constitution of the United States, and the Constitution of this State, against every aggression, either foreign or domestic, and that they will support the government of the United States in all measures warranted by the former.

That this Assembly most solemnly declares a warm attachment to the Union of the States, to maintain which it pledges all its powers; and that for this end, it is their duty, to watch over and oppose every infraction of those principles, which constitute the only basis of that Union, because a faithful observance of them, can alone secure it's existence and the public happiness.

That this Assembly doth explicitly and peremptorily declare, that it views the powers of the federal government, as resulting from the compact, to which the states are parties, as limited by the plain sense and intention of the instrument constituting the compact; as no further valid than they are authorized by the grants enumerated in that compact, and that, in case of a deliberate, palpable, and dangerous exercise of other powers, not granted by the said compact, the states who are parties thereto, have the right, and are in duty bound, to interpose for arresting the progress of the evil, and for maintaining, within their respective limits, the authorities, rights and liberties appertaining to them.

That the General Assembly doth also express its deep regret, that a

Sources: This is based upon the Resolutions in the House of Delegates, General Assembly of Virginia, December 21, 1798, prepared by James Madison for the General Assembly. See *The Papers of James Madison*, vol. 17, edited by David B. Mattern et al. (Charlottesville: University Press of Virginia, 1991), 188–90. See also, George Anastaplo, ed., *Liberty, Equality & Modern Constitutionalism: A Source Book,* vol. 2 (Newburyport, Mass.: Focus Publishing Company, 1999), 26–36.

spirit has in sundry instances, been manifested by the federal government, to enlarge its powers by forced constructions of the constitutional charter which defines them; and that implications have appeared of a design to expound certain general phrases (which having been copied from the very limited grant of powers in the former articles of confederation were the less liable to be misconstrued) so as to destroy the meaning and effect of the particular enumeration, which necessarily explains and limits the general phrases, and so as to consolidate the states by degrees into one sovereignty, the obvious tendency and inevitable consequence of which would be, to transform the present republican system of the United States, into an absolute, or at best a mixed monarchy.

That the General Assembly doth particularly protest against the palpable and alarming infractions of the Constitution, in the two late cases of the "alien and sedition acts," passed at the last session of Congress; the first of which exercises a power no where delegated to the federal government, and which by uniting legislative and judicial powers, to those of the executive, subverts the general principles of free government, as well as the particular organization, and positive provisions of the federal constitution; and the other of which acts, exercises in like manner, a power not delegated by the constitution, but on the contrary expressly and positively forbidden by one of the amendments thereto; a power, which more than any other, ought to produce universal alarm, because it is levelled against that right of freely examining public characters and measures, and of free communication among the people thereon, which has ever been justly deemed, the only effectual guardian of every other right.

That this state having by its Convention which ratified the federal Constitution, expressly declared, "that among other essential rights, the Liberty of Conscience and of the Press cannot be cancelled, abridged, restrained or modified by any authority of the United States," and from its extreme anxiety to guard these rights from every possible attack of sophistry or ambition, having with other states recommended an amendment for that purpose, which amendment was, in due time, annexed to the Constitution, it would mark a reproachful inconsistency, and criminal degeneracy, if an indifference were now shewn to the most palpable violation of one of the Rights, thus declared and secured, and to the establishment of a precedent which may be fatal to the other.

That the good people of this commonwealth, having ever felt and continuing to feel, the most sincere affection for their bretheren of the other states, the truest anxiety for establishing and perpetuating the union of all, and the most scrupulous fidelity to that constitution which is the pledge of mutual friendship, and the instrument of mutual happiness, the General Assembly doth solemnly appeal to the like dispositions of the other states, in confidence that they will concur with this commonwealth in declaring, as it doth hereby declare, that the acts aforesaid are unconstitutional, and that the necessary and proper measures will be taken by each, for co-operating with this state, in maintaining unimpaired the Authorities, Rights, and Liberties, reserved to the States respectively, or to the people.

That the Governor be desired to transmit a copy of the foregoing Resolutions to the executive authority of each of the other states, with a request, that the same may be communicated to the Legislature thereof, and that a copy be furnished to each of the Senators and Representatives representing this state in the Congress of the United States.

Appendix I

Report of a House of Delegates Minority on the Virginia Resolutions (1799)

FELLOW CITIZENS:

Opposing as we did, resolutions of the General Assembly, passed on the 24th day of December [1798] [Appendix H, above], we cannot remain silent under the unprecedented example exhibited in support of them, by a detailed display of those reasons which influenced their adoption. We lament their existence; and we deprecate the deviation from our [Virginia] legislative usage which their adoption has produced. . . .

. . . The act intituled "An act in addition to the act intituled as 'An act for the punishment of certain crimes against the United States,'" and which is commonly called the sedition law [Appendix G, above], subjects to a fine not exceeding two thousand dollars, and to imprisonment not exceeding two years, any person who shall write, print, utter, or publish, or cause or procure to be written, printed, uttered or published, any false, scandalous, malicious writing or writings against the government of the United States, or either house of the Congress of the United States, or the President of the United States, with intent to defame the said government, or either house of Congress, or the said President, or to bring them, or either of them, into contempt or disrepute, or to excite against them, or either or any of them, the hatred of the good people of the United States, or to stir up any sedition within the United States, or to excite any unlawful combination therein for opposing or resisting any law of the United

Sources: This is based upon the Report of the Minority, Virginia House of Delegates, General Assembly of Virginia, January 22, 1799, in response to the resolutions prepared by James Madison for the General Assembly. This Minority Report was evidently prepared either by John Marshall or by Henry Lee. See *Journal of the House of Delegates of Virginia,* vol. 6, 90, 93–95 (1798–1799). See also, George Anastaplo, ed., *Liberty, Equality & Modern Constitutionalism: A Source Book,* vol. 2 (Newburyport, Mass.: Focus Publishing Company, 1999), 26–36.

States, or any act of the President of the United States, done in pursuance of such law, or of the powers in him vested by the constitution of the United States, or to resist, oppress, or defeat any such law or act, or to aid, encourage, or abet hostile designs, of any foreign nation, against the United States, their people, or government; the person accused is to be tried by jury, and may give in evidence the truth of the matter contained in the libel.

To constitute the crime, the writing must be false, scandalous, and malicious, and the intent must be to effect some one of the ill purposes described in the act.

To contend that there does not exist a power to punish writings coming within the description of this law, would be to assert the inability of our nation to preserve its own peace, and to protect themselves from the attempts of wicked citizens, who, incapable of quiet themselves, are incessantly employed in devising means to disturb the public repose.

Government is instituted and preserved for the general happiness and safety—the people therefore are interested in its preservation, and have a right to adopt measures for its security, as well against secret plots as open hostility. But government cannot be thus secured, if, by falsehood and malicious slander, it is to be deprived of the confidence and affection of the people. It is vain to urge that truth will prevail, and that slander, when detected, recoils on the calumniator. The experience of the world, and our own experience, prove that a continued course of defamation will at length sully the fairest reputation, and will throw suspicion on the purest conduct. Although the calumnies of the factious and discontented may not poison the mind of a majority of the citizens, yet they will infect a very considerable number, and prompt them to deeds destructive of the public peace, and dangerous to the general safety.

This the people have a right to prevent: and therefore, in all the nations of the earth, where presses are known, some corrective of their licentiousness has been deemed indispensable. But it is contended that though this may be theoretically true, such is the peculiar structure of our government, that this power has either never been confided to, or has been withdrawn from the legislature of this union.—We will examine these positions. The power of making all laws which shall be necessary and proper for carrying into execution all powers vested by the constitution in the government of the United States, or in any department or officer thereof, is by the concluding clause of the eighth section of the first article, expressly delegated to congress. This clause is admitted to authorize the congress to pass any act for the punishment of those who would resist the execution of the laws, because such an act would be incontestably necessary and proper for carrying into execution the powers vested in the government. If it authorizes the punishment of actual resistance, does it not also authorize the punishment of those acts, which are criminal in themselves, and which obviously lead to and prepare resistance? Would it not be strange, if, for the purpose of executing the legitimate powers of the government, a clause like that which has been cited should be so construed as to permit the passage of laws punishing open resistance, and yet to forbid the passage of laws punishing acts which constitute the germs from which resistance springs? That the government must look on, and see preparations for resistance which it shall be unable to control, until they shall break out in open force? This would be an unreasonable and improvident construction of the article under consideration. That continued calumnies against the government have this tendency, is demonstrated by uninterrupted experience. They will, if unrestrained, produce in any society convulsions, which if not totally destructive of, will yet be very injurious to, its prosperity and welfare. It is not to be believed that the people of the western part of Pennsylvania could have been deluded into that unprovoked and wanton insurrection, which called forth the militia of the neighbouring states, if they had not been at the same time irritated and seduced by calumnies with which certain presses incessantly teemed, into the opinion that the people of America, instead of supporting their government and their laws, would join in their subversion. Those calumnies then, tended to prevent the execution of the laws of the union, and such seems to be their obvious and necessary tendency.

To publish all malicious calumnies against an individual with an intent to defame him, is a wrong on the part of the calumniator, and an injury to the individual, for which the law affords redress. To write or print these calumnies is such an aggravation of the crime, as to constitute an offense against the government, and the author of the libel is subject to the additional punishment which may be inflicted under an indictment. To publish malicious calumnies against the government itself, is a wrong on the part of the calumniator, and an injury to all those who have an interest in the government. Those who have this interest and have sustained the injury, have the natural right to an adequate remedy. The people of the United States have a common interest in their government, and sustain in common the injury which affects that government. The people of the United States therefore have a right to the remedy for that injury, and are substantially the party seeking redress. By the 2d section of the 3d article of the constitution, the judicial power of the United States is extended to controversies to which the United States shall be a party; and by the same article it is extended to all cases in law and equity arising under the constitution, the laws of the United States, and treaties made or which shall be made under their authority. What are cases arising under the constitution, as contradistinguished from those which arise under the laws made in pursuance thereof? They must be cases triable by a rule which exists independent of any act of the legislature of the union. That rule is the common or unwritten law which pervades all America, and which declaring libels against governments to be a punishable offense, applies itself to and protects any government which the will of the people may establish. The judicial power of the United States, then, being extended to the punishment of libels against the government, as a common law offence, arising under the constitution which creates the government, the general clause gives to the legislature of the union the right to make such laws as shall give that power effect.

That such was the contemporaneous construction of the constitution, is obvious from one of the amendments which have been made to it. The 3d amendment [that is, the First Amendment] which declares, that Congress shall make no law abridging the liberty of the press, is a general construction made by all America on the original instrument admitting its application to the subject. It would be certainly unnecessary thus to have modified the legislative powers of Congress concerning the press, if the power itself does not exist.

But altho' the original constitution may be supposed to have enabled the government to defend itself against false and malicious libels, endangering the peace, and threatening the tranquility of the American people, yet it is contended that the 3d amendment to that instrument, has deprived it of this power.

The amendment is in these words,—"Congress shall make no law respecting an establishment of religion, or prohibiting the free exercise thereof, or ABRIDGING the freedom of speech or of the press."

In a solemn instrument, as is a constitution, words are well weighed and considered before they are adopted. A remarkable diversity of expression is not used, unless it be designed to manifest a difference of intention.

Congress is prohibited from making any law RESPECTING a religious establishment, but not from making any law RESPECTING the press. When the power of Congress relative to the press is to be limited, the word RESPECTING is dropt, and Congress is only restrained from the passing any law ABRIDGING its liberty. This difference of expression with respect to religion and the press, manifests a difference of intention with respect to the power of the national legislature over those subjects, both in the person who drew, and those who adopted this amendment.

All ABRIDGMENT of the freedom of the press is forbidden, but it is only an ABRIDGMENT of that freedom which is forbidden. It becomes then necessary in order to determine whether the act in question be un-constitutional or not, to inquire whether it does in fact ABRIDGE the freedom of the press.

The act is believed not to have that operation, for two reasons.

1st. A punishment of the licentiousness is not considered as a restriction of the freedom of the press.

2d. The act complained of does not punish any writing not before punishable, nor does it inflict a more severe penalty than that to which the same writing was before liable.

1st. If by freedom of the press is meant a perfect exemption from all punishment for whatever may be published, that freedom never has, and most probably never will exist. It is known to all, that the person who writes or publishes a libel, may both be sued and indicted, and must bear the penalty which the judgment of his country inflicts upon him. It is also known to all that the person who shall libel the government of the state, is for that offense, punishable in the like manner. Yet this liability for punishment for slanderous and malicious publications, has never been considered as detracting from the liberty of the press. In fact the liberty of the press is a term that has a definite and appropriate signification, completely understood. It signifies a liberty to publish, free from previous restraint, any thing and every thing at the discretion of the printer only, but not the liberty of spreading with impunity false and scandalous slanders which may destroy the peace and mangle the reputation of an individual or of a community.

If this definition of the term be correct, and it is presumed that its correctness is not to be questioned, then a law punishing the authors and publishers of false, malicious and scandalous libels can be no attack on the liberty of the press.

But the act complained of is no abridgement of the liberty of the press, for another reason.

2d. It does not punish any writing not before punishable, nor does it inflict a heavier penalty than the same writing was before liable to.

No man will deny, that at common law, the author and publisher of a false, scandalous and malicious libel against the government or an individual, were subject to fine and imprisonment, at the discretion of the judge. Nor will it be denied, that previous to our resolution, the common law was the law of the land throughout the United States.

We believe it to be a principle incontestably true, that a change in government does not dissolve obligations previously created, does not annihilate existing laws, and dissolve the bonds of society; but that a People passing from one form of government to another, retain in full force all their municipal institutions not necessarily changed by the change of government. If this be true, then the common law continued to be the law of the land after the revolution, and was of complete obligation even before the act of our Assembly for its adoption. Whether similar acts have been passed by the legislature of other states or not, it is certain that in every state the common law is admitted to be in full force, except as it may have been altered by the statute law. The only question is, whether the doctrines of the common law are applicable to libels against the government of the United States, as well as to libels against the governments of particular states. For such a distinction there seems to be no sufficient reason. It is not to a magistrate of this or that description that the rules of the common law apply. That he is a magistrate, that he is cloathed with the authority of the laws, that he is invested with power by the people, is a sufficient title to the protection of the common law. The government of the United States is for certain purposes as entirely the government of each state, chosen by the people thereof, and cloathed with their authority, as the government of each particular state is the government of every subdivision of that state; and no satisfactory reason has been heretofore assigned why a general rule common to all, and punishing generally the malicious calumniators of magistrates, should not be as applicable to magistrates chosen for the whole, as to those chosen for its different parts.

If then it were even true that the punishment of the printer of malicious falsehoods affected the liberty of the press, yet the act does not abridge that liberty, since it does not substitute a harsher or severer rule of punishment than that which before existed.

On points so extremely interesting, a difference of opinion will be entertained. On such occasions all parties must be expected to maintain their real opinions, but to maintain them with moderation and with decency. The will of the majority must prevail, or the republican principle is abandoned and the nation is destroyed. If upon every constitutional question which presents itself, or on every question we choose to term constitutional, the construction of the majority shall be forcibly opposed, and hostility to the government excited throughout the nation, there is an end of our domestic peace, and we may ever bid adieu to our representative government.

The legislature of Virginia has itself passed more than one unconstitutional law, but they have not been passed with an intention to violate the constitution. On being decided to be unconstitutional by the legitimate authority, they have been permitted to fall. Had the judges deemed them constitutional, they should have been maintained. The same check, nor is it a less efficient one, exists in the government of the Union. The judges of the United States are as independent as the judges of the state of Virginia, nor is their any reason to believe them less wise and less virtuous. It is their province, and their duty to construe the constitution and the laws, and it cannot be doubted, but that they will perform this duty faithfully and truly. They will perform it unwarmed by political debate, uninfluenced by party zeal. Let us in the mean time seek a repeal of any act we may disapprove, by means authorized by our happy constitution, but let us not endeavor to disseminate among our fellow citizens the most deadly hate against the government of their own creation, against the government, on the preservation of which we firmly believe the peace and liberty of America to depend, because in some respects its judgement has differed from our own.

Various other points are noticed in the address alike calculated, to excite your resentment, and provoke your resistance. Seriously do we regret the expression of such sentiments by a body so respectable.

At a time when all ought to unite in repelling any evidence of the existence of division in the United States, on which division our enemy calculates and with the knowledge of which our enemy has had the presumption to upbraid us, it cannot but inflict a deep wound in the American mind to find the commonwealth of Virginia, exhibiting through her legislature irresistible testimony of the degrading charge. . . .

Appendix J

Thomas Jefferson, the First Inaugural Address (1801)

Friends and Fellow-Citizens:

Called upon to undertake the duties of the first executive office of our country, I avail myself of the presence of that portion of my fellow-citizens which is here assembled to express my grateful thanks for the favor with which they have been pleased to look toward me, to declare a sincere consciousness that the task is above my talents, and that I approach it with those anxious and awful presentiments which the greatness of the charge and the weakness of my power so justly inspire. A rising nation, spread over a wide and fruitful land, traversing all the seas with the rich productions of their industry, engaged in commerce with nations who feel power and forget right, advancing rapidly to destinies beyond the reach of mortal eye—when I contemplate these transcendent objects, and see the honor, the happiness, and the hopes of this beloved country committed to the issue, and the auspices of this day, I shrink from the contemplation, and humble myself before the magnitude of the undertaking. Utterly, indeed, should I despair did not the presence of many whom I here see remind me that in the other high authorities provided by our Constitution I shall find resources of wisdom, of virtue, and of zeal on which to rely under all difficulties. To you, then, gentlemen, who are charged with the sovereign functions of legislation, and to those associated with you, I look with encouragement for that guidance and support which may enable us to steer with safety the vessel in

Sources: This is based upon Thomas Jefferson's First Inaugural Address as President, March 4, 1801. See *Inaugural Addresses of the Presidents of the United States* (Washington, D.C.: Government Printing Office, 1874), 13–16.

which we are all embarked amidst the conflicting elements of a troubled world.

During the contest of opinion through which we have passed the animation of discussions and of exertions has sometimes worn an aspect which might impose on strangers unused to think freely and to speak and to write what they think; but this being now decided by the voice of the nation, announced according to the rules of the Constitution, all will, of course, arrange themselves under the will of the law, and unite in common efforts for the common good. All, too, will bear in mind this sacred principle, that though the will of the majority is in all cases to prevail, that will to be rightful must be reasonable; that the minority possesses their equal rights, which equal law must protect, and to violate would be oppression. Let us, then, fellow-citizens, unite with one heart and one mind. Let us restore to social intercourse that harmony and affection without which liberty and even life itself are but dreary things. And let us reflect that, having banished from our land that religious intolerance under which mankind so long bled and suffered, we have yet gained little if we countenance a political intolerance as despotic, as wicked, and capable of as bitter and bloody persecutions. During the throes and convulsions of the ancient world, during the agonizing spasms of infuriated man, seeking through blood and slaughter his long-lost liberty, it was not wonderful that the agitation of the billows should reach even this distant and peaceful shore; that this should be more felt and feared by some and less by others, and should divide opinions as to measures of safety. But every difference of opinion is not a difference of principle. We have called by different names brethren of the same principle. We are all Republicans, we are all Federalists. If there be any among us who would wish to dissolve this Union or to change its republican form, let them stand undisturbed as monuments of the safety with which error of opinion may be tolerated where reason is left free to combat it. I know, indeed, that some honest men fear that a republican government can not be strong, that this Government is not strong enough; but would the honest patriot, in the full tide of successful experiment, abandon a government which has so far kept us free and firm on the theoretic and visionary fear that this Government, the world's best hope, may by possibility want energy to preserve itself? I trust not. I believe this, on the contrary, the strongest Government on earth. I believe it the only one where every man, at the call of the law, would fly to the standard of the law, and would meet invasions of the public order as his own personal concern. Sometimes it is said that man can not be trusted with the government of himself. Can he, then, be trusted with the government of others? Or have we found angels in the form of kings to govern him? Let history answer this question.

Let us, then, with courage and confidence pursue our own Federal and Republican principles, our attachment to union and representative government. Kindly separated by nature and a wide ocean from the exterminating havoc of one quarter of the globe; too high-minded to endure the degradations of the others; possessing a chosen country, with room enough for our descendants to the thousandth and thousandth generation; entertaining a due sense of our equal right to the use of our own faculties, to the acquisitions of our own industry, to honor and confidence from our fellow-citizens, resulting not from birth, but from our actions and their sense of them; enlightened by a benign religion, professed, indeed, and practiced in various forms, yet all of them inculcating honesty, truth, temperance, gratitude, and the love of man; acknowledging and adoring an over-ruling Providence, which by all its dispensations proves that it delights in the happiness of man here and his greater happiness hereafter—with all these blessings, what more is necessary to make us a happy and a prosperous people? Still one thing more, fellow-citizens—a wise and frugal Government, which shall restrain men from injuring one another, shall leave them otherwise free to regulate their own pursuits of industry and improvement, and shall not take from the mouth of labor the bread it has earned. This is the sum of good government, and this is necessary to close the circle of our felicities.

About to enter, fellow-citizens, on the exercise of duties which comprehend everything dear and valuable to you, it is proper you should understand what I deem the essential principles of our Government, and consequently those which ought to shape its Administration. I will compress them within the narrowest compass they will bear, stating the general principle, but not all its limitations. Equal and exact justice to all men, of whatever state or persuasion, religious or political; peace, commerce, and honest friendship with all nations, entangling alliances with none; the support of the State governments in all their rights, as the most competent administrations for our domestic concerns and the surest bulwarks against antirepublican tendencies; the preservation of the General Government in its whole constitutional vigor, as the sheet anchor of our peace at home and safety abroad; a jealous care of the right of election by the people—a mild and safe corrective of abuses which are lopped by the sword of revolution where peaceable remedies are unprovided; absolute acquiescence in the decisions of the majority, the vital principle of republics, from which is no appeal but to force, the vital principle and immediate parent of despotism; a well-disciplined militia, our best reliance in peace and for the first moments of war, till regulars may relieve them; the supremacy of the civil over the military authority; economy in the public expense, that labor might be lightly burthened; the honest payment of our debts and sacred preservation of the public faith; encouragement of agriculture, and of commerce as its handmaid; the diffusion of information and arraignment of all abuses at the bar of the public reason; freedom of religion; freedom of the press, and freedom of person under the protection of the habeas corpus, and trial by juries impartially selected. These principles form the bright constellation which has gone before us and guided our steps through an age of revolution and reformation. The wisdom of our sages and blood of our heroes have been devoted to their attainment. They should be the creed of our political faith, the text of civic instruction, the touchstone by which to try the services of those we trust; and should we wander from them in moments of error or of alarm, let us hasten to retrace our steps and to regain the road which alone leads to peace, liberty, and safety.

I repair, then, fellow-citizens, to the post you have assigned to me. With experience enough in subordinate offices to have seen the difficulties of this the greatest of all, I have learnt to expect that it will rarely fall to the lot of imperfect man to retire from this station with the reputation and the favor which bring him into it. Without pretensions to that high confidence you reposed in our first and greatest revolutionary character [that is, George Washington], whose preeminent services had entitled him to the first place in his country's love and destined for him the fairest page in the volume of faithful history, I ask so much confidence only as may give firmness and effect to the legal administration of your affairs. I shall often go wrong through defect of judgment. When right, I shall often be thought wrong by those whose positions will not command a view of the whole ground. I ask your indulgence for my own errors, which will never be intentional, and your support against the errors of others, who may condemn what they would not if seen in all its parts. The approbation implied by your suffrage is a great consolation to me for the past, and my future solicitude will be to retain the good opinion of those who have bestowed it in advance, to conciliate that of others by doing them all the good in my power, and to be instrumental to the happiness and freedom of all.

Relying, then, on the patronage of your good will, I advance with obedience to the work, ready to retire from it whenever you become sensible how much better choice it is in your power to make. And may that Infinite Power which rules the destinies of the universe lead our councils to what is best, and give them a favorable issue for your peace and prosperity.

Appendix K

Schenck v. *United States* Leaflet (1917)

[Side One]

LONG LIVE THE CONSTITUTION
OF THE UNITED STATES
Wake Up, America! Your Liberties Are in Danger!

The 13th Amendment, Section 1, of the Constitution of the United States says: "Neither slavery nor involuntary servitude, except as a punishment for crime whereof the party shall have been duly convicted, shall exist within the United States, or any place subject to their jurisdiction."

The Constitution of the United States is one of the greatest bulwarks of political liberty. It was born after a long, stubborn battle between king-rule and democracy. (We see little or no difference between arbitrary power under the name of a king and a few misnamed "representatives.") In this battle the people of the United States established the principle that freedom of the individual and personal liberty are the most sacred things in life. Without them we become slaves.

For this principle the fathers fought and died. The establishment of this principle they sealed with their own blood. Do you want to see this principle abolished? Do you want to see despotism substituted in its stead? Shall we prove degenerate sons of illustrious sires?

Sources: This is based upon a leaflet, distributed by the Socialist Party in Philadelphia, which was the basis of the prosecution in *Schenck* v. *United States,* 249 U.S. 47 (1919). This 1917 leaflet was printed in two stages, as described in the Opinion of the United States Supreme Court in the *Schenck Case.* (The direction "(OVER)" was placed at the foot of each side of the leaflet.) See *Briefs and Records,* United States Supreme Court, *Schenck* v. *United States* (1919). See also George Anastaplo, *The Constitutionalist: Notes on the First Amendment* (Dallas: Southern Methodist University Press, 1971; Lanham, Md.: Lexington Books, 2005), 296–300.

The Thirteenth Amendment to the Constitution of the United States, quoted above, embodies this sacred idea. The Socialist Party says that this idea is violated by the Conscription Act. When you conscript a man and compel him to go abroad to fight against his will, you violate the most sacred right of personal liberty, and substitute for it what Daniel Webster called "despotism in its worst form."

A conscript is little better than a convict. He is deprived of his liberty and of his right to think and act as a free man. A conscripted citizen is forced to surrender his right as a citizen and become a subject. He is forced into involuntary servitude. He is deprived of the protection given him by the Constitution of the United States. He is deprived of all freedom of conscience in being forced to kill against his will.

Are you one who is opposed to war, and were you misled by the venal capitalist newspapers, or intimidated or deceived by gang politicians and registrars into believing that you would not be allowed to register your objection to conscription? Do you know that many citizens of Philadelphia insisted on their right to answer the famous question twelve, and went on record with their honest opinion of opposition to war, notwithstanding the deceitful efforts of our rulers and the newspaper press to prevent them from doing so? Shall it be said that the citizens of Philadelphia, the cradle of American liberty, are so lost to a sense of right and justice that they will let such monstrous wrongs against humanity go unchallenged?

In a democratic country each man must have the right to say whether he is willing to join the army. Only in countries where uncontrolled power rules can a despot force his subjects to fight. Such a man or men have no place in a democratic republic. This is tyrannical power in its worst form. It gives control over the life and death of the individual to a few men. There is no man good enough to be given such power.

Conscription laws belong to a bygone age. Even the people of Germany, long suffering under the yoke of militarism, are beginning to demand the abolition of conscription. Do you think it has a place in the United States? Do you want to see unlimited power handed over to Wall Street's chosen few in America? If you do not, join the Socialist Party in its campaign for the repeal of the Conscription Act. Write to your congressman and tell him you want the law repealed. Do not submit to intimidation. You have a right to demand the repeal of any law. Exercise your rights of free speech, peaceful assemblage and petitioning the government for a redress or grievances. Come to the headquarters of the Socialist Party, 1326

Arch Street, and sign a petition to congress for the repeal of the Conscription Act. Help us wipe out this stain upon the Constitution!

Help us re-establish democracy in America.

Remember, "eternal vigilance is the price of liberty."

Down with autocracy!

Long live the Constitution of the United States! Long live the Republic!

Books on Socialism for Sale at:

SOCIALIST PARTY BOOKSTORE AND HEADQUARTERS

1326 ARCH ST. Phone, Filbert 3121

(OVER)

[Side Two]
ASSERT YOUR RIGHTS!

Article 6, Section 2, of the Constitution of the United States says: "This Constitution shall be the *supreme law of the Land.*"

Article 1 (Amendment) says: "Congress shall make no law respecting an establishment of religion, or *prohibiting the free exercise thereof.*"

Article 9 (Amendment) says: "The enumeration in the Constitution of certain rights, shall not be construed to deny or disparage others retained by the people."

The Socialist Party says that any individual or officers of the law entrusted with the administration of conscription regulations, violate the provisions of the United States Constitution, the Supreme Law of the Land, when they refuse to recognize your right to assert your opposition to the draft.

If you are conscientiously opposed to war, if you believe in the commandment "thou shalt not kill," then that is your religion, and you shall not be prohibited from the free exercise thereof.

In exempting clergymen and members of the Society of Friends (popularly called Quakers) from active military service, the examination boards have discriminated against you.

If you do not assert and support your rights, you are helping to "deny or disparage rights" which it is the solemn duty of all citizens and residents of the United States to retain.

Here in this city of Philadelphia was signed the immortal Declaration of Independence. As a citizen of the "cradle of American Liberty" you are doubly charged with the duty of upholding the rights of the people.

Will you let cunning politicians and a mercenary capitalist press wrongly and untruthfully mould your thoughts? Do not forget your right to elect officials who are opposed to conscription.

In lending tacit or silent consent to the conscription law, in neglecting to assert your rights, you are (whether unknowingly or not) helping to condone and support a most infamous and insidious conspiracy to abridge and destroy the sacred and cherished rights of a free people. **You are a citizen, not a subject!** You delegate your power to the officers of the law to be used for your good and welfare, not against you.

They are your servants. Not your masters. Their wages come from the expenses of government **which you pay.** Will you allow them to unjustly rule you? The fathers who fought and bled to establish a free and independent nation here in America were so opposed to the militarism of the old world from which they had escaped; so keenly alive to the dangers and hardships they had undergone in fleeing from political, religious and military oppression, that they handed down to us "certain rights which must be retained by the people."

They held the spirit of militarism in such abhorrence and hate, they were so apprehensive of the formation of a military machine that would insidiously and secretly advocate the invasion of other lands, that they limited the power of Congress over the militia in providing only for the calling forth of "the militia to execute laws of the Union, suppress insurrections and repel invasions." (See general powers of Congress, Article 1, Section 8, Paragraph 15.)

No power was delegated to send our citizens away to foreign shores to shoot up the people of other lands, no matter what may be their internal or international disputes.

The people of this country did not vote in favor of war. At the last election they voted against war.

To draw this country into the horrors of the present war in Europe, to force the youth of our land into the shambles and bloody trenches of war-crazy nations, would be a crime the magnitude of which defies description. Words could not express the condemnation such cold-blooded ruthlessness deserves.

Will you stand idly by and see the Moloch of Militarism reach forth across the sea and fasten its tentacles upon this continent? Are you willing to submit to the degradation of having the Constitution of the United States treated as a "mere scrap of paper?"

Do you know that patriotism means a love for your country and not hate for others?

Will you be led astray by a propaganda of jingoism masquerading under the guise of patriotism?

No specious or plausible pleas about a "war for democracy" can becloud the issue. Democracy cannot be shot into a nation. It must come spontaneously and purely from within.

Democracy must come through liberal education. Upholders of military ideas are unfit teachers.

To advocate the persecution of other peoples through the prosecution of war is an insult to every good and wholesome American tradition.

"These are the times that try men's souls."

"Eternal vigilance is the price of liberty."

You are responsible. You must do your share to maintain, support and uphold the rights of the people in this country.

In this world crisis where do you stand? Are you with the forces of liberty and light or war and darkness?

[OVER]

Appendix L

The Universal Declaration of Human Rights (1948)

The Universal Declaration of Human Rights

Preamble

Whereas recognition of the inherent dignity and of the equal and inalienable rights of all members of the human family is the foundation of freedom, justice and peace in the world,

Whereas disregard and contempt for human rights have resulted in barbarous acts which have outraged the conscience of mankind, and the advent of a world in which human beings shall enjoy freedom of speech and belief and freedom from fear and want has been proclaimed as the highest aspiration of the common people,

Whereas it is essential, if man is not to be compelled to have recourse, as a last resort, to rebellion against tyranny and oppression, that human rights should be protected by the rule of law,

Whereas it is essential to promote the development of friendly relations between nations,

Whereas the peoples of the United Nations have in the Charter reaffirmed their faith in fundamental human rights, in the dignity and worth of the human person and in the equal rights of men and women and have determined to promote social progress and better standards of life in larger freedom,

Sources: This is based upon a 1948 resolution of the United Nations General Assembly. See General Assembly Resolution 217A (III), 3 (1) U.N. GAOR Resolutions 71, U.N. Doc. A/810 (1948) (December 10, 1948).

Whereas Member States have pledged themselves to achieve, in co-operation with the United Nations, the promotion of universal respect for and observance of human rights and fundamental freedoms,

Whereas a common understanding of these rights and freedoms is of the greatest importance for the full realization of this pledge,

Now therefore,

The General Assembly

Proclaims this Universal Declaration of Human Rights as a common standard of achievement for all peoples and all nations, to the end that every individual and every organ of society, keeping this Declaration constantly in mind, shall strive by teaching and education to promote respect for these rights and freedoms and by progressive measures, national and international, to secure their universal and effective recognition and observance, both among the peoples of Member States themselves and among the peoples of territories under their jurisdiction.

Article 1

All human beings are born free and equal in dignity and rights. They are endowed with reason and conscience and should act towards one another in a spirit of brotherhood.

Article 2

Everyone is entitled to all the rights and freedoms set forth in this Declaration, without distinction of any kind, such as race, colour, sex, language, religion, political or other opinion, national or social origin, property, birth or other status.

Furthermore, no distinction shall be made on the basis of the political, jurisdictional or international status of the country or territory to which a person belongs, whether it be independent, trust, non-self-governing or under any other limitation of sovereignty.

Article 3

Everyone has the right to life, liberty and security of person.

Article 4

No one shall be held in slavery or servitude; slavery and the slave trade shall be prohibited in all their forms.

Article 5

No one shall be subjected to torture or to cruel, inhuman or degrading treatment or punishment.

Article 6

Everyone has the right to recognition everywhere as a person before the law.

Article 7

All are equal before the law and are entitled without any discrimination to equal protection of the law. All are entitled to equal protection against any discrimination in violation of this Declaration and against any incitement to such discrimination.

Article 8

Everyone has the right to an effective remedy by the competent national tribunals for acts violating the fundamental rights granted him by the constitution or by law.

Article 9

No one shall be subjected to arbitrary arrest, detention or exile.

Article 10

Everyone is entitled in full equality to a fair and public hearing by an independent and impartial tribunal, in the determination of his rights and obligations and of any criminal charge against him.

Article 11

1. Everyone charged with a penal offence has the right to be presumed innocent until proved guilty according to law in a public trial at which he has had all the guarantees necessary for his defence.

2. No one shall be held guilty of any penal offence on account of any act or omission which did not constitute a penal offence, under national or international law, at the time when it was committed. Nor shall a heavier penalty be imposed than the one that was applicable at the time the penal offence was committed.

Article 12

No one shall be subjected to arbitrary interference with his privacy, family, home or correspondence, nor to attacks upon his honour and reputation. Everyone has the right to the protection of the law against such interference or attacks.

Article 13

1. Everyone has the right to freedom of movement and residence within the borders of each State.

2. Everyone has the right to leave any country, including his own, and to return to his country.

Article 14

1. Everyone has the right to seek and to enjoy in other countries asylum from persecution.

2. This right may not be invoked in the case of prosecutions genuinely arising from non-political crimes or from acts contrary to the purposes and principles of the United Nations.

Article 15

1. Everyone has the right to a nationality.

2. No one shall be arbitrarily deprived of his nationality nor denied the right to change his nationality.

Article 16

1. Men and women of full age, without any limitation due to race, nationality or religion, have the right to marry and to found a family. They are entitled to equal rights as to marriage, during marriage and at its dissolution.

2. Marriage shall be entered into only with the free and full consent of the intending spouses.

3. The family is the natural and fundamental group unit of society and is entitled to protection by society and the State.

Article 17

1. Everyone has the right to own property alone as well as in association with others.

2. No one shall be arbitrarily deprived of his property.

Article 18

Everyone has the right to freedom of thought, conscience and religion; this right includes freedom to change his religion or belief, and freedom, either alone or in community with others and in public or private, to manifest his religion or belief in teaching, practice, worship and observance.

Article 19

Everyone has the right to freedom of opinion and expression; this right includes freedom to hold opinions without interference and to seek, receive and impart information and ideas through any media and regardless of frontiers.

Article 20

1. Everyone has the right to freedom of peaceful assembly and association.

2. No one may be compelled to belong to an association.

Article 21

1. Everyone has the right to take part in the government of his country, directly or through freely chosen representatives.

2. Everyone has the right of equal access to public service in his country.

3. The will of the people shall be the basis of the authority of government; this will shall be expressed in periodic and genuine elections which shall be by universal and equal suffrage and shall be held by secret vote or by equivalent free voting procedures.

Article 22

Everyone, as a member of society, has the right to social security and is entitled to realization, through national effort and international co-operation and in accordance with the organization and resources of each State, of the economic, social and cultural rights indispensable for his dignity and the free development of his personality.

Article 23

1. Everyone has the right to work, to free choice of employment, to just and favourable conditions of work and to protection against unemployment.

2. Everyone, without any discrimination, has the right to equal pay for equal work.

3. Everyone who works has the right to just and favourable remuneration ensuring for himself and his family an existence worthy of human dignity, and supplemented, if necessary, by other means of social protection.

4. Everyone has the right to form and to join trade unions for the protection of his interests.

Article 24

Everyone has the right to rest and leisure, including reasonable limitation of working hours and periodic holidays with pay.

Article 25

1. Everyone has the right to a standard of living adequate for the health and well-being of himself and of his family, including food, clothing, housing and medical care and necessary social services, and the right to security in the event of unemployment, sickness, disability, widowhood, old age or other lack of livelihood in circumstances beyond his control.

2. Motherhood and childhood are entitled to special care and assistance. All children, whether born in or out of wedlock, shall enjoy the same social protection.

Article 26

1. Everyone has the right to education. Education shall be free, at least in the elementary and fundamental stages. Elementary education shall be compulsory. Technical and professional education shall be made generally available and higher education shall be equally accessible to all on the basis of merit.

2. Education shall be directed to the full development of the human personality and to the strengthening of respect for human rights and fundamental freedoms. It shall promote understanding, tolerance and friendship among all nations, racial or religious groups, and shall further the activities of the United Nations for the maintenance of peace.

3. Parents have a prior right to choose the kind of education that shall be given to their children.

Article 27

1. Everyone has the right freely to participate in the cultural life of the community, to enjoy the arts and to share in scientific advancement and its benefits.

2. Everyone has the right to the protection of the moral and material interests resulting from any scientific, literary or artistic production of which he is the author.

Article 28

Everyone is entitled to a social and international order in which the rights and freedoms set forth in this Declaration can be fully realized.

Article 29

1. Everyone has duties to the community in which alone the free and full development of his personality is possible.

2. In the exercise of his rights and freedoms, everyone shall be subject only to such limitations as are determined by law solely for the purpose of securing due recognition and respect for the rights and freedoms of others and of meeting the just requirements of morality, public order and the general welfare in a democratic society.

3. These rights and freedoms may in no case be exercised contrary to the purposes and principles of the United Nations.

Article 30

Nothing in this Declaration may be interpreted as implying for any State, group or person any right to engage in any activity or to perform any act aimed at the destruction of any of the rights and freedoms set forth herein.

Appendix M

George Anastaplo, On the Alcatraz Imprisonment of a Convicted Soviet Spy (1954)

Preface (2006)

I had occasion, in 1987, to comment upon a meeting with Morton Sobell, the man sentenced by Judge Irving Kaufman to thirty years imprisonment upon being convicted on espionage charges in 1951 as a codefendant with Ethel and Julius Rosenberg. (The Rosenbergs were sentenced to death at that time and executed in 1953.) My 1987 comment follows:

I introduced myself to Morton Sobell after a lecture appearance he made on the University of Chicago campus last month. He remembered that I had worked on a brief prepared by one of his lawyers, Stephen Love, who had asked me in 1954 to help him try to get Mr. Sobell out of Alcatraz, where he had been vindictively exiled by the Bureau of Prisons. Mr. Sobell remembers my efforts now more kindly than he had responded to them then—for I had heard that he had not been pleased by the line of argument I had developed in my memorandum, which had appealed to the good faith and the professional integrity of the Bureau of Prisons personnel. (There was not then the case law to support the administrative law review that might be available in comparable circumstances today.) Also, he associated me with Malcolm Sharp, of the University of Chicago Law School, whose efforts on his behalf he remembered fondly.

I invited Mr. Sobell to breakfast in our home on October 10, 1987, which I believe was the following morning. It was a long and lively conversation, which I rather enjoyed (as did, I believe, my wife). It is remarkable how "American" and good-natured this

convicted Soviet spy is. One would expect someone who has pro-
tested his innocence for three decades to be embittered, if he was
innocent, or to be devious, if guilty, neither of which does he appear to be.

Whatever Mr. Sobell had been guilty of, it had clearly been
done for "ideological" reasons. Certainly, he is appalled by what is
happening in contemporary espionage, as we learn from periodic
exposures of Americans who are willing (even eager) to betray
their country merely for money, with no pretense of any cause
being served by them.

The willingness of Americans to spy for money reflects, for
Mr. Sobell as for me, a general corruption. Consider the Navy
communications expert who has betrayed his country *by selling*
military secrets to the Russians. He engaged in seventeen years
of profitable (and even tax-free!) espionage, initiated by himself,
evidently recruiting members of his family for his enterprise.

I found Mr. Sobell to be a decent man, however ingenuous he
can be when he deals with political things. In fact, I suspect it was
his ingenuousness that got him mixed up in the early 1940s with
people who were so vulnerable to charges of subversion, if not
also of espionage. It should be noticed that serious spies have always, or so it is said, steered clear in this country of identification
with the Communist Party. And, I recall, the American Communist Party was very much disturbed initially by the Rosenberg-
Sobell indictments, not wanting to be publicly associated with
such deadly business. This contributed to the lack of availability
of experienced criminal defense counsel for these defendants, although (Mr. Sobell told me) some of the regular counsel for the
Communist Party did offer the Rosenbergs and him help behind
the scenes.

A change in times is reflected in the fact that such a relaxed
conversation could be carried on by my wife and me with someone with Mr. Sobell's record, and carried on with no efforts at
concealment. . . .

This comment may be found, with informative notes, in George Anastaplo, *On Trial: From Adam & Eve to O.J. Simpson* (Lanham, Md.: Lexington
Books, 2004), 415–16.

Stephen Love, a prominent Roman Catholic lawyer in Chicago, did not succeed in getting Sobell moved out of Alcatraz at that time. He had been sent there in late 1952 and remained there until 1958. He was released from prison in 1969. A useful account of life as an Alcatraz prisoner ("a living death") is provided by Morton Sobell, *On Doing Time* (New York: Charles Scribner's Sons, 1974).

My 1954 Alcatraz memorandum is provided here in its entirety, except for its appendices. There is an occasional minor stylistic improvement. The references in the memorandum to appendices are to the appendices in the memorandum itself, *not* to appendices in this *Reflections* volume.

George Anastaplo, *Memorandum with Respect to the Imprisonment of Morton Sobell in Alcatraz* (prepared for Attorney Stephen Love), October 17, 1954

Introduction

Since your time may be limited before you see Mr. Sobell tomorrow, I would like to point out that suggestions are made in the text below with respect to topics about which you should question him. Generally, it might be well to ask him what he knows about the classification system, what he has heard about its application to him, and that sort of thing. More specifically, questions and subjects are suggested below for your consideration: under Point 3, at page 5; under Point 10, at page 11; under Point 11, at page 11; under Point 19, at page 16. (The references are to the pages of double-spaced text [of the original (1954) manuscript]; the page numbers in the Appendices are preceded by the letter "A".)

If I had more time, as the adage goes, I would be able to cut down what is said below. As it is, the various points, suggestions and observations are arranged somewhat haphazardly. There are some repetitions; some important points are not emphasized or developed enough perhaps. What I have done is to present a great number of suggestions, with no argument that any of them would be at all effective at this time. And I have worked on the assumption, in my analysis and research, that Sobell is guilty of the acts charged. One more assumption is that you will be a far better judge than I am of the strong points.

There are, in effect, two memoranda here. First, there is the collection of points (pages 4–17, below) which collects my impressions of the various possibilities in the case (i.e., the objective being to have Sobell moved out of Alcatraz). Secondly, there is the collection of materials, from which I have worked, brought together in the Appendices (pages A1–A52, below). Not all of the material has been or can be commented upon. But it *is* there and, I believe, it gives one some idea of what to look for.

I believe, furthermore, that all the materials provided in the Appendices have some bearing on this problem. These materials (including the references to other cases, articles, literature) should give you some notion about whether this matter is worth pursuing. And if it is worth further consideration, I trust enough is there for a lawyer to work with and from. In any event, I believe that what is gathered here may be of some use even if nothing further is done with this aspect of the case in the courts.

As you will see, I have been most concerned with the "substantive" aspect of this matter. I have figured that the appropriate procedure would probably be available should it be shown that there were "rights" or "privileges" or "standards" wrongly dealt with. And, in fact, I suggest that the various cases (in Appendix H) include ideas about the procedures that might be available.

A word about the cases is in order. I had not really briefed them upon reading them. So, in reporting them below (Appendix H), I have had to rely to a considerable extent upon a reconstruction at a time when many of them are jumbled together in my head. I decided to say something about them, however, both to provide whoever else might work on this matter with some idea of what is covered and to illustrate what I have concluded about the cases. That conclusion is that they do not "really" say what they might be thought to say: it is far from clear to me that the courts have altogether abdicated supervision of the Attorney General's exercise of power in the administration of the prisons. They do seem to say that; but yet, they also seem to satisfy themselves that the Attorney General's action in a particular case is defensible or reasonable or even perhaps "possibly reasonable anyway." Combined with the classification problem and developing further the principles found in the English cases (Appendix I), this business of what the cases really hold might offer whatever hope there is in this matter.

You will soon realize that I have not probed very deeply into any problem, except as to the existence of the "rules and regulations" with respect to classification (Appendices C, F, and G provide considerable material on this). I have tried, instead, to give enough coverage of the entire picture so that you might be in a position to tell whether this would be worth pursuing as a legal matter.

I know you will stress, in your conversation with your client, the odds against anything developing with respect to this aspect of the matter. Still, this particular memorandum might at least allow him to feel that the matter is not being ignored and that some efforts are being made along certain lines. There is, even aside from the content, something "solid" about it. In addition, it might not be harmful for one in his position to have the satisfaction of being able to produce information that he is asked about (e.g., about the classification system and such things), even though it may not do him much good at this time.

What follows now, starting at the top of page 4 [of the original 1954 manuscript] are various points for your consideration in evaluating the relative value of the various possible courses of action in this matter.

1. As to whether a classification system exists in Federal Prisons

(a) There is a definite, and longstanding, Congressional mandate or policy in support of a classification system. "Classification" means more than sorting out prisoners according to the place of detention; it also includes sorting them out for the kind of work they will do and the kind of training they are to receive. The various meanings of the term ("classification") are used interchangeably in the literature; I will use the term, however, to refer to the process of sorting out prisoners according to the place where they are detained. There are many references, in Appendices A, B, C, and F (at least) to the establishment of a classification set-up. There can be little doubt that such a set-up was desired by Congress and that Congress thought it had been established (particularly with respect to Alcatraz—Appendix G).

(b) There is considerable evidence—if evidence it can be called—supporting the position that the Bureau of Prisons, its Director, and the Attorney General have been operating under a Classification system. The evidence is both in terms of what they have said they were doing (such as what Johnston, the Alcatraz warden, says; Appendix F) and in terms of what they have done and how what they have done is to be explained. It is pretty likely that nothing in the way of printed regulations, explaining how prisoners are to be tested and sorted, will be found, even though the policy is pretty well formulated. (There is a reference in *Stroud* v. *Swope,* 187 F.2d 850 [1951], I believe, to a Manual Bulletin No. 96, dated February 23, 1944, issued by the Director of Prisons and relating to the question of the extent to which a convict is to be permitted to carry on any business he has outside the prison. It is likely that there are other such manuals—at least ninety-five others?—and it is possible that one of them might relate to classification [in our sense of the word].) In the absence of printed regulations, it would seem appropriate to establish the existence of *de facto* regulations by evidence of what is done and said. The material in the Appendices indicates that this could be established. Such a procedure might be acceptable to establish rules that have been violated in a particular instance.

2. As to whether a classification system exists with respect to Alcatraz

Even if there is no overall classification system, it seems that one does exist for Alcatraz Prison. That prison is one of the most definitely and unequivocally defined in the system; in its definition has been found its justification (to make up for its inconvenience, cost, reputation, conditions, etc.). Both Director Bates and Director Bennett, the two directors of the Bureau of Prisons, have classified it as something for the desperate, hardened and otherwise perhaps unmanageable offender; various Attorneys General have done the same thing. There is little doubt that the character of the prison population, over a period of twenty years, could be established in this manner.

3. As to how Sobell fits into the system

It could easily be shown that Sobell does not fit into any of the categories that have ever been listed (over a period of twenty years) as appropriate for confinement in Alcatraz. The various elements looked to—character, previous activities, prison record, previous behavior, etc.—would show him to be "ineligible" for admission to Alcatraz. Sprinkled throughout the appendices below are the various criteria—or rather, the various restatements of the criteria—that make one eligible for Alcatraz (see, for instance, for one of the most comprehensive statements, Warden Johnston's, in Appendix F). It is important, before any more work or time is spent on this aspect of the problem, that a thorough check be made of Sobell's background and record (including by putting the question to Sobell himself) to make sure there is nothing in it that would justify commitment to Alcatraz. (Espionage itself would not seem sufficient; as witness the cases of Gold and Greenglass; nor does the combination of espionage and perjury make one eligible, as witness the Hiss situation, which is so regarded.) It would be well to read the Johnston statement (Appendix F) before talking to Sobell; this would suggest that he should be questioned about whom he had talked to in quarantine, where quarantine was for him, for how long, what prisons he had been in, for how long, the names of fellow prisoners (for their testimony is sometimes acceptable, it seems, in establishing the character of practices), how his experiences compare with those of his fellow prisoners, what his companions at Alcatraz are there for (as many as he knows about), and all that sort of thing. It might be useful, also, when the motives of the Bureau Director or the Attorney General are examined (as they might have to be in such a case), to have before you some report of what officials have been questioning him about, what inquiries have been made, what inquiries are made now, whether any promises have been made, etc. etc. It might be a good idea, as well, to get an affidavit at this time, particularly about what he has been and is being questioned about and about his conversations with prison and other federal officials. Any differences between his treatment and that of his fellows should be noted.

Thus, it would help if it could be shown that

(a) Sobell did not fit into the Alcatraz scheme of things,

(b) there must be some other reason, aside from the legitimate ones of safekeeping, for keeping him there.

Unless these two point can be shown, along with the point above as to the Alcatraz classification system (which is implied in (a)), there would not seem to be any grounds for legal action for removal to another prison.

4. Aspects of the incarceration that are unfair or improper

Thus, the situation described must be most unusual; if so, it can then be shown to lead to unfairness or to a severity toward the prisoner and his family. That is, it is a departure from the norm that makes a difference, that affects adversely the prisoner's comfort, safety, finances (as well as those of his family), and his ability to contact friends and counsel. Furthermore, it might be argued, such an incarceration deprives him of an opportunity to rehabilitate himself in a normal prison environment.

5. As to the legal effects of a classification system

Do these regulations (established by speeches, reports and experience) have the force or status of law? Can they be likened to the regulations of an administrative agency? I have not had an opportunity to research the problem of just how much an administrative or regulatory body has to live up to its own "gratuitous" regulations. But it would seem that such regulations, especially when they follow Congressional policy statements and when they have been in force for two decades, would have some force and could be relied upon in some manner (more on that below).

Then there is the 1849 English case, *Cobbett* v. *Grey*, described in Appendix I below (pp. A46–A50). In some ways, the two situations are parallel. The question would be as to what there is in American law that would permit an action (perhaps in equity) along the lines of the action for trespass in English law. It could be argued that it is not unthought of that regulations, made pursuant to statute, should be the basis for an action when the regulations are ignored—especially when there is involved an imprisonment in "the wrong place." This is only to suggest that there might be the possibility of an action along the lines of the English case

6. How an explicit classification system is disregarded

But the Government will have analogies much closer to home, these (for instance) relating to the Board of Medical Examiners and the Springfield, Missouri Medical Center. Congress had specified how prisoners were to be tested before commitment to the mental hospital (Appendix A, p. A4); but it seems that the Attorney General has been able to bypass the procedure successfully on several occasions (various cases, Appendix H). Still, it could be argued, that the procedure (unwritten) as to Alcatraz is even more definite than the procedure (written by Congress) for the medical hospitals. And it could be further argued that some flexibility might have to be permitted in the handling of mental cases, from the nature of the disturbances, whereas only about 250 or so prisoners are ever out at Alcatraz at the same time and they sort of "nominate themselves." Perhaps.

7. As to the power to review the Attorney General's discretion

The cases are pretty definite in their statements to the effect that the Attorney General's powers in dealing with prisoners are sweeping, even unlimited. But the cases themselves should be studied with some care.

Comment has been provided with some of those which have been briefed (ever so roughly) in Appendix H. The cases, when looked at closely, are not as strong as they first might seem (and some of them, it turns out upon closer examination, have no relation to the point for which they have been cited). In fact, it perhaps could be shown that in every case where the unlimited discretion of the Attorney General was upheld, there were factors (usually noticed by the court) which suggest that the Attorney General's decision was reasonable under the circumstances. It should be remembered, moreover, that in practically all these cases (most of them, at least) the papers before the District Courts were prepared by the prisoners themselves.

It is just possible that a court might stop to listen if

(a) it is pointed out that there was another element in each case upon which the decision turned (and not just the unlimited discretion point);

(b) a very strong case is made showing that there is absolutely no reasonable, defensible basis for the Attorney General's action in this case. The question of the Attorney General's "motive" might become very important here.

There might be, for every court, a certain reluctance really to say, when faced with a situation where there is *no* reasonable basis for the decision, that the discretion is unlimited. Especially might this be so when the statute provides that the Attorney General may classify prisoners, and that he shall provide suitable quarters. What should happen when the evidence is clearly to the effect that there has been such a classification and such a definition of "suitableness" that it seems that Sobell and Alcatraz do not go together?

8. Some dents in the idea of unlimited discretion

Even while the courts talk about unlimited discretion, there are cases with language to the effect that prisoners cannot be kept, for instance, from counsel. And there are other deprivations evaluated in terms of what is reasonable.

Even more could be set up: e.g., the Attorney General can, in the terms of the statute, do with a witness who is in his custody what he can do with a convict, so far as transferring him is concerned. What if he is holding a material witness and decides to ship him out to Alcatraz until his turn to testify comes up. Is such discretion unlimited here? What if the defendant claims this is intimidation of witnesses? What if this is done to a person charged with a crime who protests such pressure?

Or what if the Attorney General decided to make every prisoner go to religious services regularly in prison and to the same service? Perhaps it would be admitted then that his discretion is not unlimited, so far as the handling of prisoners is concerned. But then, how about putting among a group of desperadoes a man who is not a desperado (when these men have been collected because of their desperado-traits)?

9. Request for recommendations and reports of the Classification Board

Perhaps one way of getting something going would be to make a request of the Director of Prisons for the findings or conclusions of the Classification Board. (Perhaps the request could be made of the Assistant Director in charge of classifications—see Warden Johnston's speech, p. A27.) Perhaps a request could also be made for the "classification manual" that Director Bennett mentioned in his 1938(?) Report and for the instructions and charts for the marshal he mentioned in his 1951 Report.

Such a request, if made in court, could be coupled with evidence about what the policy must be, what the decision of the Classification Board should have been with respect to Sobell, and what then must be influencing the Attorney General (improper influencing, that is) in committing Sobell to Alcatraz in the face of what is presumed to be the Classification Board finding. If the unusualness of confinement at Alcatraz is stressed as well as the strength of Sobell's case, then a court may be more inclined to risk the flood of petitions that might otherwise come if a loophole is permitted in the law relating to the supervision by courts of prison activities. (It might also be pointed out that there are only 250 men in Alcatraz and that there is little doubt about the appropriateness of most of the commitments—but if this were said publicly, Sobell might not be so popular there!)

There is just a possibility, if they have no report and if they feel a court might insist upon one, that the Attorney General may not want to get involved in this kind of controversy. That is, they may not want to take a chance on setting a precedent of supplying such reports. And, in a sense, they would be taking more of a chance in this case than in almost any other case they might have (except for the medical hospitals—where, I believe, they do make some kind of a showing of "unsoundness" even if they do not have a formal hearing): for there is the most clear-cut policy with respect to Alcatraz, and it may be that Sobell simply does not fit into the rationale they have for the system. Such a challenge, as to the appropriateness of a prison, could not be made for most of the other prisons; thus, why run the risk on the weakest case of being required some day to furnish reports on the 19,750 others (or of having to turn down such requests from other prisons)? (I say "weakest," of course, if there is set to one side the fact that Sobell has been convicted of espionage.)

They might be even more reluctant to run this risk of setting a precedent on reports when it is pointed out

(a) that they want to leave Alcatraz one of these days anyway (and Alcatraz, as has been said, is their most vulnerable point, if they have any, with respect, to "standards" having been set)—there *is* talk of closing down the place;

(b) besides, they may figure that by now they have gotten about all they are going to get out of Sobell anyway—so why run a risk of something that may bother them for years in their prison administration!

10. As to the "prisoners' mail box"

Has Sobell made use of this device? The operation of it should be asked about so that this "administrative remedy" could be exhausted if any action is planned. Perhaps a request for change of prison should go through "channels" first, rather than by legal action (if by legal action at all).

11. As to the frustration inherent in the Attorney General's procedure

Perhaps it could be pointed out to the Attorney General (or to an appropriate court) that the procedures being engaged in by the Attorney General are so indefensible (as proper police methods) that their results would not be defensible in a court of law if any attempt were ever made to rely upon them. It would be in their interest, therefore, if they think they might get something out of Sobell that they can use, to get it from him while he is not in a prison which is so conspicuously inappropriate for him and which only makes it likely that there will be claims of coercion and pressure in any court case. (This assumes, of course, they are interested not only in leads but also in evidence for use in court.)

Furthermore, it might be argued, that if such methods are so bad that their results could be challenged in court, then it would be appropriate to do something (before the results are reached) to stop the use of such methods at this time. Perhaps the "classification" point could be restated in this manner: just as there is no reasonable penological basis for the classification of Sobell for Alcatraz, neither is there any reasonable criminal-investigatory basis for such a classification (for that would suggest the third-degree methods which are not considered reasonable). It would be desirable, then, to have an affidavit as to what is being asked about, by whom, and about the effect of the routine at Alcatraz, the questioning, the entire situation with Sobell and his wife. (Mr. [Malcolm] Sharp could develop this point more for you.) See pp. A44–45.

12. As to a possible tort action against the United States

Would this be possible on the theory of the English case (Appendix I)? Even it if is not possible, it might be well to make some kind of a record on this aspect of this matter. Thus, the materials would have been brought together for later use if they are needed; such materials (bearing on "imprisonment in the wrong place" and for indefensible purposes) might be useful for influencing public opinion; in addition, such a claim (with the measure of damages including the extra expenses to the Sobell family for visiting, attorney's costs, and the extra anguish resulting from incarceration in Alcatraz), even if not legally valid, might be of value (if put on the record somehow) should there come a time when Sobell is shown to be innocent, or is thought to have suffered too much (even though guilty of certain acts)—that is, if there should ever be any move to compensate him. All this, it should be noted, is quite unlikely; but it is something to consider. On the other side, there are the resentment and hostility likely to be aroused by certain kinds of actions; and a prisoner *is* in a particularly vulnerable condition.

13. Does equity follow the law with respect to a tort action
against the United States

If a tort action (continuing) lies for false imprisonment (or wrongful imprisonment), could an injunction be based upon it? Could an injunction be secured even though a tort action would not be possible?

14. Editorial support on the basis of a strong record

If it could be shown what is happening with respect to Sobell at Alcatraz, why and how much a departure that is from accepted procedure, then there might be a possibility of working up some newspaper support.

Particularly is this so with respect to a newspaper like *The New York Times* which has, over the years, accepted Alcatraz as an institution, but not without a few qualms (and a look now and then at Devil's Island). Some of the editorials referred to in Appendices D and E suggest an arguing point.

15. Talking to Director Bennett and others
on the basis of a strong record

"A strong record" refers to a good case showing that Sobell is being treated in a most unusual manner and that Alcatraz is not being used properly. Although such a case probably would have little standing in court, it might still be a good point from which to work when talking to officials of the Bureau and to the Attorney General's office. Especially is this so if it is realized that it is known just how much this case is a departure from accepted procedures and how hard it is to defend. In short, it might be a point to consider in negotiations.

This might be a particularly good point when talking to career men who take pride in the fact that they have seen the federal prisons improve considerably during their regime. It could be pointed out that what is being done to Sobell only casts adverse reflection upon what they have done generally and is not something they should acquiesce in. It seems that there is a humanitarian streak in some of them; and Director Bennett or Director Bates has insisted that "we do not take the law into our own hands." It may be possible, that is, so to formulate the position as to induce one or two of the insiders in the Bureau or the Department to argue for Sobell's transfer. Perhaps it would help in negotiations and conversations if the other side realizes that you know as much about the prison set-up, and this departure from the usual routine, as they do.

There might also be taken into account, when discussing the point, the effect of this sort of thing on the purpose of Alcatraz. Some of the psychological value of the place is distorted if those who do not "belong" there are sent there; the space is not being used for those who are really dangerous (but it should be noted, the place is not full now); there is injected an additional (and unnecessary) note of arbitrariness into the prison system; the good faith of the prison officials is thereby questioned. (And there is also the unnecessary expense—but is this really *de minimis,* so long as only one prisoner is involved?) In short, some of the officials might be bothered, if pressed enough, to justify this departure in their total scheme of things.

16. "A strong case" and Judge Kaufman

Since I am mentioning various possibilities, and not just probabilities, it is appropriate to note that Judge Kaufman might also be approached to see what he would do to recommend a change of locale for Sobell. He would still have some influence, perhaps even some say, in the matter. If he has any doubts about the whole case, or if he wants to show that he is not without some consideration even for a convicted spy, then he might be interested in the possibility of such an intervention, especially if a "strong case" is made out. Who knows?

17. Use of the "strong case" in other facets of the case

A "strong case" as to what is now being done to Sobell might be of value in pointing out arguments in other aspects of the case. That is, what is being done now in contravention of accepted practice and custom could be said to be indicative and representative of what has been going on throughout the case. Thus, this is simply another "case in point."

18. "Cruel and unusual punishment" aspect

There might possibly be a toehold here in the Eighth Amendment. I know of no case where this has been tried with respect to Alcatraz involving a prisoner who really does not "belong" there. If the "strong case" is built up—with no loophole justifying a departure in this instance from accepted practice—then would it be "unusual"—"unusual" enough for the Eighth Amendment to apply? Warden Swope said, in 1953, that there "is always that small minority needing an Alcatraz" (p. A26). Does Sobell, on the basis of any criterion, fit into that minority of 250 prisoners?

19. As to the argument that Sobell was put in Alcatraz
for his own protection

It should not be too difficult to show that a convict is no safer in Alcatraz than elsewhere, perhaps worse off (unless, of course, the need is to separate him from a particular person). Thus, the place is filled with the most desperate of criminals; even Al Capone was stabbed there; and there is trouble quite frequently (Appendices D and E). Nor is there any indication that Alcatraz prisoners are any less "patriotic" than those in other prisons (thus, they have been known to attack a fellow-convict who advocated, during wartime, a slowdown in the Army laundry). And there is the question of what threats Sobell has received, if any, either in Alcatraz or before he got there. What basis is there at all to the safety claim of the Bureau (if the claim is made in seriousness)?

20. As to the kind of action

As indicated before, the cases and their comments (Appendix H) give some idea about the procedural questions raised by this matter. It should be noted, however, that it would be preferable, if any legal action is taken, that Washington rather than San Francisco be preferred. It is obvious in the cases that the courts in prison jurisdictions are most reluctant to have anything to do with prisoners' cases.

I have found nothing definitively foreclosing a declaratory judgment suit. As for an injunction, the cases toward the end of Appendix H suggest the difficulties. (You might consider an action, perhaps seeking an injunction, back against those at the last prison who let Sobell go to Alcatraz. But that may be rather stale now; besides, all roads lead to Washington and to the Attorney General's office.) Habeas corpus may be ruled out, except if it is stressed that this is essentially a false—i.e., wrongful place of—imprisonment. Once again, it should be noted, the procedural problems are better handled in the cases themselves, the comments upon them and in the description of the various points already considered.

21. Miscellaneous

(a) There does not seem to be any significant change of language in the 1948 Prisons legislation from what there was in the 1930 legislation. Thus, the cases that came up in the Thirties and the Forties would probably still have force. Relevant excerpts from the two pieces of legislation are set forth in Appendices A and B.

(b) What may have changed in the last two decades, and which may have some effect on the cases, is the status of the classification policy, particularly with respect to Alcatraz. It is now definitely established; perhaps that could not be said until enough time had run.

(c) It does not seem that Alcatraz was set up by Congressional legislation but rather by negotiation between the War Department (which had it) and the Justice Department (and Attorney General Cummings—who wanted it). Then Congress seems to have "ratified" the acquisition by appropriating money for its operation every year.

(d) Finally, Alcatraz is the place which led Attorney General Murphy to come back with a public denunciation of it as "horrible."

o - o - o - o - o - o - o

Table of Contents for the Appendices of the
1954 Sobell Memorandum

Photocopies are available from George Anastaplo of the original 1954 Sobell Memorandum, including its ten appendixes (not included here). Copies of the complete 1954 Sobell Memorandum will be offered to the law libraries of the United States Supreme Court, the University of Chicago, Loyola University of Chicago, and the United States Department of Justice.

Appendix N

George Anastaplo, An Obscenity-Related Case from Dallas (1989–1990)

George Anastaplo, Memoranda with Respect to the Regulation of "Sexually-Oriented" Businesses in Dallas, Texas (1989)

Introduction (prepared in 2006)

I was able, while teaching in the Loyola University of Chicago School of Law program in Rome, Italy, during the Summer of 1989, to provide a half-dozen memoranda for Analeslie Muncy, City Attorney for Dallas, Texas. It was hoped that these memoranda would be of use to her and her associates as they prepared for the oral argument she was scheduled to make before the United States Supreme Court, during its October Term, 1989, in the case of *FW/PBS, Inc. et al.* v. *City of Dallas et al.*

The controversy in this case has been introduced in this way in the Syllabus provided in the *United States Reports* at 493 U.S. 215 (1990):

Respondent city of Dallas adopted a comprehensive ordinance regulating "sexually-oriented businesses," which are defined to include "adult" arcades, bookstores, video stores, cabarets, motels, and theaters, as well as escort agencies, nude model studios, and sexual encounter centers. Among other things, the ordinance requires that such businesses be licensed and includes civil disability provisions prohibiting certain individuals from obtaining licenses. Three groups of individuals and businessmen involved in the adult entertainment industry filed separate suits challenging the ordinance on numerous grounds and seeking injunctive and declaratory relief. The [United States] District Court [in Dallas] upheld the bulk of the ordinance but struck down several subsections, and the city [of Dallas] subsequently amended the ordinance in conformity with the court's judgment. The [United States] Court of Appeal [for the Fifth Circuit] affirmed, holding, *inter alia,* that the ordinance's licensing scheme did not violate the First Amendment despite its failure to provide the procedural safeguards set forth in *Freedman* v. *Maryland,* 380 U.S. 51 [1965], and that its civil disability provisions and its provision requiring licensing for "adult motel owners" renting rooms for fewer than 10 hours were constitutional.

My six Summer 1989 memoranda are provided here in their entirety (with an occasional stylistic improvement). (A few clarifying phrases and even sentences are added.) These memoranda suggest how the regulation of business establishments providing pornography, obscenity, and related "services" has come to be thought about among us. I add at this time a seventh memorandum that notices what the Supreme Court did in this 1990 case and how matters now seem to stand in this field of constitutional law.

Memorandum No. 1 [June 13, 1989]. A Reminder of First Principles

I.

I have not had access to the record or to all of the briefs in this case. Even so, it does seem to me, upon reviewing the ordinance, the opinions of the District Court and the Court of Appeals, and the briefs and other such materials available to me, as well as a number of relevant United States Supreme Court opinions—it does seem to me that it is likely that the City of Dallas will prevail in this litigation, *PW/PBS Inc.* v. *City of Dallas* [1989–1990]. That is, the Supreme Court is not likely, considering its precedents and present inclinations, to invalidate the Dallas ordinance in any of its essential features. Particularly helpful here are the careful District Court opinion and its informed affirmation by the Court of Appeals. (I plan to discuss in a subsequent Memorandum for the City of Dallas, No. 4, the dissenting opinion in the court of appeals.)

The most vulnerable part of the ordinance, it also seems to me, is its inclusion of the offense of obscenity among the significant prior convictions that are listed. I suspect, however, that that offense should not matter much in practice, partly because obscenity convictions are fairly difficult to secure these days and partly because those charged with obscenity offenses are apt to be vulnerable in other respects also. If, therefore, the presence of the obscenity element should come to seem troublesome in oral argument, its suppression can be conceded without sacrificing much if anything of what Dallas is trying to do. Certainly it would be prudent to concede the point, and thereby remove it from the Supreme Court's consideration, if it should seem to threaten the strength and comprehensiveness of the Court's determination of the overall issue.

If Dallas's case is as strong as I believe it to be, then one should ask what the most good may be that Dallas can do for itself and for communities elsewhere in the way that it conducts itself before the Supreme Court. Critical to the contribution that Dallas can make is that it now proceed with utmost confidence—that is, that it be aware of how sound its case is in the present circumstances.

A proper (but not reckless) show of strength by Dallas means, among other things, that it should try to get the Supreme Court to go even further than it needs to go in this case, perhaps even to begin to reconsider the supposed privileged status of pornography and related materials and activities under the First Amendment. Thus, the Court should be encouraged, and given an opportunity, to reconsider various positions it has taken in recent decades, positions which make it difficult for communities to do what communities are entitled if not even obliged to do for the sake of the general welfare. Or, put another way, Dallas should encourage the Court to reconsider the relevance of the First Amendment in this kind of litigation, but it should do this without making it seem that its own case depends on that reconsideration. The sad fact is that the Supreme Court's position, as developed in recent decades, does encourage sleazy types to exploit the First Amendment when they should not be able to do so. There are various highly questionable enterprises that a self-confident community should be able to put out of business in a routine manner. Indeed, but for the Supreme Court's mistaken reading of the First Amendment, most of those businesses would, in most parts of the country, remain under-the-counter and otherwise virtually harmless aberrations, not the prominent and otherwise offensive empires that they have become. Some members of the Court, perhaps even a majority, may not dislike hearing this said frankly.

In short, we have in the United States these days a bizarre state of affairs which can be traced back to the way that the Supreme Court has read the First Amendment. The Court in *Near* v. *Minnesota,* 283 U.S. 697 (1931), it should be remembered, was confident that indecency could be routinely suppressed by government. (See, e.g., 283 U.S., at 716.) The Supreme Court should be reminded of this, especially since Dallas's opponents make so much of *Near.* (*Near* is discussed by me in Memorandum No. 2.)

II.

It is important in this litigation that Dallas claim the high ground, that it not permit itself to be portrayed as narrowminded or repressive. Thus, the City should recognize and make clear that *it,* rather than its opponents, is truly on the side of liberty. It is the City which is promoting good character and public decency, without which liberty is meaningless or of little use, if not even dangerous. And it is the City which promotes a general respect for law and the judicial process, without which liberty is not likely to be supported for long by the citizen-body at large. It is difficult to maintain a proper respect for courts when they are seen as repeatedly interfering with sensible and restrained efforts to promote decency.

What is essential in interpreting the First Amendment is the recognition that discussion of public issues should be unfettered, no matter how unpopular the positions taken may be. A mature community *can* be taught to appreciate the necessity of such respect for dissenting opinions, something which recent atrocities in Peking have dramatized. Properly unfettered discussion among us includes the arguments, by professional purveyors of sleaze, that it is good, or at least not bad, that they should be allowed to operate unimpeded. We do need to hear what can be said both on behalf of such stuff and about the risks of trying to regulate it.

It is sometimes argued that regulation of any type of expression can endanger the continued freedom to discuss political issues fully. But Dallas could usefully make the counterargument that the extension to all forms of expression of the high privileges of political discussion tends to cheapen the First Amendment and thus makes vulnerable the extensive and unfettered freedom we do need for genuine self-government. In this way too, Dallas should insist, it is truly on the side of liberty, much more so than those who exploit the First Amendment for base commercial interests by pandering to tastes and conduct that sound communities have always recognized to be indecent, destructive, and hence subject to public regulation.

III.

One sees, in opinions by the Supreme Court and even more by defenders of the commercial purveyors of pornography, frequent references to the Framers of the First Amendment and their intentions on behalf of all forms of expression. It would be salutary for Dallas to remind the Supreme Court that such a reading of these Framers is a gross distortion. There is no defensible way that the Framers of the First Amendment can be understood to have intended the sort of immunity for pornography and for sexual expression, as well as for commercial speech generally, that has developed in recent decades.

The typical citizen today still finds it difficult to accept much of what the Supreme Court has had to say about the extension of freedom of the press to indecent expression in various forms. The opinion of the typical citizen is reflected in the efforts repeatedly made by communities all over the United States to curb public indecency and related corrupting influences. The Framers of the First Amendment would almost certainly have found themselves on the side of decent citizens here, whatever reservations they may have had about the prudence of certain kinds of regulation. Here too, that is, Dallas should recognize that it is on the side of the best in our constitutional tradition—and the Supreme Court should be encouraged to return to the principles upon which the Framers depended in developing both the Constitution and the First Amendment.

One consequence of the Court's questionable First Amendment doctrines is that communities are obliged to resort to all kinds of contrived measures for the sake of public morals and citizen morale, measures which are obviously designed to curb the rapidly growing commercialization of vice in this country. It is unfortunate that communities are not permitted to do directly and more efficiently the kinds of things on behalf of the general welfare that our Eighteenth Century Framers had assumed that they would continue to be able to do. Even so, the restrained Dallas measures do attempt to deal with obvious social problems, working from the commonsensical observation that persons with certain kinds of criminal records have identified themselves as in need of being corralled for the good of the community, if not also for their own good, when they propose to engage in businesses which are known to be peculiarly subject to abuse.

The dubious character and effects of "sexually-oriented businesses" have been recognized by the Supreme Court in what it has permitted to be done by way of regulations and restrictions of all kinds, ranging from measures concentrating these businesses in one area in a city to measures scattering them among many areas. There are obvious connections, and hence a rational relation, between the abuses to which "sexually-oriented businesses" are prone and the kinds of disqualifying prior offenses listed in the Dallas ordinance. To attempt to rein in the persons identified in the ordinance is hardly likely to limit the publication and circulation of the materials available through such "sexually-oriented businesses." But it can discourage those who want to work for, or to profit from, these businesses from being or using the sort of people who are most likely to permit if not even to encourage the abuses all too commonly associated with such businesses.

It should be emphasized by Dallas that the conduct, past or anticipated, that its ordinance is primarily concerned with *not* "expressive" activity. To emphasize "expressive" activity in the fashion that Dallas's opponents are attempting to do is but another instance of an attempt to exploit the First Amendment for purposes quite foreign to its original intention. (It would be as if denial of a driver's license because of drunken-driving convictions should be understood as interfering with that form of expression seen either in driving an automobile or in drinking freely.) It is along these lines, I suggest, that Dallas should proceed in that part of its argument devoted to the explication and application of first principles with respect to the First Amendment.

Memorandum No. 2 [June 14, 1989]. On the Relevance of
Near v. *Minnesota* (1931)

I.

The City of Dallas, in its briefs and oral argument, should be particularly concerned, so far as cases are drawn upon, with *Near* v. *Minnesota,* 283 U.S. 697 (1931). That is the vital precedent in this field; all else is either elaboration or ephemeral. *Near* is often said to deal with a classic prior restraint measure. (This is not so, strictly speaking, but it is not likely to serve any useful purpose to try to correct the general misconception here. Prior restraint, also known as previous restraint, depends in its "pure" form upon a system of censorship pursuant to which all publications are required to be approved in advance of each issuance. This means, among other things, that the manuscript of each proposed publication by any publisher must be submitted to the authorities for inspection and approval. That certainly is not what happened in *Near.*) Whether *Dallas* truly resembles *Near* is itself a serious question. In *Near* a publication had been enjoined, and it was enjoined because of what its would-be publishers had said on other occasions. In *Dallas,* the amount of publication need not be decreased because of the enforcement of the ordinance, nor need the number of "adult" bookstores be reduced. Rather, the Dallas ordinance attempts to curb identifiable persons who can be expected, because of their conduct in recent years, to promote or at least to permit the unseemly public sexual conduct that "sexually-oriented businesses" have been shown to depend upon for much of their income. I offer in this memorandum a series of suggestions, keyed to passages in *Near* as found in Volume 283 of the *United States Reports.* These suggestions bear upon the circumstances and arguments of the City of Dallas in this litigation. Critical to a proper reading of *Near* here is the recognition that the Supreme Court in that case was confident that indecency could properly be suppressed by government. (See, e.g., 283 U.S., at 716.) Indeed, it can be said, the *Near* Court would have been offended by any reading of its Opinions that denied not only the power but also the duty of government to curb indecency and to protect and advance morality.

II.

In *Near,* a publication itself is aimed at without regard to the criminal record otherwise of the publisher. The action of the State is directed against those who have published scurrilous articles on public issues. The distinctions from *Dallas* are many and significant:

P. 703: The prohibition placed upon the offending person in *Near* is perpetual; in *Dallas,* the licensee or his employee can cure his disability by behaving himself for a few years.

P. 704: It is obvious that the offender in *Near* had addressed serious political issues, albeit in a virulently anti-Semitic way: "There is no question but that the articles made serious accusations against the public officers named and others in connection with the prevalence of crimes and the failure to expose and punish them." (See, also, p. 710.) The traditional prior-restraint abuses, which the Framers of the First Amendment were very much aware of, were primarily in connection with efforts to suppress unorthodoxy with respect to politics and religion. The only political issue in *Dallas* is whether such legislation as is resorted to by Dallas is useful, effective, etc.—and no attempt has been made, or ever should be made, to curb the right of any party in Dallas to discuss fully *that* issue. No one claims, or can claim, that any political or religious discourse would be in any way restrained by the Dallas ordinance.

P. 705: No one in Dallas is being kept, by the Dallas ordinance, from repeating the crimes they have committed heretofore. But an attempt *is* made to keep out of certain licensed activities certain persons whose recent criminal records strongly suggest that they will be easily tempted to do more harm not unlike that which they have done before. (It is like disqualifying for employment in the office of the municipal tax collector anyone who has recently been convicted of embezzlement or it is like disqualifying as a school-bus driver anyone who has been recently convicted of drunken driving.) (Please notice that each of the comments I make about the *Dallas* situation should be read in the context of the passage in *Near* to which I cite before I make my comment.)

P. 712: Unlike the *Near* situation, there is no indication in *Dallas* that the materials and activities of "sexually-oriented businesses" would not be widely available in Dallas if its ordinance should be vigorously enforced. Nor is there any indication that any person who is curbed in Dallas cannot contribute to distribute similar materials elsewhere in the State of Texas. Indeed, it seems that such persons can even prepare such materials (as "wholesalers") for distribution by "retailers" in Dallas. The only possible effect of the Dallas ordinance on the amount and variety of such materials in Dallas is that it could encourage some of the disqualified would-be vendors to promote "take-home" video materials, permitting those who are addicted to sleaze to enjoy it among themselves and in circumstances where public conduct is not affected as much or as immediately. The hope is, of course, that the Dallas ordinance will curb certain public conduct (that is, misconduct) on the premises of the businesses, not that it will reduce the amount or variety of the materials available to the market served by "sexually-oriented businesses." In *Near*, on the other hand, the State action, if upheld, would have eliminated the major source of a particular set of arguments found offensive by the authorities.

P. 713: The *Near* publisher was brought before a judge upon a charge of conducting a business of publishing scandalous and defamatory matters. This is, the Court says, of "the essence of censorship." But censorship is not at all the issue in *Dallas:* previous misconduct *in publishing* is a small, even negligible, part either of the past offenses or of the future activity being licensed. (Indeed, one troublesome feature of the Dallas ordinance, from the point of view of someone interested in the cause of public decency and personal morality, is that its licensing of "sexually-oriented businesses" can be construed as a tacit legitimation by the State of a dubious way of life. On the other hand, the ordinance does assert that the community is entitled to be concerned about such matters, however ineffectual various of its measures may turn out to be. The Supreme Court is asked, in *Dallas,* to ratify that community concern.

P. 715: The statute in *Near* did not deal with punishments, except in the form of contempt sanctions if an injunction should be ignored. (See, also, p. 711.)

P. 716: The *Near* Court observes that there are few exceptions to the constitutional ban on previous restraints. The second of the list of exceptions, having to do with the community's legitimate concern with decency, provides dramatic testimony to the inapplicability of *Near* to the *Dallas* situation: "No one would question but that a government might prevent actual obstruction to its recruiting service or the publication of the sailing dates of transports or the number and location of troops. On similar grounds, the primary requirements of decency may be enforced against obscene publications."

P. 716: Censorship is the key problem in *Near.* We have noticed that if Near could not publish his newspaper, his position would not be available to any significant degree in the community (and anyone else who did attempt to set it forth would anticipate similar sanctions). We have also noticed that suppression of a publication is neither the intended nor the likely consequence of the Dallas ordinance, where no limitation is placed (except for zoning) upon the routine operations of licensed "adult" bookstores. The *Near* Court is properly troubled by the "grave importance" of the prospects of the suppression, as a public nuisance, of a newspaper "guilty" of having presented a recklessly unpopular position of public issues. (See, e.g., p. 707.)

P. 717: Particularly troublesome for the *Near* Court is when the censorship before it is directed at the publication of the censure of public officers. The Framers of the First Amendment are recalled for their efforts to prevent ever again the kind of measures resorted to by the British government to keep American patriots from enlightening their fellow-citizens about the issues of the day. There is no question but that citizens in Dallas are left free to criticize their public officers, including those responsible for the preparation, enactment and enforcement of the ordinance under examination in this litigation. Not only that—and by this the Framers would be astonished—there is no question but that this ordinance does nothing to make the materials distributed by "sexually-oriented business-es" any less generally available than they would otherwise be. What the ordinance does attempt to curtail, however modestly, are those modes of operating such businesses that encourage crime, offend public decency, and otherwise subvert the general welfare.

P. 718: The importance of censorship for the *Near* Court may be seen in its willingness to risk abuses rather than to censor the offence in ad-vance. (See, also, p. 719.)

P. 720: The *Near* Court insists that a publisher does not lose his right to publish by exercising that right. In *Dallas,* even the person denied a license because of specified criminal conduct for which he has been re-cently convicted continues to have the "right," or at least the power, to engage in the conduct that had led to his conviction. No license had been required then, or is required now, for *that* activity. The only question is whether Dallas is empowered to act on the informed opinion that one's recent conduct in certain matters bears on one's qualifications as licensee in a line of business that is particularly susceptible of abuse. It should be emphasized that the line of business for which licenses are required is *not* primarily that of publishing.

P. 721: It can be wondered to what extent, or in what way, may the Dallas ordinance be susceptible to the criticism implied by the following observation by the *Near* Court: "Equally unavailing is the insistence that the statute is designed to prevent the circulation of scandal which tends to disturb the public peace and to provoke assaults and the commission of crimes." It should be again noticed that it is not the circulation of materi-als that is aimed at by the Dallas ordinance but primarily all-too-common illegal conduct on the premises of "sexually-oriented businesses." A good-faith effort is made by the City to curb those persons who, experience shows, are most likely to yield to the temptations and failings of such busi-nesses. It could be useful to indicate to the Supreme Court, if the Dallas ordinance *has* been in operation for most if not all prospective licensees since its enactment, whether the circulation of any kind of publication has been noticeably reduced in Dallas because of the enforcement thus far of the ordinance. Such representation could prove a telling response to the censorship concerns that are being voiced.

III.

I have attempted in this memorandum to suggest obvious and important distinctions between the *Near* and *Dallas* situations that the Supreme Court should be encouraged to notice. But this should not be done in such a way as to concede that the two situations *do* so resemble each other that it is necessary to pry them apart. The Court needs to be assured that there is no effective suppression of the dissemination of *any* "ideas" by the Dallas ordinance, an ordinance which is designed to keep the cesspool as clean as possible or at least to keep the cesspool from seeping into the rest of the community. That is, an effort is being made to contain the sleaze which is the stock-in-trade of "sexually-oriented businesses"—so to contain it as not to permit it to corrupt life generally. What Dallas is trying to do, then, is to keep the sleaze among those who believe they want it. The Supreme Court should be given an opportunity to help communities all over the United States to make conscientious efforts to keep the nation's cesspools under control. This is perhaps the most profound environmental issue of our time.

Memorandum No. 3 [June 16, 1989]. On the Relevance of Various Other Cases

I.

It is evident, from the draft I have seen of part of the Brief by the City of Dallas, that there may be little I can add to the City's analysis and use of various precedents provided by the United States Supreme Court. Thus, the Dallas brief deals more than adequately with *Freedman* v. *Maryland,* 380 U.S. 51 (1965), a case in which there *was* a genuine prior-restraint problem raised, with individual movies having to be reviewed systematically by the Maryland authorities. It should be obvious to anyone studying both *Freedman* and *Dallas* that the *latter* licensing arrangement has little if anything to do with controlling or curtailing individual publications.

It is also evident, upon considering what the Supreme Court permitted to be done in *City of Renton* v. *Playtime Theatres, Inc.,* 475 U.S. 41 (1986), that if the *Renton* arrangement is constitutional, then the *Dallas* arrangement must certainly be as well. It was recognized in *Renton* that the city's effort was not to suppress the expression of unpopular opinions but rather to control various neighborhood and other effects of a deleterious character. (p. 48) It was important for the *Renton* Court that the messages involved there were still permitted to be distributed. (pp. 48–49) These reassurances are available for the Court in considering the *Dallas* situation as well, indeed even more so, since nothing need be shut down in Dallas because of the ordinance under review.

II.

I have, in Memorandum No. 2, provided an analysis of the relevance of *Near* v. *Minnesota* (1931) with a view to the current litigation. Perhaps it would be useful for me to provide, in much the same way but briefly, an analysis of *Fort Wayne Books* v. *Indiana,* 109 Sup. Ct. 916 (1989), in which two suits are considered. Insofar as the State is restrained in *Fort Wayne Books,* it is because of improper procedures and premature seizure of assets. That case, if anything, provides considerable support for what Dallas is trying to do, and not only because the *Fort Wayne* Court permitted much harsher sanctions than any contemplated by the Dallas ordinance.

I collect here, using the format of Memorandum No. 2, some suggestions about the reading of *Fort Wayne Books* in the light of the current *Dallas* litigation:

P. 921: *Fort Wayne Books* relied upon convictions for selling obscene publications in order to justify RICO-type forfeitures. The concern throughout is with the sale and possession of obscene materials, something that is almost incidental to *Dallas.*

P. 921: The seizure orders were issued on the basis of an *ex parte* hearing. Even so, the padlocking of premises and the hauling away of the contents of stores could be justified by the Supreme Court in *Fort Wayne Books. Dallas* involves, by comparison, a remarkably mild and orderly process.

P. 924: If RICO-type sanctions apply to obscenity in the way and to the extent permitted in *Fort Wayne Books,* then the much milder *Dallas* restrictions are not apt to be overturned.

Pp. 924–925: There was, in *Fort Wayne Books,* no vagueness problem in having an obscenity law and in relying upon violations of that law for RICO-type purposes. The Court rejected the tacit invitation to overturn *Miller* v. *California,* 413 U.S. 15 (1973).

Pp. 925–926: It was decided in *Fort Wayne Books* that the self-censorship caution inspired in some booksellers because of the sanctions exacted against a few booksellers did not invalidate the legislation being applied. There is even less of a "chilling" effect in the *Dallas* situation, partly because the authorities' judgments are less subjective.

P. 927: The reversal with respect to one of the suits in *Fort Wayne Books* is because of the harsh action that was taken on the basis on inadequate procedures. There are no comparable confiscations in *Dallas,* which has, besides, fairly detailed procedures even for the denial of a license.

P. 929: No one in *Dallas* is deprived of any property he has, being left free to use his property elsewhere (and even in Dallas, within a reasonable time, once specified disabilities are cured). The "prior restraint" concern of the Court in *Fort Wayne Books* is with respect to closing down bookstores or other such establishments on the basis merely of probable cause. The overriding concern in *Fort Wayne Books,* much more so than is possible in *Dallas,* is with the propriety of State interference with the circulation of published materials. Even so, the harsh measures reviewed in *Fort Wayne Books* were permitted by the Supreme Court, whatever reservations it had about the procedures relied upon in one of the suits.

P. 932 (Stevens dissent): It is pointed out that there was no charge in *Fort Wayne Books* that anyone had engaged in sexual misconduct on petitioners' premises. But if such misconduct should be the primary concern of a law, as in *Dallas,* might not even Justice Stevens and his dissenting colleagues be expected to uphold the State action?

P. 939 (Stevens dissent): A curious concession is made by Justice Stevens in *Fort Wayne Books:* "Perhaps all, or virtually all, of the protected films and publications that petitioners offer for sale are so objectionable that their sales should only be permitted in secluded areas." This kind of concession means, in effect, that measured efforts to deal with the activities and consequences of "sexually-oriented businesses" might well find a sympathetic response even from one or more of the dissenters in *Fort Wayne Books.*

It should be evident, upon a careful study of the *Dallas* situation, that what is involved there is not even a minimal and hence justified abridgment of the freedom of the press but rather a controversy which has nothing to do with the First Amendment at all. The activities being proceeded against can properly be proceeded against by the State, and can be anticipated by the State, whether carried on in a "sexually-oriented business" or in a churchyard. Is it not evident that the parties in opposition to the City of Dallas here are much more concerned with self-interest and self-gratification than they are with the First Amendment and freedom of the press? The common sense of the Supreme Court should be appealed to here, especially by suggesting to the Court that the true friends of liberty are not likely to be those who cynically exploit the language of liberty for personal gain.

III.

Another case in which the Supreme Court upheld measures far more onerous than those seen in *Dallas* is *Arcara* v. *Cloud Books, Inc.*, 478 U.S. 697 (1986). Common sense prevailed on that occasion, with the Court looking behind the First Amendment curtain to see what it was that the respondents were really up to with their "bookstore." *Arcara,* too, can be used to justify various features of the Dallas ordinance and its implementation.

Particularly applicable to the *Dallas* situation, with its emphasis upon the disqualification of potential licensees who have recently displayed themselves as unfit to exercise the privilege they seek, is the following passage in *Arcara* (p. 697): "Again in *United States* v. *Albertini,* 472 U.S. 675 (1985), we considered a protestor's conviction for re-entering a military base after being subject to an order barring him from entering that establishment based on his previous improper conduct on the base." The Court's reliance here upon *Albertini* is encouraging to the Dallas cause, since the Court relied upon recent misconduct in justifying present exclusion. Is not this essentially what is to be seen in the licensing arrangement challenged in *Dallas,* but with the difference that the *Dallas* approach is substantially more orderly and otherwise predictable than that upheld in *Albertini* and confirmed in *Arcara*?

Memorandum No. 4 [June 15, 1989]. On Judge Thornberry's
Dissenting Opinion

The dissenting opinion by Judge Thornberry in *Dallas* is adequately anticipated by the United States District Court opinion and is adequately dealt with by the majority opinion of his colleagues on the United States Court of Appeals. Even so, it might be of use to those preparing the brief and oral argument for the City of Dallas to have the Thornberry dissent commented upon, if not responded to critically, paragraph by paragraph. I work from the paragraphing as set forth in the *Federal Reporter,* 2d Series (837 F.2d 1298, at 1306–1312 [1988]).

Paragraph 1: This case is *not* primarily about Dallas's restricting "the speech of its citizens." Restrictions on "speech" are insignificant, if not even non-existent, in this kind of situation. Nor is it so that "prior case law" militates against the sort of controls imposed by the City of Dallas.

Paragraph 2: This is a limited dissent, and that is based upon a perceived First Amendment interference. It is odd that "obscenity" is now so defined by the courts that obvious obscenity is not covered. But no matter: the position of the City of Dallas does not depend on what is determined to be obscene.

Paragraph 3: The man denied a license continues to be able to speak freely and to have his ideas marketed by others. He may engage in the restricted business elsewhere in the State. And may he not even operate an ordinary bookstore in Dallas in which *some* of his stock-in-trade includes the sort of things which dominate "adult" bookstores?

Paragraph 4: The objection implied here applies to all licensing systems, including many about which there can be no serious constitutional question.

Paragraph 5: The *Freedman* process is not needed in *Dallas,* since the circumstances are different. Potential licensees in *Freedman* are less likely than those in *Dallas* situations to appeal from a denial of license, since the denial does not relate to one's business but only to a particular film (and for that, an appeal may be uneconomic, making stringent routine procedures a desirable safeguard against State abuse). Also, *Freedman* is more like the classic prior restraint situation, a system of censorship, than is *Dallas.* Besides, effective judicial review is available in the *Dallas*-type situation, where the parties challenging the ordinance or its application can do what the parties did here.

Paragraph 6: Is this a sound characterization of the majority position with respect to the *Freedman* requirement? In any event, the *Fernandes* situation dealt primarily with a First Amendment activity, whereas the *Dallas* situation does so no more than incidentally, if at all.

Paragraph 7: Speech has little if anything to do with the *Dallas* situation. The conduct aimed at would be evident even to someone who does not know the English language—and would be evident to the ordinary Texan even if the language used for the transactions should be ancient Sanskrit.

Paragraph 8: The "content neutrality" of the Dallas ordinance, which Judge Thornberry insists upon, should be pointed up. *Fernandes* is not the problem. The Supreme Court should be asked to appreciate what "content neutrality" means here: that is, ideas are not being persecuted or suppressed, but rather conduct which sometimes masquerades as speech.

Paragraph 9: *Fernandes* is critically different. Any control of religious solicitations poses a sensitive problem. There is not usually, in such solicitations, the dubious side-effects of the "sexually-oriented business." In any event, key concessions can be made at this stage of the litigation: Dallas should be prepared, if pressed, to offer guarantees of automatic judicial review, either by concession of counsel or by amendment of the ordinance.

Paragraph 10: The majority point quoted here reflects an awareness of the *Freedman* observation about the difficulty of appealing single-instance rejections.

Paragraph 11: This again assumes that it is First Amendment rights that are aimed at or are in fact regulated in *Dallas*. The common sense invoked by Judge Thornberry should be applied to a proper description of what is truly being done here.

Paragraph 12: It is not a licence to "engage in sexually-oriented speech" but a licence to engage in sexually-oriented businesses. This is a critical distinction. No license is needed in Dallas for any *speech* or publication itself, no matter how sexually-oriented it may be.

Paragraph 13: *Renton* and *Young* take care of the zoning problem. Dallas is entitled to supplement that approach, if it should want to. (No time should be wasted during oral argument justifying the zoning aspects of the ordinance. That is too well settled in the case law. If the Court is now prepared to overturn *that,* nothing Dallas can say is likely to deter the Court.)

Paragraph 14: Whatever the District Court did with "sexually-oriented speech," that is not a phrase that needs to be used here. (See my comment on Paragraph 12, above.) Again, the "content-neutral" concession should be made use of. *Does* licensing have a far more restrictive effect on speech than zoning? Zoning can keep certain activities completely out of an area, while routine licensing need not do so at all.

Paragraph 15: The Dallas ordinance does not prevent anyone from speaking. It does keep designated persons out of certain businesses for a limited time.

Paragraph 16: Judge Thornberry exposes here his awareness that the Supreme Court is open to the *Dallas*-type legislation.

Paragraph 17: What does the "standard of review" have to do with the issue of whether anyone may have his right to speech extinguished? It must be rare that such extinction can be justified. Be that as it may, the

Judge is talking about some other case: no one is completely banned by the Dallas ordinance "from speaking."

Paragraph 18: Again: the procedural safeguards that can be conceded by Dallas at this stage of the litigation can take the wind out of any sails dependent on *Freedman*. But, it can also be said, those safeguards have been provided, in effect, by this case. In any event, Dallas should not permit this controversy to be turned into a *Speiser* problem, for that could be troublesome. (See, on the continuing vitality of *Speiser* v. *Randall*, 357 U.S. 513 (1958), my 1986 *John Marshall Law Review* article on Justice Brennan.)

Paragraphs 19, 20, and 21: Concessions can also be made by Dallas about the health, fire and building departments and their inspections. The provisions bearing upon the roles of these departments are not essential to the ordinance. The city does not want to seem to be in the business of harassment. There may be seen here how harassment can be categorized— and this can be anticipated for the oral argument.

Paragraph 22: One can see here, as elsewhere, the problems created by the Supreme Court's loose talk about the First Amendment. It should be stressed by Dallas that it is not First Amendment activity that is being regulated by the City but rather conduct for which one's past is a reliable test. (See the driver's license example used in the concluding paragraph of my Memorandum No. 1.)

Paragraph 23: *Are* bookstores singled out by the Dallas ordinance? Judge Thornberry is troubled by *Arcara*. He cannot get around it, exposing thereby the weakness of his own position. (See Memorandum No. 1, Section III.)

Paragraph 24: *Is* "impressive" evidence needed in support of this kind of ordinance? The District Court adequately anticipated this concern by showing what the City of Dallas did draw upon. Should not the Supreme Court be informed that the amount of "legislative history" relied upon in developing this ordinance is considerably more than that available for most ordinances passed by the City Council? (Are illustrations of this available, of which a public record is available?) Besides, the Court should be reminded, this is not the only matter that the Dallas City Council was concerned about during the year that it enacted this ordinance!

Paragraph 25: May not zoning laws effectively keep one out of a city permanently, whereas this ordinance bans a person for two to five years? And, it should be said more than once, this ordinance, in its previous-convictions aspect, need not reduce at all the number of "sexually-oriented businesses" operating in the city.

Paragraph 26: What does Judge Thornberry see as permissible in the service of the laudable struggle "to fight crime and urban blight"? Certainly, whatever legitimate complaint there may be about procedures and potential harassment can be readily cured for the Dallas ordinance.

The most disinterested case to be made against the Dallas ordinance is found in Judge Thornberry's dissenting opinion. Yet even that learned critique of the ordinance stands, in effect, as a testimonial to the constitutional soundness of the Dallas ordinance, especially as one comes to appreciate how forced and otherwise unpersuasive most, if not all, of what this dissenter had to say is.

Memorandum No. 5 [June 22, 1989]. On the Amicus Briefs

I.

It is a sad commentary on the state of American constitutional law today that nationally known law firms are available to advance the cause they serve here. I happen to know respectable people in both of the Chicago law firms responsible for these unfortunate *amicus* briefs. The ultimate question, though, is not the integrity of the particular firms but rather what has happened to First Amendment law in this country, particularly because of woefully inadequate interpretations by the United States Supreme Court. What the Court has done is to encourage, if not even to oblige, firms of the caliber enlisted here to resort to the dubious arguments they do. This is *not,* by the way, a situation in which lawyers conscientiously make themselves available to clients accused of crimes, something which we want lawyers always to be prepared to do. Rather, we see here that lawyers are being used to promote and perpetuate highly questionable businesses and business practices.

Much is made in these *amicus* briefs of the defense of high ideals, especially the right to discuss ideas freely. But what is truly being served here is gratification, or rather the right of some entrepreneurs to profit from catering to the base gratifications of others. The customers of the "sexually-oriented businesses" regulated by the Dallas ordinance are hardly interested in ideas but rather in sexual satisfaction, the sooner the better—and this tends to lead to dubious *conduct* on the premises of these businesses. The Jenner brief (for PHE, Inc.) warns of the vast "wasteland" that is apt to evolve if the Dallas ordinance is allowed to remain in force. (p. 13) But "wasteland" applies much more to what the Supreme Court has done and what various entrepreneurs (including PHE, Inc.) do in exploiting the Court's errors, not to what more or less helpless City authorities are trying to do in order to weed out an unhealthy growth or at least to keep it within bounds. I have, in my first four memoranda, commented on various points made in the *amicus* briefs.

II.

The Jenner brief attempts, at pages 21–24 and elsewhere, to distinguish the Dallas situation from the situations found in several Supreme Court cases which have upheld diverse forms of regulation of "sexually-oriented businesses." The effort in the Jenner brief is quite forced, indicating how troublesome those cases are for the Jenner clients. (Consider, for example, what is done with *Young* v. *American Mini Theatres,* 427 U.S. 50 (1976), at page 17.) The Jenner brief suggests that other means than those found in the Dallas ordinance should have been used by the city. No doubt, similar arguments were made in opposition to those "other means" when *they* first came up for review by the Supreme Court. That is, some *other* means are always to be preferred, which means that nothing that a city thinks of is ever likely to be permitted—and this, in turn, means that the community's concerns are not being taken seriously.

It is silly to believe that what Dallas has done is a significant step toward complete censorship of the press. And yet, this is suggested at page 15 of the Sonnenschein brief (on behalf of the American Booksellers Association and others). But, it can be said, Dallas, rather than having embarked on a course of censorship, has tacitly recognized and thus legitimated the operations being regulated by its ordinance. Those citizens who heartily detest such operations might be tempted to criticize the Dallas City Council for accommodating itself as much as it has to "sexually-oriented businesses." Here too, however, the ultimate fault rests with the United States Supreme Court, repeatedly ruling out as it has more straightforward measures.

III.

One consequence of what the Supreme Court has permitted, if not encouraged, is that common-sense distinctions are fudged which in other circumstances would be insisted upon. In both the Sonnenschein and the Jenner *amicus* briefs, the law firms' clients are sometimes presented as if they are covered by the Dallas ordinance. It is, however, a mistake to speak, as in the Sonnenschein brief, of the risks run by the Sonnenschein clients of losing their licenses because of one (perhaps inadvertent) misdeed by them under the Dallas ordinance. It is repeatedly lamented in that brief that the Sonnenschein clients would have to be licensed under the ordinance, but this is hardly likely. Thus, it is assumed in the Sonnenschein brief, as at page 5, that virtually all bookstores and video stores must secure a license from the City of Dallas. This pervasive misconception should be pointed out to the Supreme Court.

Of course, the Sonnenschein brief recognizes that its clients do not run what are known as "adult" bookstores. (See Sonnenschein brief, pages 2, 5, 20, 20–21.) What, then, has been the experience thus far with the Dallas ordinance? Have "mainstream" bookstores and the corner newsstands considered themselves obliged to secure licenses? Have the Dallas authorities moved against any of them for not having licenses? Certainly, Dallas must be able to give assurances, if need be during oral argument as well as in its brief, about the many bookstores and other vendors that this ordinance obviously does *not* apply to.

Is there not a general abdication of common-sense judgment in the way that the two *amicus* briefs describe the Dallas ordinance and its potential applicability? Should not the courts, as well as the City of Dallas, be relied upon to exercise as much common sense as anyone else in these matters? Consider how the Jenner and Sonnenschein clients will argue once the Dallas ordinance is upheld by the Supreme Court: it is obvious, they would then say, that this kind of ordinance was never intended to apply to *them*—and of course they would be right.

IV.

Further fudging of obvious distinctions and even more systematic subversion of common sense may be seen in the fear expressed in the *amicus* briefs about the effects of such ordinances as this on literary innovation. Great artists are apt to be crippled—and we are reminded of the vulnerability of works such as Joyce's *Ulysses* and Chaucer's *Canterbury Tales*. (See, e.g., Jenner brief, p. 12.) The threats to "our finest works of literature and art" are thus exposed. (See Jenner brief, p. 4.)

The briefs tacitly acknowledge, however, that the Supreme Court knows the difference between Joyce and Chaucer, on the one hand, and

the typical stock-in-trade of the businesses dealt with by the Dallas ordinance, on the other hand. The typical customer of "sexually-oriented
businesses" would be miserable if obliged to read Joyce, Chaucer and the
like. The *amicus* briefs do have the grace of at least *not* pretending that the
typical stock-in-trade items of "sexually-oriented businesses" have any pretensions to art. These briefs, in tacitly acknowledging the rather obvious
difference between great art and obvious trash, draw upon standards that
the Supreme Court can be depended upon to keep in mind in assessing
any city which presumes to try to do much more than Dallas attempts to
do here. If anything, the kinds of publications featured in the "sexually-
oriented businesses" that these *amicus* briefs defend make future serious
art *less* likely. That is, Dallas should be firm in pressing these questions:
Who really stands for genuine art? Does not art, if it is to endure, depend
on discipline and decency, neither of which is respected or advanced by
the "sexually-oriented businesses" regulated by the Dallas ordinance?

It is salutary to notice again, as I have in earlier memoranda, that what
we are seeing in the opposition to the Dallas ordinance is an insistence
upon the immunization of those activities of "sexually-oriented businesses" which cater to sexual appetites in the most unseemly manner. This is
done by attempting to place under the protection of the First Amendment
any activity which happens to have any "expressive" element involved in
it, however minimal. This is not to deny that the Dallas approach may
well be ineffectual, considering how strong the blight is which it is trying
on its own to resist—but "ineffectuality" should not be routinely translated as "unconstitutionality." Besides, it may be good for the morale of
concerned communities that they be permitted to try to do *something* to
deal with the obvious causes and manifestations of degradation.

V.

One critical assumption throughout the Jenner brief is that obscenity
convictions should be treated differently from all other convictions. The
brief argues, in effect, that obscenity should never be considered a crime.
But *that* is not an issue in this litigation.

If obscenity is a crime, however infrequently obscenity convictions are
secured, then disabilities can properly follow from it as from other crimes,
so long as the disabilities are plausibly connected with the activities for
which a man has been convicted. Various unwelcome things do follow
from felony convictions for dealing in obscenities: the convicted man may

go to prison; he may lose his right to vote. Both of these consequences are probably more serious than being denied a license to operate a "sexually-oriented business."

It is not a question, despite what the Jenner brief indicates, of whether additional punishment can be imposed for a crime. The denial of a license, pursuant to the Dallas ordinance, is not a punishment for crime. (It would be unconstitutional on several counts for any legislature to add *punishments* to whatever has been done to one after trial, conviction and sentencing.) A critical element in the landmark case of *Near* v. *Minnesota* (1931) was that the suppression of future publication by the petitioner was the principal, if not the only, punishment levelled against him for his past offences. Dallas is hardly out to punish the many people in the State of Texas who are convicted of the disqualifying offences that it lists in its ordinance. Instead, it does no more than select from many possible offences those which seem most likely to suggest that the offender should not be trusted with the operation of these "sexually-oriented businesses" which are highly susceptible of serious abuse.

VI.

The Jenner brief several times says that Dallas is attempting to suppress "speech crimes." That is, the brief does not take seriously the emphasis placed by Dallas upon the *conduct* that is aimed at, especially conduct which experience shows to be associated with the operations of certain kinds of businesses. The conduct, or effects, aimed at by the Dallas ordinance may be seen as the proper object of the zoning laws that have been repeatedly upheld by the Supreme Court. I have already suggested that it can be important for the Dallas brief to point out that the Dallas ordinance need have no effect at all upon the amount and variety of publications available in Dallas. (Here, too, the experience thus far, if any, under the ordinance may be relevant.) On the other hand, the kind of zoning regulations already approved by the Supreme Court is much more apt to curtail distribution of published materials, since it can interfere with market arrangements in a locality. That is, zoning regulations do interfere, sometimes drastically, with the allocations and uses of resources that entrepreneurs would otherwise make. Licensing may increase marginally the cost of doing business, but it is not likely, in the form seen in the Dallas ordinance, to have much effect on the allocations and uses of resources. In short, a fairly simple economic analysis can be used to demonstrate that zoning restrictions are much more apt than licensing to reduce the availability of publications in a market.

However unfounded the Jenner brief may be in its insistence upon "speech crimes" as being critical to the Dallas ordinance, that insistence does have the salutary effect of implicitly calling into question what the Supreme Court has done with the First Amendment. One consequence of the judicial confusion here has been to encourage lawyers to label a wide variety of activities as "speech crimes" in the hope of taking advantage of the First Amendment. Related to this distortion is the sophistical character of that argument in the Jenner brief which suggests that political discussion is threatened by the Dallas ordinance, or at least by the principle upon which it might be upheld. Also threatened, we have seen it suggested, are great works of literature. But, it can be answered, it is not future "expressive" crime (political or otherwise, artistic or otherwise) that is regulated but rather blatant conduct associated with a certain kind of business enterprise. (Compare Jenner brief, p. 5.) Nor is there here an effort to keep a man from committing again the crime for which he has already been convicted; rather, an effort is made to keep a vulnerable situation (the premises of, *and the activities in,* "sexually-oriented businesses") under control. (Compare Jenner brief, p. 6.)

VII.

I again suggest that it can be helpful for Dallas to indicate what has happened in Dallas since the ordinance was enacted (if the operations of the ordinance have not been enjoined pending review). Who has, and who has not, been licensed? What effect has there been on the stuff circulated in the city? And what has been said to, and done by, the Dallas authorities with respect to most of the bookstores in Dallas? But, it may be said, the concern is not with how Dallas is acting now but rather with how it may act once this ordinance is upheld. There will be time enough to correct matters, however, if Dallas should ever be so shortsighted as to attempt to embark on a generally repressive program on the basis of this ordinance. In any event, we do *not* have here the kind of situation found in the *Pentagon Papers Case* (1971): the restrictions that had been placed upon the *New York Times* and the *Washington Post* meant, in practice, that publication of the Pentagon Papers would be delayed for some time. Considering the plentiful supply of the stuff about which the *amicus* briefs are immediately concerned, there is little likelihood of any serious harm if the

Dallas ordinance should be allowed to operate until the prophesied dire consequences actually begin to appear.

Be all this as it may, it is silly for the *amicus* briefs to appear to stand in this case for "individual dignity" and the finest literature, considering what the sleazy operators aimed at in the Dallas ordinance are after, do, and produce. (See, e.g., Jenner brief, p. 24.) Common sense obliges the observer to recognize the degradation such operators routinely promote and cater to. There is a need here for Dallas to exhibit full self-confidence in presenting itself as a champion of personal dignity, as well as a champion of liberty and of genuine art, by trying in its limited way to protect and promote a disciplined life which respects age-old standards of decency.

Memorandum No. 6 [June 29, 1989]. Comments on the June 1989
Draft of the Dallas Brief (pages 1–24)

I.

I have made a number of suggestions on the copy of the draft brief sent me, most of which suggestions have been anticipated by the five memoranda already provided. But some of my suggestions are new on this occasion, such as the one at page 17 of the draft brief: it is now apparent to me that whoever does get one of the Dallas licenses will probably acquire as well the stock-in-trade of anyone who has been rejected as an applicant for a license, which means that the amount of materials distributed by "sexually-oriented businesses" in the Dallas area is not likely to be cut down because of the failure of any particular applicant to secure a license.

I have noticed that considerable use has been made of points, or at least phrasings, provided in my memoranda. I venture to suggest that even more use be made of the materials I have provided. Thus, for example, the memorandum on the *Near* case should be mined for additional observations, especially since this is likely to be the case upon which much will turn for Dallas.

More should be made of the fact that it is not unusual to have various kinds of criminal conduct bear upon one's eligibility to engage in specified (including certain licensed) activities. A note could well provide citations to an extensive list of such activities.

The *amicus* briefs open the door to your reporting of the experience thus far with the Dallas ordinance. That is, those briefs anticipate all kinds of dire effects upon "mainstream" bookstores if the ordinance should go into effect. It is important to notice both what is *not* licensed in Dallas and what the effects have already been with applications and rejections. The *amicus* briefs should have their gloomy predictions met with readily available facts. One point is critical to make: assurances should be given that no book dealer, licensed or unlicensed, faces the danger of that harassment which takes the form of a threat to prosecute (and thereafter to close down) a conscientious dealer who should happen to be accused of any one of thirteen crimes. The Supreme Court should not be allowed to believe that this is the way that Dallas might conduct itself once this ordinance is upheld. That is, one concern the Supreme Court will have is that hostile city authorities might find it convenient to find, if not even to create, disqualifying offenses in order to silence dealers who do not toe some political or ideological line.

II.

One way to deal with the fears that the Supreme Court might have about harassment is to claim for yourselves the highest ground available, rather than to allow the other side (and especially the *amicus* briefs) to do so alone. Dallas should not permit itself to be characterized as merely repressive and narrowminded. I believe I have provided more than enough materials that can be drawn upon, especially in the beginning and at the end of your brief, to present Dallas as at least as highminded as the people and their lawyers on the other side.

A proper use of the materials I have provided along these lines can help make your brief livelier than such briefs tend to be. It will not hurt to seem somewhat "opinionated" here: that is, the Justices may well appreciate a brief that is not stodgy and unduly cautious. You can show that you stand for a robust freedom of speech by exercising some of it yourselves. It may not hurt even to say that that is what you are doing.

In any event, Dallas should present itself, in this case, as the true friend both of liberty and of artistic integrity. A sound reading of the First Amendment should be insisted upon. You use *United States* v. *O'Brien*, 391 U.S. 367 (1968)—but you do not go far enough with it, even though it is very much on your side. In that case the Supreme Court upheld prosecution of unlawful conduct even though that conduct was intended and described by its perpetrator as a form of political speech and thus especially entitled to First Amendment protection. In *Dallas,* on the other hand, no such conduct is the immediate target of the ordinance's regulation: no expressive activity is in the forefront of the scent under consideration in the current litigation.

It needs to be said that the country can benefit from recognition by the Supreme Court of the community's duties and hence power to serve the common good. Related to such recognition is an informed awareness of the original purpose and early uses of the First Amendment.

It is important that communities be permitted, partly through the laws they make and enforce, to take moral positions. Moral statements on the part of a community can be salutary even in circumstances where the efforts resorted to by the community are apt to be ineffective.

III.

I believe that some members of the Supreme Court may need reassurances that a highminded and yet historically sound reading of the First Amendment is supported by respectable scholarly authority. It may be of some use, therefore, to cite to the observation about the First Amendment in my *Encyclopedia Britannica* article on Censorship (the Fifteenth Edition, beginning with the 1985 printing) and in my Johns Hopkins University Press book, *The Constitution of 1787* (1989).

Also useful here is what I say in *The Constitutionalist* (Southern Methodist University Press, 1971) about prior restraints. See, for example, the note devoted therein to the Helen Vlachou memorandum. (These and other materials should be available from the Politics Department at the University of Dallas.) I presume to mention these texts partly because at least three members of the Supreme Court know my work and evidently think it worthy of some attention. Besides, it is obviously because of this work by me that you have solicited my memoranda.

It is important that you deal carefully with the problem considered in *Speiser* v. *Randall,* 357 U.S. 513 (1978). That important case, for which Justice Brennan wrote the Opinion of the Court, continues to have considerable appeal for much of the Court. I again refer you to my 1986 *John Marshall Law Review* article on Justice Brennan and *Speiser.* Related to all this is my 1988 article on Justice Brennan in the *Cardozo Law Review.*

Finally, it would be prudent to say something about the parts of the ordinance that the District Court has invalidated. A proper recognition of, and deference to, what the District Court did in refining the ordinance can serve to reassure the Supreme Court that the Dallas authorities appreciate what a sensible constitutionalism calls for at this time. Heaven only knows, however, what may usefully be said about the recent "Dial-a-Porn" decision by the Supreme Court [492 U.S. 115 (1989)]: it is indeed a sorry reading of the First Amendment that keeps the community from stopping something so rank and unwholesome as the multi-billion-dollar telephonic pornography industry. If you are asked about the implications of that recent decision, you can at least observe that it does assure us that nothing Dallas can do to its local sleazy operations is likely to affect in the foreseeable future the amount and "quality" of "sexually-oriented" materials generally available these days to the American consumer.

Memorandum No. 7 [January 1, 2006]. Seventeen Years Later

I.

Except for what is said in Memorandum No. 3 (of June 16, 1989) and in Memorandum No. 6 (of June 29, 1989), I do not know—nor did I ever need to know—what was done with my six memoranda either in preparing the City of Dallas briefs or during the October 4, 1989, oral argument before the United States Supreme Court.

Moreover, even though I have studied the Justices' five Opinions in this matter, I cannot be sure precisely what the Supreme Court did with this case. The Syllabus provided in the *United States Reports* indicates the complexity of the judicial responses on this occasion (493 U.S., at 215, 219 [1990]):

Held:The judgment is affirmed in part, reversed in part, and vacated in part, and the cases are remanded. . . . O'Connor, J., announced the judgment of the Court and delivered the Opinion of the Court with respect to Parts I and IV, in which Rehnquist, C.J., and White, Stevens, Scalia, and Kennedy, JJ., joined, the opinion of the Court with respect to Part III, in which Rehnquist, C.J., and While, Scalia, and Kennedy, JJ., joined, and an opinion with respect to Part II, in which Stevens and Kennedy, JJ. joined. Brennan, J., filed an opinion concurring in the judgment, in which Marshall and Blackmun, JJ., joined, *post,* p. 238. White, J., filed an opinion concurring in part and dissenting in part, in which Rehnquist, C.J., joined, *post,* p. 244. Stevens, J., *post,* p. 249, and Scalia, J., *post,* p. 250, filed opinions concurring in part and dissenting in part.

I had made much, in my second memorandum (and in Section I of my sixth memorandum), of *Near* v. *Minnesota,* 283 U.S. 697 (1931), and, in my third memorandum, of *Fort Wayne Books* v. *Indiana,* 489 U.S. 46 (1989). These cases were barely referred to by the Justices in the *Dallas Case,* perhaps because they had been effectively neutralized by the City's representations. On the other hand, the O'Connor Opinion, as well as two other Opinions, did much more than I did with *Freedman* v. *Maryland,* 380 U.S. 51 (1965), a case concerned with providing "adequate procedural safeguards" whenever prior restraints (or previous restraints) are relied upon by the authorities. (Of the three other cases referred to in my Memorandum No. 3, only one of them is referred to in the Justices' Opinions in *Dallas: City of Renton* v. *Playtime Theatres, Inc.,* 475 U.S. 41 [1986].)

Critical to my 1989 memoranda was a series of suggestions about what was wrong with what the Supreme Court had been saying about First Amendment matters well before this case. I offered what I considered a commonsensical assessment of these matters, an assessment that I believed was consistent with a proper reading of the First Amendment.

An argument can *perhaps* be made that the Supreme Court's actions on this 1990 occasion justified the prediction I ventured to make in my first 1989 memorandum, that the Court was "not likely . . . to invalidate the Dallas ordinance in any of its essential features." But the Justices' Opinions needed considerable clarification in the light of the circumstances in which the Dallas authorities found themselves.

The City of Dallas did seem to be left with options that, if pursued, could have allowed the City to regulate, much as it had hoped to do, the activities addressed by its legislation theretofore. (I do not now recall, if I ever knew, precisely what was done in Dallas along those lines in the early 1990s.) Particularly to be guarded against by governments, understandably anxious to curtail unsavory activities, are measures that are not highly disciplined or that are obviously unfair. Thus, my six 1989 memoranda included repeated suggestions about how those in authority should restrain themselves even in Pursuit of the Good if they are not to arouse due process and other old-fashioned concerns that the Law must take seriously.

Indeed, such suggestions may be essential for those of us who want to see the First Amendment flourish.

II.

As I have indicated in this volume of *Reflections on Freedom of Speech and the First Amendment,* it is not likely that the issues addressed a generation and more ago will be as important in the years ahead as they once seemed to be. Technological developments during the past decade or so have made far more accessible to everyone some of the erotic services provided by the businesses that the Dallas City Council had attempted to regulate.

The relevant developments here are now worldwide in scope, so much so that they can make any local efforts seem trivial, if not even pathetic, by comparison. Illustrative of these developments are the operations described in an extensive account, which begins on the front page of the *New York Times* of December 19, 2005, about how an American adolescent (living originally in California) was sexually exploited for almost a decade by dozens of men all over the country. The scope evident here of the child pornography routinely available on the Internet is, depending on one's perspective, either appalling or exhilarating.

Thus, it may become virtually impossible, at least while we remain as generally permissive as we insist on being, to police effectively what is now being readily done among us, much of it in the name of "freedom of expression" and "self-fulfillment." Everyone involved in the *Dallas Case* litigation, authorities and purveyors alike, can be thought of as having once lived in an age of relative innocence, even though there was already in operation the extensive "Dial-a-Porn" industry described in *Sable Communications of California, Inc. v. FCC,* 492 U.S. 115 (1989).

At the other extreme from the manifestations of that ugly permissiveness among us described at length in that December 19, 2005, *New York Times* article to which I have referred is that devastating repressiveness over decades in North Korea described in still another front-page story in the same issue of the newspaper. An adult refugee from that "country" is quoted as saying, "When you've had the kind of life I've had, it's difficult to believe in anything." Should not properly self-confident men and women be able, in their mature freedom, both to identify and to insist upon a healthy balance between the two extremes (of a corrupting permissiveness and a crippling repressiveness) described in these (and in many other) reports available to us?

III.

It still seems to me unfortunate that the wide-ranging "freedom of expression" formula should have come to be substituted, by sophisticated moderns, for the traditional, more disciplined "freedom of speech [and] of the press" protected by the First Amendment. That substitution did seem to be taken for granted again by the United States Supreme Court in the 1990 *Dallas Case.*

The Court was commendably more old-fashioned, however, in its concern about anything that looked like an unregulated "prior restraint." The centuries-old suspicion of prior restraints was *never* limited primarily to the protection of political discourse, as the traditional freedom of speech and of the press had properly been. This suspicion applied, rather, to interference with all kinds of publications, including alleged obscenity that might not otherwise be considered covered by freedom of speech protection.

Thus, the Court properly insisted in its 1990 *Dallas Case* Opinion that licensing schemes require procedural safeguards. (*Freedman* v. *Maryland* is very much relied upon here.) Whatever the scope of the First Amendment, and whether it should have anything to do with the kind of activities that were very much the concern of the Dallas City Council, there can be no doubt but that these and like matters, including what may be done about them, can properly be discussed by any self-governing citizenry.

The accents of such a citizenry may be heard in the following comments in Justice O'Connor's Opinion for the Court in the *Dallas Case* (at 493 U.S. 237):

> It is not clear [that whether motel owners] have . . . standing to challenge the ordinance on the ground that the ordinance [discouraging room rentals of less than 10 hours] infringes the associational rights of their motel patrons. . . . But even if the motel owners have such standing, we do not believe that limiting motel room rentals to [at least] 10 hours will have any discernible effects on the sorts of traditional bonds to which we [have] referred. . . . Any "personal bonds" that are formed from the use of a motel room for fewer than 10 hours are not those that have "played a critical role in the culture and traditions of the Nation by cultivating and transmitting shared ideals and beliefs." . . . We therefore reject the motel owners' challenge to the ordinance.

The last words quoted, in the five 1990 Supreme Court Opinions in the *Dallas Case,* draw (at 493 U.S. 264) on an observation by Chief Justice Earl Warren (dissenting in *Jacobellis* v. *Ohio,* 378 U.S. 184, 199 [1964]), about the proper means "to reconcile the right of the Nation and of the States to maintain a decent society and, on the other hand, the right of individuals to express themselves freely in accordance with the guarantee of the First and Fourteenth Amendments." We can thus be reminded, still another time, that the critical tension here, and elsewhere in such matters, may be (especially in a determinedly permissive modernity) between the Individual and the Citizen.

Photocopies are available from George Anastaplo of the original 1989 Dallas Memoranda. Copies of these 1989 Memoranda will be offered to the law libraries of the United States Supreme Court, the University of Chicago, Loyola University of Chicago, Southern Methodist University, and the University of Texas.

Appendix O

Cases and Other Materials Drawn On

Cases

Abrams v. *United States*, 250 U.S. 616 (1919).
Bar Admission Cases, 366 U.S. 36, 82 (1961).
Barron v. *Mayor and City of Baltimore*, 32 U.S. 243 (1833).
Bates v. *State Bar of Arizona*, 433 U.S. 350 (1977).
Brandenberg v. *Ohio*, 395 U.S. 444 (1969).
Brown v. *Board of Education*, 347 U.S. 483 (1954).
Buckley v. *Valeo*, 424 U.S. 1 (1976).
Cohen v. *California*, 403 U.S. 15 (1971).
Communist Party of the United States v. *Subversive Activities Control Board*, 367 U.S. 1 (1961).
Debs v. *United States*, 249 U.S. 211 (1919).
Dennis v. *United States*, 183 F.2d 201 (1950).
Dennis v. *United States*, 341 U.S. 494 (1951).
Dred Scott v. *Sandford*, 60 U.S. 393 (1857).
Erie Railroad Company v. *Tompkins*, 304 U.S. 64 (1938).
FW/PBS, Inc. v. *City of Dallas*, 493 U.S. 215 (1990).
Gertz v. *Robert Welch Inc.*, 418 U.S. 323 (1974).
Gitlow v. *New York*, 268 U.S. 552 (1925).
Jacobellis v. *Ohio*, 378 U.S. 184 (1964).
Johnson, Texas v., 491 U.S. 397 (1989).
Korematsu v. *United States*, 323 U.S. 214 (1944).
Marbury v. *Madison*, 5 U.S. 137 (1803).
Miller v. *California*, 413 U.S. 15 (1973).
Near v. *Minnesota*, 283 U.S. 697 (1931).
New York Times v. *Sullivan*, 376 U.S. 254 (1964).

New York Times v. *United States,* 403 U.S. 713 (1971).

Paris Adult Theatre I. v. *Slaton,* 413 U.S. 49 (1973).

Pentagon Papers Case, 403 U.S. 713 (1971).

Progressive Magazine, United States v., 467 F Supp. 990 (1979).

Randall v. *Sorrell,* United States Supreme Court, No. 04-1528 (June 26, 2006).

Regina v. *Hicklin,* 3 Q.B. 360 (1868).

Rosenberg v. *United States,* 346 U.S. 293 (1953).

Schenck v. *United States,* 249 U.S. 47 (1919).

Somerset v. *Stewart,* 98 Eng. Rep. 499 (1772).

Spies v. *Illinois,* 122 Ill. 1 (1887).

Texas v. *Johnson,* 491 U.S. 397 (1989).

Tinker v. *Des Moines Independent Community School District,* 393 U.S. 503 (1969).

Virginia State Board of Pharmacy v. *Virginia Citizens Council,* 425 U.S. 748 (1976).

Whitney v. *California,* 274 U.S. 357 (1927).

Wickard v. *Filburn,* 317 U.S. 111 (1942).

Yarbrough, Ex parte, 110 U.S. 651 (1884).

Zenger, Case of John Peter (1735). See George Anastaplo, *The Constitutionalist: Notes on the First Amendment* (Dallas: Southern Methodist University Press, 1971; Lanham, Md.: Lexington Books, 2005), 826; *Encyclopedia of the American Constitution* (New York: Macmillan, 1986), 2088.

Other Materials

Alschuler, Albert W. *Law without Values: The Life, Work, and Legacy of Justice Holmes.* Chicago: University of Chicago Press, 2000.

Ames, Fisher. *Works.* Indianapolis: Liberty Classics, 1983.

Anastaplo, George. *The Amendments to the Constitution: A Commentary.* Baltimore: Johns Hopkins University Press, 1995.

————. *The American Moralist: On Law, Ethics, and Government.* Athens, Ohio: Ohio University Press, 1992.

————. Bibliography. In *Leo Strauss and His Legacy: A Bibliography,* ed. John A. Murley. Lanham, Md.: Lexington Books, 2005, 29, 733–855, 871.

————. *The Constitutionalist: Notes on the First Amendment.* Dallas: Southern Methodist University Press, 1971; Lanham, Md.: Lexington Books, 2005.

———. "Did Anyone 'In Charge' Know What He Was Doing? The Thirty Years' War of the Twentieth Century." In George Anastaplo, *Campus Hate-Speech Codes, Natural Right, and Twentieth-Century Atrocities.* Lewiston, N.Y.: Edwin Mellen Press, 1999, 49.

———. "Modern Greece." *Encyclopedia Britannica,* 15th ed. Chicago.

———. "On Plato's *Apology.*" In George Anastaplo, *Human Being and Citizen: Essays on Virtue, Freedom, and the Common Good.* Athens: Ohio University Press, 1975, 8.

———. *On Trial: From Adam & Eve to O.J. Simpson.* Lanham, Md.: Lexington Books, 2004.

———. *Reflections on Constitutional Law.* Lexington: University Press of Kentucky, 2006.

———. "September Eleventh, The ABCs of a Citizen's Responses: Explorations," 29 *Oklahoma City University Law Review* 165–382 (2004) (supplemented by a collection of periodic assessments in *International Law Review* [Loyola University of Chicago], vol. 4 [2006]).

Articles of Confederation and Perpetual Union (1776–1789).

Bacon, Francis. *New Atlantis.*

Berns, Laurence. "On an Oral Argument in December 1960, before the United States Supreme Court." In *The Constitutionalist: Notes on the First Amendment,* ed. George Anastaplo. Dallas: Southern Methodist University Press, 1971; Lanham, Md.: Lexington Books, 2005, 362.

Blackstone, William. *Commentaries on the Laws of England.* Chicago: University of Chicago Press, 1979.

Chafee, Zechariah. *Freedom of Speech.* Cambridge, Mass.: Harvard University Press, 1920.

Churchill, Winston S. "The Sinews of Peace." Westminster College, Fulton, Missouri, March 5, 1946.

Cohen, William. "A Look Back at *Cohen* v. *California,*" 34 *U.C.L.A. Law Review* 1595 (1987).

Confederate Constitution (1861–1865) (reprinted in George Anastaplo, *Reflections on Constitutional Law* [Lexington: University Press of Kentucky, 2006]).

Constitution of the United States and Amendments.

Declaration of Independence.

Devlin, Patrick. *The Enforcement of Morals.* London: Oxford University Press, 1965.

Dictionary of American Biography. New York: Charles Scribner's Sons, 1937.

Dry, Murray. Book Review. 6 *Constitutional Commentary* 351 (1989).

Encyclopedia Britannica, 15th ed. Chicago.

Encyclopedia of the American Constitution. New York: Macmillan, 1986.

Flanagan, Roy. *John Milton, A Short Introduction.* Blackwell, 2002.

Friedman, Milton. *Capitalism and Freedom.* Chicago: University of Chicago Press, 1962.

Gildin, Hilail. "Mill's *On Liberty,*" in *Ancients and Moderns,* ed. Joseph Cropsey. New York: Basic Books, 1964, 288.

Grant, Ulysses S. *Personal Memoirs.* New York: C.L. Webster, 1885.

Green, Thomas A. Introduction to William Blackstone, *Commentaries on the Laws of England,* vol. 4. Chicago: University of Chicago Press, 1979.

Kalven, Harry, Jr. *A Worthy Tradition: Freedom of Speech in America,* ed. Jamie Kalven. New York: Harper & Row, 1988.

Lewalski, Barbara K., *The Life of John Milton.* Blackwell, 2003.

Levy, Leonard W. *Emergence of a Free Press.* New York: Oxford University Press, 1985.

Lincoln, Abraham. *The Political Speeches and Writings,* ed. Joseph R. Fornieri. Washington, D.C.: Regnery, 2006 (rev. ed.).

Magna Carta. 1215 (reprinted in George Anastaplo, *Reflections on Constitutional Law* [Lexington: University Press of Kentucky, 2006]).

Meiklejohn, Alexander. *Free Speech and Its Relation to Self-Government.* New York: Harper & Brothers, 1948.

Murley, John A. ed. *Leo Strauss and His Legacy: A Bibliography.* Lanham, Md.: Lexington Books, 2005.

Newman, Roger K. *Hugo Black: A Biography.* New York: Pantheon Books, 1994.

Northwest Ordinance. 1787.

Plato. *Dialogues.*

Progressive Magazine. "The H-Bomb Secret: How We Got It, Why We're Telling It." November 1979.

Publius. *The Federalist.*

Shakespeare, William. Plays.

Sobell, Morton. *On Doing Time.* New York: Charles Scribner's Sons, 1974.

Steffens, Lincoln. *Autobiography.* New York: Literary Guild, 1931.

Stone, Geoffrey R. *Perilous Times: Free Speech in Wartime.* New York: W. W. Norton, 2004.

Strauss, Leo. *Natural Right and History.* Chicago: University of Chicago Press, 1953.

Wesley, John. *Thoughts upon Slavery,* 1774 (reprinted in George Anastaplo, *Liberty, Equality and Modern Constitutionalism: A Source Book,* vol. 1 [Newburyport, Mass.: Focus Publishing Company, 1999], 252).

Yeats, William Butler. "For Anne Gregory."

Index

There is appended to this Index a Roster of Documents and Cases Considered in George Anastaplo, *Reflections on Constitutional Law* (University Press of Kentucky, 2006).

Abolitionists, 74, 85–88, 90–91. *See also* Civil War; Slavery; Prudence
Abrams, Jacob, 110, 140
Abrams v. *United States* (1919), 76–77, 98, 101–7, 117, 126, 140, 300
"Abridging," meaning of, xv–xvii
Absolutes, 128, 136–37. *See also* Divine, the; Ideas; Philosophy
Accident, xi
Achilles, 4
Adam and Eve, ii, 302
Adams, John, 75
"Adult" bookstores, 154, 269. *See also* Obscenity; Pornography; Vulgarity, suppression of
Adversity, uses of, 173
Advertising, 170–76
Africans, 87. *See also* Slavery
Agamemnon, 4
Air Corps, United States Army, xiii
Albertini, United States v. *See United States* v. *Albertini*
Alcatraz Prison, 253–68
Alchemy, 18
Alcibiades, 5. *See also* Calhoun, John C.; Socrates; Sicilian Expedition
Alien and Sedition Acts (1798), 71–77, 95, 97–98, 101, 105, 123, 127; *text,* 224–25

Alien Registration Act (1946), 123–32
"All Men are created equal," 86, 89, 97. *See also* Declaration of Independence; Equality principle
Alschuler, Albert W., 301
Amendments to the Constitution, 17, 48, 57–63, 91, 98, 152, 172; *text,* 205–14
Ames, Fisher, 172, 301
Anarchy, criminal, 82, 112–13
Anastaplo, George, ii, xvii, 189n, 193n, 205n, 224n, 253, 269–70, 294, 301–3; bar admission case, xiii; *bibliographies,* xviii, 301.
Anastaplo, John, xviii
Ancients and moderns, 152
Anti-Federalists, 58. *See also* Federalists
Anytus, 3
Apollo, 4, 6
Apology of Socrates, 3–8, 20. *See also* Plato
Arcara v. *Cloud Books, Inc.* (1986), 282, 285
Areopagitica (1644), 4, 20, 53, 67, 78, 80–81, 142. *See also* Milton, John
Aristophanes, 4–5
Aristotle, ii, 4, 11, 88, 142, 159, 182
Articles of Confederation (1776–1789), 15, 57–58, 91, 137, 192n, 302
Arts, support of, 137, 159
Assembly, right of, 68–69, 83, 86; *text,* 205
Astrologers, non-licensing of, 172
Asylum, right of, 178
Atheism, 6–7. *See also* Divine, the; Prudence; Sensitivity

Greece, modern, 119, 302
Greek Colonels, 119
Green, Thomas A., 26, 303
Greenglass, David, 259. *See also Rosenberg Case*
Guantánamo. *See* Fearfulness, unseemly; *Habeas corpus;* September Eleventh

Habeas Corpus Acts (1641, 1679), 30, 55. *See also* Great Britain
Habeas corpus, writ of, xiv, 5, 46, 68, 92, 101, 118, 151, 180, 267; *text,* 198
Hades, 7
Hand, Learned, 124–26
Happiness, 13, 39, 41, 50, 137, 158–59
Harding, Warren G., 110–11
Harlan, John Marshall (1833–1911), 139
Harassment, official, 285
Harpers Ferry, Virginia, 90
Hate-speech codes, 302
Haymarket bombing. *See Spies* v. *Illinois*
Health programs, 152
Hebrew Congregation of Newport, Rhode Island, 218n. *See also* Jews, Judaism
Hening, William Waller, 218n.
Henry, Patrick, 26–35, 87
Henry I, King, 31
Henry VII, King, 15
Henry VIII, King, 14–19, 28–30, 80, 187, 215–17
Hera, 7
Heresy, 18, 80
Heroism, 16, 122, 128
High and the Low, the, 156
Hiss, Alger, 259. *See also* Cold War, the
History, 54, 111
Hitler, Adolf, 88, 102, 109, 117, 120, 122. *See also* First World War, folly of
Hoffman, Julius, 106

Holocaust, 178
"Hollywood Ten" blacklist, 160
Holmes, Oliver W., Jr., 76–77, 101–7, 108–15, 125–26, 144, 301. *See also* Alschuler, Albert W.; Realism; Relativism
Homeland Security programs, unseemliness of, 131. *See also* September Eleventh
Homer, ii, 4, 125, 134
Honor, 11, 116, 122, 156. *See also* Declaration of Independence, the
House Un-American Activities Committee, 112. *See also* Cold War, the
Human, truly, 157. *See also* Philosophy
Human beings, human rights, 177–82
Humphrey, Hubert H., 106

Iago, 82
"Ideas" versus "forces," 98–99. *See also* Good, the; Natural, nature; Philosophy
Illinois, 32, 38, 55–56, 58, 85–86, 184, 305
Immigrants, 39–40, 64–65, 123, 161
Importation of slaves, power to prohibit, 91; *text,* 198, 203
Incitement of violence, 149. *See also* Iraq Intervention (2003)
"Incorporation" of the First Amendment, 112–14. *See also* Fourteenth Amendment
Indecency, attempted regulation of, 269–99
India, 161
Indiana, 38
Indians, United States, 39–40
Individualism, attractions and liabilities, 69, 78–84, 137, 150–52, 156, 158–59, 179, 181, 184, 187, 292, 299. *See also* Conscience; Privacy rights; Self

Roster of Documents and Cases Considered in George Anastaplo, *Reflections on Constitutional Law*

There are, in George Anastaplo, *Reflections on Constitutional Law* (University Press of Kentucky, 2006), considerations of these documents: the Articles of Confederation (1776–1789), the Bill of Rights (1791), the Confederate Constitution (1861–1865), the Declaration of Independence (1776), the Emancipation Proclamation (1862–1863), *The Federalist* (1787–1788), the Gettysburg Address (1863), Magna Carta (1215), the Northwest Ordinance (1787), the Petition of Right (1628), and the United States Constitution and its Amendments (1787, 1791–1992).

Also there are, in George Anastaplo, *Reflections on Constitutional Law,* considerations of these cases: *Baker v. Carr* (1962), *Barron v. Baltimore* (1833), *Black and White Taxicab Company Case* (1928), *Bolling v. Sharp* (1954), *Brown v. Board of Education* (1954–1955), *Bush v. Gore* (2000), *Calder v. Bull* (1798), *Carey v. South Dakota* (1919), *Civil Rights Cases*

About the Author

George Anastaplo was born in St. Louis, Missouri, in 1925, and grew up in Southern Illinois. After serving three years as an aviation cadet and flying officer during and just after World War II, he earned A.B., J.D., and Ph.D. degrees from the University of Chicago. He is currently lecturer in the liberal arts at the University of Chicago (in the Basic Program of Liberal Education for Adults), professor of law at Loyola University of Chicago, and professor emeritus of political science and of philosophy at Dominican University. See http://hydeparkhistory. org. See also http://cygneis.com/Anastaplo.

His publications include a dozen books and two dozen book-length collections in law reviews. His scholarship was reviewed in seven articles in the 1997 volume of the *Political Science Reviewer.* A two-volume Festschrift, *Law and Philosophy,* was issued in his honor in 1992 by the Ohio University Press. Between 1980 and 1992 he was nominated annually for a Nobel Peace Prize by a Chicago-based committee that had as its initial spokesman Malcolm P. Sharp (1897–1980), professor emeritus of the University of Chicago Law School.

Professor Anastaplo's career is assessed in a chapter in *Leo Strauss, the Straussians, and the American Regime* (Rowman & Littlefield, 1999). A bibliography of his work is included in *Law and Philosophy* (v. II, pp. 1073–1145). See also "George Anastaplo: An Autobiographical Bibliography (1947–2001)," 20 *Northern Illinois University Law Review* 581–710 (2000); "George Anastaplo: Tables of Contents for His Books and Published Collections (1950–2001)," 39 *Brandeis Law Journal* 219–87 (2000–2001). See as well the massive bibliography in political philosophy compiled by John A. Murley, Rochester Institute of Technology, *Leo Strauss: A Bibliographical Legacy* (Lexington Books, 2005), pp. 733–855.